Sampford Peverell during the First World War

*By Peter Bowers, Clive Cotton, Heather Culpin
and Allan Weller*

A Sampford Peverell Society publication

Previous publications by the Sampford Peverell Society

The Schools of Sampford Peverell, by Carole Bond, Christopher Chesney, Christine Mason, Jacky McKechnie, Jenny Parsons, Peter Bowers and Vivienne Heeley, published by the Sampford Peverell Society, 2015

A Village Childhood, Denis Cluett, edited by Sampford Peverell Society, and published by Charles Scott-Fox, 2007

Sampford Peverell: The Village, Church, Chapels and Rectories, Editor and publisher Charles Scott-Fox, 2007

Supported by
The National Lottery®
through the Heritage Lottery Fund

heritage
lottery fund

Printed by Hedgerow Print Ltd

Published by the Sampford Peverell Society 2018

Copyright © Sampford Peverell Society

ISBN: 978-0-9933171-1-8

*This book is dedicated to the memory of
all those Sampford Peverell men and women
who lost their lives in, or whose lives were
changed forever by, the First World War*

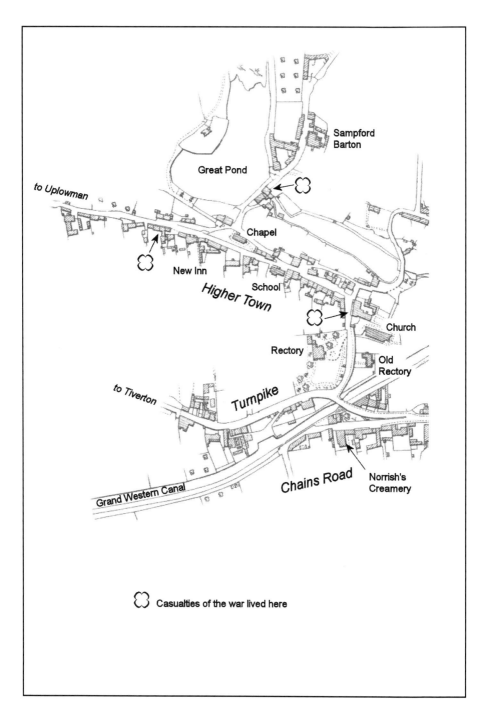

Sampford Barton

Great Pond

to Uplowman

Chapel

New Inn

Higher Town

School

Church

Rectory

Old Rectory

to Tiverton

Turnpike

Grand Western Canal

Chains Road

Norrish's Creamery

✿ Casualties of the war lived here

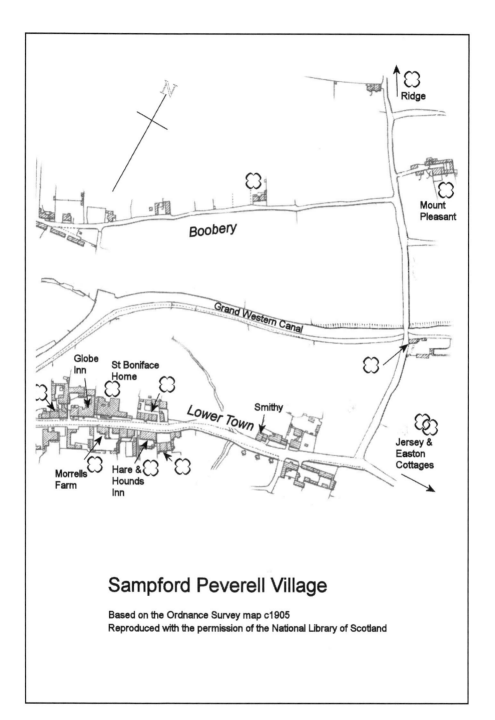

Sampford Peverell Village

Based on the Ordnance Survey map c1905
Reproduced with the permission of the National Library of Scotland

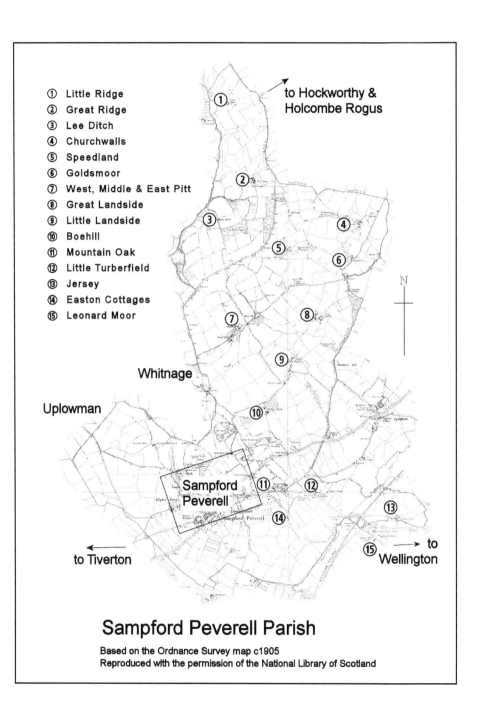

① Little Ridge
② Great Ridge
③ Lee Ditch
④ Churchwalls
⑤ Speedland
⑥ Goldsmoor
⑦ West, Middle & East Pitt
⑧ Great Landside
⑨ Little Landside
⑩ Boehill
⑪ Mountain Oak
⑫ Little Turberfield
⑬ Jersey
⑭ Easton Cottages
⑮ Leonard Moor

to Hockworthy &
Holcombe Rogus

N

Whitnage

Uplowman

Sampford
Peverell

to Tiverton

to
Wellington

Sampford Peverell Parish

Based on the Ordnance Survey map c1905
Reproduced with the permission of the National Library of Scotland

Contents

Introduction and acknowledgements

The aim of this book is to paint a picture of Sampford Peverell and its residents just before, during, and just after, the First World War. For those who do not know Sampford Peverell, it is a village in Devon, near the town of Tiverton, and midway between Exeter in Devon and Taunton in Somerset. We have tried to find out as much as possible about the people who lived in the parish in the second decade of the twentieth century, and especially those closely connected with the parish who played an active role in the war.

We begin with an imaginary walk around the village to visualize how it looked at that time. We then go on to look at various aspects of village life in 1914 to 1918, especially in relation to the war. This is followed by events in the village in the immediate aftermath of the war.

The next section of the book provides more information about those men connected to Sampford Peverell who gave their lives during the war. We have tried to find out who they were (there were more than the names on the original church plaque), and we wanted to find out as much about them as we could: their families, their lives before the war, and their service.

We also wanted to write about all those connected with the village who served in the war and survived. Their experience of war must have changed them and those around them. It is also interesting to see where they served. Before the First World War most of the residents of Sampford Peverell would rarely have left the area, let alone the country. The war led to more than one hundred of them going abroad: not just to France and Belgium, but also to Greece, Turkey, Iraq, Egypt, Palestine and India. With so many involved we have not gone into as much detail here as for those who died, but where we have more information we are putting it on our website where it is available for anyone to read (details below).

We have used a large number of sources, which are listed elsewhere, but we are particularly grateful to those people with close connections to those who served and who were willing to share with us documents, letters, photos and other memorabilia. Among these are:

Ken Bass, who provided information on Arthur Bass

Angelo Binaccioni, who provided information on James Trevellyan and Ernest Johnson

Terry and Debbie Burns, Wendy Trump and their families who provided information on Albert Osmond, William Saunders and others.

Marilyn Clatworthy, who provided information on Walter (Sid) Ridler

Stan Trevelyan, who provided information on Stanley Trevelyan

Christine Twose, who provided information on William Henry Osmond

We are grateful to local members of the Royal British Legion, led by Keith Astbury, who have visited the graves of some of our men and supplied us with information and photos.

We would also like to thank Rachel Jasinska, who read the first draft of this book and gave us very useful feedback, Richard Horrocks who created the maps, and Christine Butler who did the typesetting and arranged the pictures for us.

Further thanks are owed to the Heritage Lottery Fund whose award of a grant under their 'First World War: then and now' programme provided funding for our project 'Sampford Peverell: the Great War Remembered' of which this book forms a part.

If any more information comes to light after the publication of this book we will add it to our website which is here:

https://spsocresearch.weebly.com/ww1.html

The village before the war

This is an attempt to picture the village of Sampford Peverell as it was just before the First World War, by taking an imaginary walk along the principal roads of the village. Many of today's buildings did not exist then, and some of the buildings in the village in 1914 have since been demolished or replaced, but we will try to picture it as it was. To help us, we will use the 1910 Land Survey, the 1911 census, land tax returns, trade directories, and old photographs. Denis Cluett's memories of life in the village in the early 1900s provide a vivid first-hand account of a boy's life in Sampford Peverell before and during the war, and some of the best anecdotes come from this source, which is worth reading alongside this book[1]. Current (2018) addresses are occasionally given in brackets and in italics. Descriptions of buildings, rooms, outhouses and water supply come from the 1910 Land Valuation Survey. This was a survey conducted between 1910 and 1915 of every property in the country, to assess the value of the land for tax purposes. The results were recorded in 'Field Books' which included detailed descriptions of buildings and their occupants, and properties were cross-related to a map, which has helped us work out who lived where and what their property was like. The original books and maps are held in the National Archives.

Now imagine that you are standing in Sampford Peverell in 1914.

Before we set off, there are a few basics that you should know. Sampford Peverell is a village of some 140 properties (in 2018 there are 520) but there are a lot of children around. About 60 boys live at St Boniface Home, a Church of England home for 'waifs and strays' who have come from broken homes or situations of severe poverty. Apart from them, there are another 120 or so youngsters under 14, and the average age of the whole population here is under 30 years old. Everywhere you go you will hear people speak with a broad Devon accent, because about three-quarters of them were born in the county.

With very few exceptions, once children reach the age of 14 they leave school and go out to work. For boys and men, agriculture is the most common employment, but there are also shop workers, craft workers, or

---

[1] Denis Cluett and Sampford Peverell Society., *A Village Childhood : Memories of Living in Rural Devon before the Age of the Motor Car*, Sampford Peverell Society Publication (Great Britain: Charles Scott-Fox, 2007).

those working on the railway, in the quarry, or at the creamery. All the jobs are within walking distance of home, except for a few professionals such as the doctor, the Rector and the vet, who will need to travel to perform their duties. Of girls and women, about 70% have occupations, for instance as domestic servants, dairymaids, shop-workers or seamstresses, and those who don't have paid jobs still work hard looking after the house and family. Some take in piece-work, such as sewing or laundry, which they can do at home while still running the house.

Now, ladies and gentlemen, before we set off make sure you are wearing stout boots, as there are very few pavements, the roads are surfaced with rolled, crushed stones, and horses and livestock use the road regularly! Cars are a rarity, so you will see a few bicycles and a lot of horse-drawn vehicles: you'll notice that many of the houses have stables. There are some elegant properties in the village but many of the cottages are old and in poor repair. The village has plenty of shops and three pubs. If you need a drink of water at any time use one of the many village pumps. Most families have to fetch water from the nearest pump, and those who live near the pond or canal use water from them for everything other than drinking. If you need to use a toilet most cottages have an 'earth closet', which is an outside toilet, consisting of a kind of large bucket under a seat. Earth is sprinkled into the bucket after each use, and the bucket is regularly emptied, sometimes being used as garden fertiliser. Most villagers keep animals such as pigs or hens in an outhouse. A lot of human and animal waste ends up in the stream, the pond or the canal, so don't drink the water from those!

Don't worry if it gets dark - there are oil-fuelled street lamps which Fred Vickery goes around lighting every evening in the winter months. Of course, inside the houses people use candles or oil lamps for their light. The kitchen is the main room in every home as it has a cooking range, fuelled by wood or coal, that helps to keep it warm. People cook, eat, wash and socialize in the kitchen, especially in winter when all the other rooms are very cold. They have baths in the kitchen too, in a metal bathtub filled with water which has been heated on the range, perhaps sharing with other members of the family. But we can keep warm with a brisk walk.

From the Canal Bridge along Higher Town

Higher Town is a very busy and heavily populated road. We'll start at the lower end, by the canal bridge. If we watch the canal from here we may see barges carrying lime, or people walking along the canal towpath to get to

The canal c 1905 with the (one storey) Old Rectory on the left.

Halberton or Burlescombe, and we may catch sight of Joe Barrie in his boat on the canal gathering waterlilies, which he will sell on to townsfolk.

On the right we pass the Old Rectory, occupied by Mrs Rossiter, widow of the former rector. It was built in around 1500 AD. The main building has only one floor because the upper floor, which was in a poor state of repair, was removed by an earlier Rector – much to the annoyance of his successor, Revd Ireland! Perhaps it will be re-instated one day. This section of the Old Rectory has a large room and a kitchen. The taller side section has one large room with three bedrooms over it, and there is also a small lean-to coach house and a WC.

After the Old Rectory we go past the Church, restored in the 19th century by Revd Ireland, and come to High Cross House, a large residence with a central front door (*2018: since divided into two houses - 3 and 5 Higher Town*). It is owned by Mrs Rossiter, but is rented out to Mr Frederic Coupland-Smith, a gentleman of private means, who lives here with his son, Frederic, a pupil at Blundell's School. Mr Coupland-Smith's wife seems to like travelling independently, but she also lives here occasionally. Downstairs the house has a drawing-room, dining-room, smoking-room, kitchen and scullery. There are six bedrooms upstairs plus two servants' rooms, a bathroom and an indoors WC. The property also has several outbuildings including a stable, and across the road there is a tennis court belonging to the house. There are also two servants living here: a general domestic servant, and a groom. It is quite a grand establishment.

High Cross House c 1912

Turning left and crossing the top of Boobery we come to Cross Hill (*2018: 7 Higher Town*), yet another property owned by Mrs Rossiter. The tenant is John Henry Smith, headmaster of the village school, who lives here with his wife and two children. It has several rooms downstairs, three bedrooms, and takes its water from the public pump.

There are a few cottages going uphill from Cross Hill, including Paulett. A serious fire in 1902 destroyed a house and shop in this row of cottages and three years later a new house was built on another part of the same plot, which was given the name 'Paulett House'. It is described as a modern stone, plastered and slated butcher's shop and house. The ground floor consists of a shop, plus a private entrance leading to a sitting room, 2 kitchens, and a stone and tile washhouse. There is a stable and traphouse (a trap is a small horse-drawn carriage) in the rear. It also has four bedrooms, cellars in the basement, and a small lawn but no garden. The butcher in Paulett House is James Salter, who has a slaughterhouse in Boobery near Quay Head. Mr Salter is on the Parish Council.

A little further uphill we pass another cottage and come to Halls, (*2018: 11a Higher Town*). This is occupied by William Dunn, known as 'Cocky' Dunn, a boot and shoe maker. He is in his seventies and works behind the window in the shop on the side of the house. He is happy to have people watching him work but he doesn't say much, possibly because his mouth is usually full of small brass tacks. Cocky fills his mouth with these and pushes them out between his teeth one at a time while he hammers them into the sole at a tremendous rate. Cocky Dunn is also the village barber and is on the Parish Council.

Continuing up the right-hand side of Higher Town we come to London House (*2018: 21 Higher Town*). It was a shop for much of the nineteenth century, then became a pub called the London Inn between 1899 and 1906 but fell into disuse. In 1910 it was a Men's Club, and in 1913 it changed use again and became the Post Office, managed by Mrs Rosa Jennings, the sub-postmistress. She took over the Post Office after the retirement of her husband, Joseph, in 1902. He died in 1913, causing her to leave the previous Post Office premises in Lower Town. Mrs Jennings is very familiar with Post Office work, having helped her former husband in the business her whole life. Mrs Jennings is ably assisted by a team of postmen, including Tom Parkhouse. Letters arrive from Tiverton three times a day and are also dispatched three times a day. If you want to communicate with someone outside the village, you have the choice of sending a letter or a telegram. If your communication is of a personal nature, you should post a letter, as the contents of telegrams are not regarded as being strictly confidential!

The cottages in Back Street (behind Halls) and further up the road are all fully occupied, as are those in the road leading to Sampford Barton Farm. This road runs alongside the Great Pond, a lovely feature which provides a head of water for the mill, which is now only used occasionally as there is no longer a full-time miller. Most of the cottages, including Mill Cottage, are owned by the farm, and are occupied by farm workers. The Barton itself is a large farmhouse, close to the site of a former castle, and is the home of Mrs Pedler, a widow of private means, her son John, a farmer and County and Parish Councillor, her daughter Edith, and a servant, Harriet Hayward. Mrs Pedler has several other adult children who have left home. One of the cottages in this area, occupied by Thomas Goffin and his wife Ida, is sometimes called 'Pond Cottage' and sometimes 'Pump House' because it gets its drinking water from a pump in the road and other water from the pond. The pump is also used by a number of other homes in the area.

Back on Higher Town, just before we get to the Methodist Chapel there is a thatched cottage which includes a big archway over the road that goes down towards the pond. There is a room over the archway, and the cottage is nicknamed 'Marble Arch'.

Marble Arch, with the New Inn in the background on the left

There are only a few more cottages further along Higher Town on the right (north) side but let's walk up to the last cottages on the left. This is a group of three cottages around a yard, occupied by the Hurford, Tapp and Ridler families. Mr Ridler works for Henry Wood, the saddler. The Tapps' cottage has a kitchen, bake house, larder and 3 bedrooms, and adjoining the road there is a linhay: an open-fronted two-storey barn. The Hurfords' cottage has two kitchens and three bedrooms, and the Ridlers' has a kitchen and two bedrooms. Each cottage has a good garden, and there is a shared earth closet.

Walking back along the south side of Higher Town we pass about a dozen more cottages including one with a former Bible Christian chapel attached (*2018: 30 Higher Town*), and a footpath that runs down to Turnpike, before arriving eventually at the New Inn (*2018: 22 and 22a Higher Town*) where we can pause for some refreshments. Despite its name it is the oldest of the three pubs in the village, known to have been an inn since the 1750s or earlier. It is owned by the Furze and Co brewery of Uffculme, and the licensee is Robert Tambling, who is also a market gardener. Mr Tambling is assisted by his wife Elizabeth. The inn has all the usual facilities including stables, a bake house and a skittle alley.

Feeling refreshed we can now continue down the hill, passing the Methodist chapel on our left, until we come to Charles Thomas's bakery on our right (*2018: 18 Higher Town*), a property also known as the Ghost House. It used to be run by William Thomas who died recently, but now it is run by his son Charles, Charles' mother, Elizabeth, his sister, Minnie, and two other assistants in the bakery and shop. They sell tinned and cottage loaves and small milk loaves which children love to eat hot from the oven. They also make and deliver hot cross buns at Easter.

Having bought a bun at the bakery we can continue our walk past the village school, which was built 40 years ago in 1874. It has three schoolrooms and two sets of lavatories, one for boys and one for girls. One of the schoolrooms was added recently, in 1909, to provide more room after the arrival of the boys at the St Boniface Home for Waifs and Strays. After a few more cottages we come to Holloway's store (*2018: 14 Higher Town*), a stone, cob and slate house with Baker and Grocers Shop. The ground floor has a double fronted shop, a private entrance, sitting room, kitchen pantry, bake house with loft over, coach entrance, store, a stable, and a lean-to

Higher Town, showing Halls on the left and Holloways on the right

washhouse. This large shop is owned by Samuel Holloway, a baker, grocer, and draper, assisted by his wife, Susannah, and his daughter, Millford. His teenage son Samuel Cromwell Holloway also lives with them. Millford will soon be marrying Albert Dinham, who lives in Moor End Cottage and is employed as a clerk at Norrish's Creamery in Chains Road.

The cottages downhill from Holloways are all owned by Mrs Rossiter and rented out to a number of families. Like most of the cottages in the village they have a parlour and a kitchen, or two kitchens, downstairs, and two or three bedrooms upstairs. Water is fetched from the nearest pump. They do not have bathrooms, but they usually have an earth closet outside.

Turning to the right we pass the tennis court belonging to High Cross House, constructed on land where there used to be four cottages, and then we come to the Rectory *(2018: Church House)*, occupied by the Reverend John Rees, his wife Mary, three daughters, and a servant. It is a substantial residence approached by a carriage drive, with four reception rooms, kitchen and scullery, and a verandah. On the first floor it has eight bedrooms and a WC. Adjoining it are stables for four horses, a coach house, and a 'game larder'.

This brings us back to the canal bridge ready for our next walk.

Boobery and Whitnage Road

Boobery is a quiet country lane, with few houses. There is just one side road which leads up to the disused quarry and lime kilns on Connigar Hill. Starting at High Cross House, we walk down the short steep hill and come first to Quay Head on our left at the bottom of the hill. This is quite a large property containing a kitchen, a back kitchen, two sitting rooms, and five bedrooms. It also has a lean-to wash house, a coal house, a chicken house, a pig house, a stable with a loft over it, and various other outhouses. It has an earth closet and gets its water supply from a nearby pump. Quay Head is owned by Mr Southwood, but the occupiers who rent it change frequently. Across the road and next to the stream is the slaughter house used by Mr Salter, the butcher. Boys like watching animals being slaughtered there! If they are lucky Mr Salter gives them a pig's bladder which they can inflate and use as a football. On the right we pass a coach house and, on the left, just before the sharp bend in the road, we come to a pair of fairly new brick cottages, built in 1896, which are occupied by Sampford Barton farm workers.

Barton cottages

After the bend the road straightens out and on the right we come to Boobery Cottage (*2018: where 1 and 1a Boobery are located*), which is occupied by Mr Marshall, a gentleman of private means, with his wife and brother. It is a cob and thatched house with an adjoining cottage, garden and outbuildings which include the coach house which we passed on our way here, a stable, and a hen house. On the ground floor the house contains dining and drawing rooms, and a kitchen, scullery and larder. On the first floor there are 4 bedrooms, a dressing room, a servant's room, and a lavatory with WC. On the second floor there are two attics. It has its own water supply from a pump in the scullery. The rent seems a low one for the class of house, which is considered to be quite superior. Just past Boobery Cottage there is a pair of 3-bedroom cottages and then a string of three 2-bedroom cottages. After these there are no more buildings on the right (south) side of the road, just orchards and meadows sloping down to the canal. There is, however, a pump house, half way along Boobery on that side of the road.

On our left, the north side, and opposite Boobery Cottage, there is a pair of cottages called 'Doctors and Rocas' (*2018: Smokey Lane Cottage and Rocas*). 'Doctors' has a slate roof, and 'Rocas' a thatched roof. Behind them is a garden with two earth closets, and an orchard. Just up the road from them is Mount Cottage, occupied by Mr Shattock: a double-fronted house with two sitting rooms, two small kitchens, three bedrooms, some outbuildings, and a garden and meadow. Next, we come to a cottage which is sideways on to the road: Roberts Cottage (*2018: 14 Boobery*), is occupied by the Cluett family: Walter Cluett is the chief clerk at Norrish's dairy factory, and his son Denis is a schoolboy with a flair for writing. Walter Cluett's stepson, Archie Caudwell, is an apprentice engineer in Tiverton and stays here during the week. The cob and slate house contains a sitting room, kitchen and scullery, and three bedrooms. It has a washhouse, linhay, earth closet, and an adjacent meadow. There is then a bit of a gap until we come to another cottage which is also sideways on to the road. This is Pullens Cottage (*2018: Little Spalsbury*), a two-bedroom cottage with a stable, various outbuildings and two fields of tillage, occupied by Samuel Hellyer, a market gardener.

After passing a few strips of field, we come to a pair of thatched cottages called Smoke Alley (*2018: 22 and 24 Boobery*) occupied by the Church and Tucker families. From here it is just fields until we come to Whitnage Road. If we turn left into Whitnage Road and stay on the left-hand side of the road we soon come to a pair of cottages variously known as Wink Cottages, Higher Mount Pleasant, or Mount Pleasant cottages (*2018: 10 & 12 Whitnage Road*). They belong to the owner of Boehill Barton, a large farm further up the road, and are occupied by farm workers. We will cross the road here and walk back down Whitnage Road, passing Mount Pleasant farm, which belongs to the Taylors. It consists of a house, a cottage, various outhouses, barns and animal pens, as well as surrounding fields.

Smoke Alley

We continue down Whitnage Road until we come to where Buckland Bridge crosses the canal. On the south side of the canal there is a cottage called Wharf Cottage (*2018: Fairview Cottage*), occupied by James Trevellyan, his wife, Edith, and his young daughter, Ivy. It has two kitchens, two bedrooms, a lean-to linhay, and an earth closet. It is situated in a corner of the Cricket Field, and near the cottage by the canal there is an open-air swimming pool directly connected to the canal through an arch in the wall. Both the cricket ground and swimming bath are used by the St Boniface boys. Given that a lot of sewage ends up in the canal, the swimming pool may not be very pleasant! Walking further down the road we pass another field on our left called Little Buckland, and on the right is a field known as Fairfield which is used for livestock sales on Sampford Fair days. Finally, we come to the junction with Lower Town.

Lower Town and Chains

Turning left into Lower Town from Whitnage Road, the first building we come to is Mountain Oak Farm, a four-bedroom house with a dairy, a stable, barns and outhouses. The farm also owns Easton field across the road. There is a track called Easton Lane, formerly called Sowtry Lane, crossing the field which leads to Easton Cottages: a house and a cottage (*which in 2018 no longer exist*). The house has a kitchen, wash-house, pantry, parlour and four bedrooms, but it is old and in poor repair. Adjoining it there is a cottage and a pighouse. The water supply is a well in the lane.

Back on Lower Town and continuing away from the village we come to Moor End Cottage (*2018: Moor End House*), and then Moor End Villa, a modern brick and slate dwelling house occupied by Charles Hussey, the undertaker. There are some older cottages called Moor End Cottages a little further along and set back from the road. The road splits near Moor End Cottage, with one road heading towards Westleigh and Holcombe Rogus, and the other curving round past a pair of cottages known as 'Little Turberfield Cottages, Moor End', then Little Turberfield farm and Jersey cottage, which is split into two dwellings, one of which is occupied by the Hine family. Little Turberfield Farm is owned by the Pedlers, who also own Sampford Barton, and is occupied by the Case family. As well as a five-bedroom house the farm has a variety of farm buildings, a pump house, and a cottage which is used as a dairy. The road runs down towards Sampford Siding on the Great Western Railway line, then turns left just after Spratford Brook, crosses the railway, and continues to Waterloo Cross. Trains do not stop here – the nearest station is at Tiverton Junction, in Willand.

Smithy and Pullens House on left, Turberfield House on right

The Jennings' new and old shops

Returning to Lower Town we walk back towards the village, past fields and orchards on the left, until we come to Turberfield House, occupied until recently by Dr MacDonald and his family, from New Zealand, but now occupied by Dr Mitchell Browne. The house contains a dining room, drawing room, passage, surgery, greenhouse, kitchen, scullery and larder. Upstairs there are four bedrooms, a bathroom to which water is pumped up from a pump in the yard, and three other rooms. There are a number of outhouses and linhays, including a coach house and a stable. The house also has its own orchard.

Staying on the south side of Lower Town we walk past more orchards until we come to a brand-new shop (*2018: 27 Lower Town*) which belongs to the Jennings family, built next to the old thatched cottage (*2018: 25 Lower Town*) which used to be the Jennings' shop and is now home to Mr and Mrs Jennings senior. Their son Charles is a keen photographer and is also rather eccentric: for example he likes to ride his bicycle backwards! He runs the shop which sells general groceries and newspapers, with help from his mother.

The next three cottages are set back a little from the road (*2018: 23-19 Lower Town*), and the middle one of the three is also known as the Police House. PC Fewings used to live here, and now it is occupied by PC

Lower Town – 3 cottages behind wall on left, then the Hare and Hounds, Kings Cottages and Morrells

Blackmore and his family. After these cottages we come to another pub, where we can stop for a drink or a bite to eat. This large thatched building is called the Hare and Hounds (*2018: Coronation Cottages, 17-11 Lower Town*). As well as the pub there is a yard, stabling and an orchard, but the buildings are old and in poor repair. The pub used to be run by the Dunns, but now the landlord is Allan Gunn, who lives here with his family. He also works as a thatcher.

There is a small track separating the pub from the next set of buildings, known as Kings Cottages (*2018: where 5 and 7 Lower Town are located*). It is a block of four cottages with another cottage and pasture behind. The first cottage is a coal depot, with attached coal yard, owned by George Small Ltd of Uffculme. The manager is Mr James Hill, who delivers coal by horse and wagon.

Continuing up the road, we come to Morrells House, occupied by Mrs Wallington, who runs a girls' boarding school here, with the help of her daughters. Downstairs it has the usual rooms plus a schoolroom, and upstairs there are four bedrooms, a servant's bedroom, and a WC. Outside

Looking down Lower Town, Bridge House and Red House on left, Merriemeade and Ivy Grove on right

it has a garden, another WC, a potting shed, and against the road there is a stable with a loft over it.

Just past the house is Morrells farm, and then we come to Merriemeade House (*2018: the Merriemeade pub*), occupied by the Norrish family. The nearby creamery or dairy factory in Chains Road was established by Mr R S Norrish. He died in 1907 so the business is now run by his sons, William and Richard Norrish. William and his large family live in Merriemeade House, having recently moved in from the neighbouring Ivy Grove. Downstairs Merriemeade House has two sitting rooms, two kitchens, a back kitchen, two larders, a room used as a billiard room, and a verandah. On the first floor there are eight bedrooms, a lavatory, a WC, and a bathroom with hot and cold water (a rare luxury!). On the second floor there is an attic. Outside there are various buildings including a stable and a kitchen garden with a greenhouse. The next property along, Ivy Grove, formerly known as Smiths (*2018: Cordwangles*), used to be occupied by Mr Norrish but is now occupied by Mr Williams, a shop-keeper. The property consists of a five-bedroom house, a stable, a pump house and farm buildings.

Continuing down Chains Road we come to Kerslakes (*2018: a row of three cottages*) a three-bedroom house with land, an orchard, a yard with work buildings and a stable rented out to Mr Wood, the saddler (*2018:*

Always Cottages on left, Creamery office and Creamery, Chains Cottage and Chains House on right

land now Home Orchard). Next, we come to Norrish's creamery. The modern buildings include a five-bedroom house *(2018: 6, Chains)* with two offices downstairs behind large windows, a store, a scalding room, a dairy refrigerating room, a butter room, and an engine and boiler house. A lot of local men are employed here, but no women. The chief clerk is Walter Cluett – perhaps we'll be able to see him through the office windows. The creamery produces pasteurised milk, butter, cream, and cheese, and sells its products both locally and further afield, transporting them by rail from Tiverton Junction. There are a couple of cottages across the road from it called Always Cottages. Finally, we come to the recently built Chains Cottage *(2018: 8 Chains)* and then Chains House *(2018: Chains Farmhouse),* an old house and adjoining cottage with various sheds and outbuildings. The occupants share an earth closet. They get their drinking water from a pump, and other water from the canal.

Going back to Lower Town, we'll cross the road to the bridge over the canal, where we find the former Post Office, now a private residence as the Post Office has moved to London House. It is a three-bedroom plastered house with a small front garden. Next door is Bridge Cottage or Bridge House, a plastered four-bedroomed house occupied by Mr R Saunders with a stable and outhouses behind it. The adjoining 2 Bridge House, also known

The Post Office near the canal bridge

as Red House (*2018: Red Robin House*), is a modern four-bedroom red brick house occupied by Mr W Saunders, again with a stable and various outhouses including a WC in a yard, and an adjoining garden.

Turning to face downhill we pass some open ground and come to Challis Cottage and then Taudevin's shop in Challis House, which is run by Mrs Taudevin and her son and daughter. This large, double-fronted grocer's shop is perhaps the largest and busiest shop in the village. There are four bedrooms upstairs and stable and other buildings outside. Next door is Challis, a house and butcher's shop owned by Mr Williams, with outbuildings and a slaughterhouse. We then come to another pub and stop for a drink in The Globe Inn, next to Providence House (*2018: part of the Globe*). The Globe has five bedrooms and a lavatory upstairs. Downstairs we find a dining room, bar, cellar, 2 larders, two kitchens, a pump house and a tool house. In the yard there is an attached skittle alley. Outside it has a 6-stall stable with loft and WC, a pig sty, a small garden, and an orchard. Providence House has five bedrooms and the usual downstairs rooms. It also has a pump and a stable, pig houses, a wood house, a granary, a cider press and a WC.

The next property is a very large building which used to be a school but which in 1907 became the St Boniface Home for boys, run by the 'Church

St Boniface Home

19

of England Society for Waifs and Strays' who take in boys who are homeless or whose families cannot look after them for one reason or another. The many rooms include individual and communal bedrooms, a dining room, bathrooms, and a chapel. Unusually it is lit by acetylene gas. The home houses about 60 boys aged between 7 and 14, and a number of staff members to look after them, under the direction of the Superintendent, Mr Keeley, and his wife, Lucy, who acts as the matron. The boys are regularly seen going through the village in a procession to attend the village school or church. When they reach the age of 14 they have to leave. Some find jobs in the local area, some join the army or navy, and some are encouraged to emigrate, mainly to Canada.

After St Boniface Home there is a group of eight small cottages, five in front, which are thatched, and three with slate roofs behind them. We now walk past some open ground through which runs the stream, until we come to the buildings opposite Turberfield, which all belong to Mr Down, the Veterinary Surgeon. First, there are two cottages and a smith's shop run by John Arthurs. The smithy is a big draw for local children, and as well as shoeing horses he is always busy making and mending all manner of implements, machines, and vehicles. Then we come to the main house (*2018: Pullens House, 30 Lower Town*) which has four bedrooms, a bathroom, and the vet's surgery, as well as various outhouses in a yard behind the house.

View of canal showing the backs of houses in Turnpike

Turnpike

Returning to the junction of Lower Town and Chains, we will now cross the bridge over the canal and walk along Turnpike. The first property on the left is a house and shop called Rose Cottage (*2018: Wharf House*), owned and occupied by Henry Wood, the Saddler, Parish Council Clerk, and captain of the fire brigade. There is still a huge demand for saddles and harnesses in the area. As well as the shop there is a workshop, harness room, stable, and coach house. Adjoining this property is Wharf Cottage, which is occupied by Henry Wood's daughter, Sarah Ann, and her husband, Edwin Vickery, a tailor. Its garden slopes down to the canal, where there is a small wharf. There are several more cottages along this side of Turnpike including Wharf Cottage (*2018: 4 Turnpike*): a plastered house with three bedrooms and two box rooms, which was occupied by the Reverend Rees before he moved into the Rectory. Further along Turnpike we come to Laburnum Cottage (*2018: Bowdens, 10 Turnpike*), a plaster and slate house of superior character. The last property along here is Boobiers Farm, which includes a 4-bedroom house, land and outbuildings.

Across the road, on the north side of Turnpike, there is a group of buildings formerly called Norths, and now called Ivydene. One is a 6-bedroom house which was once two cottages, one with two and one with four bedrooms (*2018: Worths, 7 Turnpike*). Adjoining the property there is a workshop, machine shop and joiner's shop. A new 3-bedroomed house has just been built in the garden of this property. Next, we come to Turnpike Cottage, occupied by Thomas Ponsford, a fly proprietor. A fly is a small carriage or horse-drawn cab, which he rents out. The property includes a stable and a lot of old sheds and adjoins the footpath which runs down from Higher Town. A pump is situated in the road here. After the footpath there are no more buildings on this side of the road until we get back to where we started, at the canal bridge.

Thank you for joining us, we hope you enjoyed the walk, and don't forget to clean your boots when you get home!

The Saunders family by the canal bridge

The village during the war

Recruiting for the war

When war was declared between Great Britain and Germany at 11pm on 4 August 1914, a recruitment campaign for the Army had to begin with all speed. The British Army of about 700,000 men, of which number about 300,000 were reservists, was small in comparison with those of France and Germany. It was expected that many more of the population of over 5 million men of fighting age would be needed.

News spread to Sampford Peverell surprisingly quickly, despite the absence of television or radio at the time. The primary means of receiving news was by newspapers, of which there were many: national papers produced in London and sent down by rail; Devon newspapers produced in Plymouth or Exeter and distributed similarly; and local newspapers printed in many of the larger towns. By this means, news of the declaration of war was received the following day, and then spread around the village by word of mouth (there being only one telephone, which was in the Post Office). The first call for volunteers appeared in the National newspapers on 6th August, under the headline 'Your King and Country needs You', in which unmarried men aged between 18 and 30

Your King and Country Need You.

A CALL TO ARMS.

An addition of 100,000 men to his Majesty's Regular Army is immediately necessary in the present grave National Emergency.

Lord Kitchener is confident that this appeal will be at once responded to by all those who have the safety of our Empire at heart.

TERMS OF SERVICE.

General Service for a period of 3 years or until the war is concluded.

Age of Enlistment between 19 and 30.

HOW TO JOIN.

Full information can be obtained at any Post Office in the Kingdom or at any Military depot.

GOD SAVE THE KING!

Western Morning News 11 Aug 1914. *Image reproduced with kind permission of The British Newspaper Archive (www.britishnewspaperarchive.co.uk) ©THE BRITISH LIBRARY BOARD. ALL RIGHTS RESERVED* were encouraged to contact their local Recruiter, via their Post Office. A day later, one of the Devon newspapers, the Western Times, was reporting on a contingent of Army Reservists parading through Exeter in the hope of attracting more recruits. At the same time, elsewhere in the county, horses and wagons were being requisitioned by the Army and railway workers were being recruited in considerable numbers. Nobody could have missed the changes that were taking place, and the ever-growing pressure on the unmarried young men to 'do their duty'.

In the event, it seems that the initial surge of volunteers rapidly overwhelmed the local Army recruitment centres, which had to register them and arrange for their training. The standards of physical fitness were raised, and a minimum height requirement set to stem the flow. However, at a national level, Lord Kitchener was adamant that more recruits were needed, and the following notice appeared in the Devon and Exeter Gazette on 1st September 1914:

> The crisis is so great, and the need for more recruits, in addition to the one hundred thousand men just raised, is so vital to the interests of the country that Lord Kitchener has inquired of the Leaders of the great political parties if they should jointly agree that their organisations would give their full co-operation in securing more men...

In the Sampford Peverell column of a local newspaper[2], it was stated that '17 [men] from this Parish are with the colours in various parts of the world', i.e. serving with the armed forces. These were men who had enrolled with the Regular Army, Territorial Army, or the Navy before the outbreak of hostilities. We have managed to identify sixteen of them.

Recruitment at the local level proved to be the most effective, as evidenced by the number of men who volunteered after an open-air meeting was held in the courtyard of St Boniface Home in Sampford on 9th September[3]. The meeting was presided over by County Councillor John Pedler, from Sampford Barton farm, with visiting dignitaries from Tiverton and various Army recruiters present. The powerful speeches made, together with the singing of the National Anthem to the accompaniment of St Boniface Home bugle band, persuaded several young Sampford men to give their names on the spot. The next day, Sergeant Beer returned to take 'nearly 20 recruits to Tiverton', including 15 who were specifically named in the report. Not all of these men were necessarily accepted because they may

---

[2] The Devon and Somerset News of 27th August
[3] Western Times, 11th Sep 1914

The Devons on parade in Tiverton in October 1914

not have met the required standards at the time, but amongst those who were recruited were the brothers Walter and Lewis Gale: Walter was to become the first Sampford-born man to die in the war. After five weeks at war, the first significant body of men from the Parish had signed up, and many more were to follow in their footsteps.

Despite this initial surge of recruits, the take-up across Devon began to dwindle. Daily tallies were reported, by county, in the newspapers. On one day, 15th October, it was reported that, for the whole of Devon, only 3 new recruits enrolled - the lowest number on any day since War recruitment began[4]. No doubt as a consequence of this, some of the required standards were dropped, and the minimum height level lowered (generally, but not universally, to 5 feet 5 inches). This did little to improve the flow of new recruits, and in September a call went out to all ex-NCOs to re-enlist.

A survey by parish of all men recruited into the Royal Navy, Army or Territorial Force carried out by Devon County Council was reported in the Exeter and Plymouth Gazette on 11 December 1914. The survey showed that just 27 Sampford Peverell men had joined up so far.

---

[4] Western Times, 17th October 1914

He did not mention, although it was

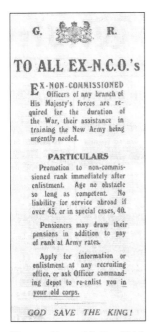

G. R.

TO ALL EX-N.C.O.'s

EX-NON-COMMISSIONED Officers of any branch of His Majesty's forces are required for the duration of the War, their assistance in training the New Army being urgently needed.

PARTICULARS

Promotion to non-commissioned rank immediately after enlistment. Age no obstacle so long as competent. No liability for service abroad if over 45, or in special cases, 40.

Pensioners may draw their pensions in addition to pay of rank at Army rates.

Apply for information or enlistment at any recruiting office, or ask Officer commanding depot to re-enlist you in your old corps.

GOD SAVE THE KING!

Western Times 30 Nov 1914. Image reproduced with kind permission of The British Newspaper Archive (www .britishnewspaperarchive.co.uk) ©THE BRITISH LIBRARY BOARD. ALL RIGHTS RESERVED

By 9th November, Lord Kitchener was able to report at the Guildhall in London[5] that 'the Kitchener Million' recruits target had been met. But it did not stop there; 'I shall want more men and still more' became his next campaign message. He did not mention, although it was reported elsewhere, that he now sought a further one million men, or that the casualty rate at that point was one in five. The situation was dire and the need for more men was desperate.

More locally, Earl Fortescue, as Lord Lieutenant of the county, called an all-party political meeting, open to the public, in Exeter on 23rd November. In it, he reinforced Lord Kitchener's message, emphasising that the county of Devon had done poorly in recruitment terms when compared with other counties. He called upon farmers, tradesmen and shopkeepers to release their sons to come forward in large numbers, making clear that they needed 'to avail themselves more of women's labour and of older boys, so that the men could be released'. With the other political leaders endorsing his conclusions, arrangements were made to set up cross-party Divisional Committees and to start canvassing to persuade the local populace to do their patriotic duty.

Despite these good intentions there are very few references in newspapers to Divisional Recruitment Committees being established in the following months and neither Devon County Council, Tiverton Rural District Council, nor Sampford Peverell Parish Council appear to have played any part in the ensuing recruitment drive[6]. It would seem that the message expressed time and again by Lord Kitchener - 'more men and still more' - was expected to be sufficient to prick the consciences of those holding back from volunteering.

Word was getting back to Sampford Peverell about conditions on the front line. The Western Times of 24th December 1914 carried this interesting

---

[5] Western Mail, 10th November 1914
[6] sources: newspaper reports of meetings; for SPPC, its own minutes

report under the Sampford Peverell heading:

> Bombardier G. Lock, of the R.F.A., had a narrow escape from a German shrapnel shell which burst close to him and killed an Indian soldier, who was walking with him along the lines. He describes the incident in a letter to his mother, who lives at Higher Town, Sampford Peverell, in the following terms: "The other day I was examining the telephone wire to find out some damage, as I could not speak to my pal, the corporal, who was in the trenches with an Indian Regiment. I was walking along with one of the Indians. I gave him a cigarette, and was just getting out a match to light it when a shrapnel shell burst overhead and killed the Indian on the spot. The bullet went through his heart, and the poor fellow never spoke. I tell you my heart was in my mouth then. There were bullets whistling all around me, and not a soul to be seen alive. To get back safely I had to crawl about a quarter of a mile on my hands and knees along a ditch." In the same letter Bombardier Lock says: "A lot of the German shells do not explode, and they are not so careless of their firing now. They seem to be getting short of ammunition. The British troops are well provided for by the Government; they get plenty of food, and when their boots get leaky they can always get a new pair."

Despite the note of reassurance at the end, such reports must have alarmed those at home.

As the war progressed during 1915, Kitchener's messages, relayed through newspaper columns throughout the country, became more personal. For example, in July 1915 'If you are physically fit, of military age and not engaged in making munitions, don't let it be said that you shirked your duty. Join the Army today.'[7] Married men were now also being encouraged to come forward, their families receiving a 'Separation Allowance' if they enrolled[8].

Alongside Kitchener's messages a new Act came into force in July 1915: The National Registration Act. This put a 'novel and onerous' responsibility upon local authorities to distribute forms to, and collect them from, every household, similar to a census[9]. The registration date was to be 15th August, and it was expected that the work of distributing and collecting the forms would be done by unpaid volunteers. Tiverton Rural District Council discussed the scheme at its July meeting and decided to enlist the help of the Volunteer Training Corps of Cullompton and Uffculme[10].

---

[7] Birmingham Mail, 22nd July 1915
[8] Taunton Courier, 2nd June 1915
[9] Exeter and Plymouth Gazette, 19th July 1915
[10] Western Times, 21st July 1915

It is not until October 1915 that there is a newspaper report concerning the Tiverton Divisional Parliamentary Recruitment Committee[11]. This committee met in Exeter, presided over by Sir Ian Heathcoat Amory, with a large attendance of interested parties. Its aim was to adopt 'Lord Derby's scheme', whereby those potential recruits not in a 'starred' occupation would be approached by appointed local canvassers to try to persuade them to volunteer. The selected canvassers were expected to be too old to fight, to have some knowledge of those whom they were going to meet, but not to bring undue influence upon them. They were to complete a record at each meeting, noting the reasons for refusal, if that was the case. They were also empowered to tell the men that if they volunteered, then they did so for the duration of the war; but if

Exeter & Plymouth Gazette 25 May 1915
Image reproduced with kind permission of The British Newspaper Archive (www.britishnewspaperarchive.co.uk) ©THE BRITISH LIBRARY BOARD. ALL RIGHTS RESERVED

they left it until pressed, then they may perhaps be expected to join for five or seven years. The exercise had to be completed by the end of November, and all records were to be sent to London.

The Exeter meeting was quickly followed by one in Tiverton[12], where appointments were made. The canvasser appointed for Sampford Peverell was Mr E Pearce, from the Parish Council. The parish was said to have 54 eligible men (this was not exceptional - Halberton had 88 and Uplowman 22). In the days that followed, 'Lord Derby's scheme' was spelt out more clearly by the politicians. In the words of a journalist writing under the appropriate pen-name of 'Miles Veteranus' for the Exeter & Plymouth Gazette[13] "...today, single as well as married men know how they stand.

---

[11] Western Times, 30th Oct 1915
[12] Exeter & Plymouth Gazette, 3rd Nov 1915
[13] 16th November 1915

The former must go first or be fetched; the latter of recruitable age should present themselves at the recruitment office. If fit, they will be attested and passed to their class in the Reserves." The intention was that those enlisted as reservists should be encouraged to join the Volunteer Training Corps (VTC), where they would receive their preliminary training. This would not only save a lot of money, but would also mean that they could be deployed more rapidly into active service as the need arose.

Lord Derby's scheme, however, was merely the precursor to what, by now, had become inevitable: conscription. On 27 January 1916 the Military Service Act was implemented, which decreed that every single or widowed male between the ages of 19 and 41 and without dependent children had to enlist for active service or as a reserve, unless he met certain exceptions. An example from the list of exceptions was 'being a regular minister of any religious denomination'. There were, however, four possible reasons why a person could apply for exemption:

- if it was in the national interest that he should be engaged in other work;
- if serious hardship would ensue;
- ill health or infirmity; or
- conscientious objection.

Should a man wish to claim exemption on any of these grounds, he would have to state his case at a local tribunal, and if successful, would be granted a certificate of exemption. For Sampford Peverell, the local tribunal was Tiverton Rural District Tribunal, which was set up in February 1916 to deal with claims of exemption and which met frequently in the months that followed.

Newspapers reported the results of each Tribunal sitting, which would have been read with great interest. The first such report to appear concerning a man from Sampford Peverell was the case of Percy Bradfield, assistant master of St Boniface Home[14]. The Master of the Home was at the Front and had been wounded, so an application was made for postponement in respect of Percy Bradfield, which was granted until such time as the Master could return and resume his duties. Nevertheless, the Tribunal made the point that the job of assistant master could be done by a man over military age, so postponement would only be for a short while. (*Percy Bradfield did join up subsequently and appears in the casualty list*).

---

[14] Devon & Somerset News, 10 February 1916

A week later a Sampford Peverell market gardener appeared at the Tiverton tribunal[15]. He had passed the army medical despite having had pleurisy when he was younger and "I quite depended on it that I should not be passed, but I made a mistake". This led to laughter in the court! He asked for exemption as his mother was an old-age pensioner and would not live with anyone else. The exemption was granted, perhaps due to his occupation as well as his dependent mother. This was one of only two exemptions granted that day out of fourteen applications.

Another Sampford Peverell man to appear before the tribunal[16] was William Saunders, who sought to have his call-up 'starred' (i.e. postponed for an indefinite period) until his father, who was suffering from the effects of an accident, could work again. His application was refused. Of the 15 other cases considered by the Tribunal on that day, and reported by the newspaper, 4 were refused, 6 were given leave for one month only, 4 were granted exemption and one decision was deferred. Even those whose objection was on conscientious grounds were not necessarily granted exemption. The message must have gone out that exemptions would be very hard to win.

Norrish and Sons' Creamery of Chains Road, Sampford Peverell, applied for exemption for 2 of its senior staff: Henry Lovell, the dairy engineer and Walter Cluett, the secretary and managing clerk. The military granted exemption to the latter but did not consider that Lovell was indispensable. During the hearing[17], Mr W H Norrish, the Creamery's proprietor, stated that 9 out of 14 men from the creamery had joined voluntarily and none had been appealed for. They had been replaced by women and boys and older men. On this occasion, the military also agreed to exemption for Mr Norrish himself.

However, after a subsequent tightening of the criteria for exemption, the military appealed the decision about Mr Norrish two

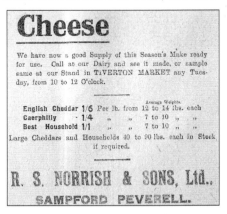

Devon & Somerset News 28 Jun 1917

---

[15] Western Morning News, 19 February 1916
[16] Western Times, 16 March 1916
[17] Devon & Somerset News 25th May 1916

years later, which was reported as follows[18]:

> Some of us would like to know where all the cheese goes' laughingly remarked the Chairman (of the Tribunal hearing) to William Henry Norrish, one of the proprietors of a creamery and milling business at Sampford Peverell. It was stated by Mr Norrish, for whom Mr L.D. Thomas appeared, that they made and dealt with large quantities of butter, a great deal of cheese also being made and disposed of.- Mr Norrish mentioned that some of the cheese went to farmers.- The Chairman: 'Because they have so many other things to eat. You don't send any cheese to Tiverton, do you?' - (Laughter) - Mr Norrish: 'Oh yes we do'. In dismissing the military appeal, the Chairman told Mr Norrish to go on making as much cheese as he could.

Appeals were heard at the Exeter Tribunal, to which 19-year-old Arthur Sidney Bass of Sampford Peverell took his case[19]. He had been refused exemption by the Tiverton Tribunal, to which he had applied as the sole employee (a cattleman) of his father, who was ill. His appeal was rejected, because his employment was listed as a carpenter on the national register. William Saunders also appealed, unsuccessfully. This is a draft of the appeal letter from his father:

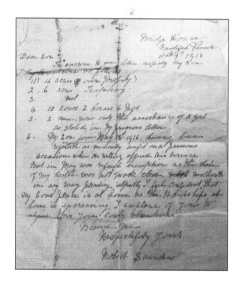

The military could also lodge an appeal, as they did in the case of Sampford Peverell's Stanley Williams, proprietor of a butcher's shop and cattle farmer who did most of his own slaughtering[20]. In this case, the conditional exemption granted to him by the local tribunal was set aside; instead, he was granted exemption, but only until the end of the year.

Stanley Williams did join up in 1917, and his land and business were taken over by his brother Edward, who was on the Parish Council. Shortly afterwards it was the 33-year-old, married, Edward's turn to face the Tribunal, because he also sought exemption. A year earlier his trade was given as cattle dealer, but now he maintained that, because he looked after

---

[18] Western Times of 18th May 1918
[19] Western Times, 29th March 1916
[20] Western Times, 14th July 1916

cattle on 75 acres of his own and his brother's land, slaughtered animals and carried on the butchery business, he was in all respects a farmer, whose work was in the national interest. After much questioning and debate amongst the Tribunal panel members, he was granted 6 months conditional exemption, to which the military said that they would appeal.

Those men who were enrolled as reservists were allocated into a 'Class' related to the year of their birth, and they were notified that they would be called up by Class. Class 1 was for those born in 1897. They were 18 years old. They were told they would not be called up until they were aged 19. Class 2 was for those born in 1896, Class 3 for 1895 and so on up to Class 23 for those born in 1875. A public proclamation was placed in prominent spots, advising the date on which a particular Class would begin call up. This was deemed to be sufficient notice, but in addition, generally, each man received an individual notification. It was the individual's responsibility to be alert to such notices and to report himself for duty. There were penalties for not reporting and for inducing or assisting a reservist to absent himself.

Nationally, conscription was not popular: 200,000 people demonstrated against it in Trafalgar Square in April 1916. By then the cost in human life was becoming apparent. Popular or not, it was beginning to achieve its objective. A second Act passed in May 1916 extended conscription to married men, and by the end of the year an additional 1.1 million men had enlisted, including some married men from Sampford Peverell. Further refinements to the system were made in 1917, reducing the number of 'certified occupations' said to be in the national interest. Employers were asked to find substitutes for staff affected in order to accommodate the change.

The recruitment need was not confined to men for the Army, as was made clear in the Army and Navy Gazette on 22 July 1916. The Admiralty recruiting officer was quoted as saying: 'the impression spread abroad that men called to the Colours under the Military Service Act cannot join the Navy is entirely erroneous'. At that time, the Navy was keen to recruit fitters and turners between the ages of 21 and 45, whether married or single, and had their own recruitment offices, of which the most convenient for Sampford Peverell men were in Exeter and Devonport. In the following year, recruitment also extended to the recently created Royal Naval Air Service[21].

---

[21] Western Morning News 19th December 1917

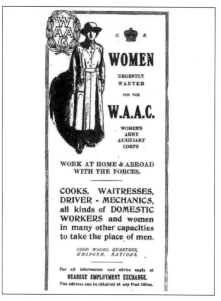

Western Morning News 19 Dec 1917. Image reproduced with kind permission of The British Newspaper Archive (www.britishnewspaperarchive.co.uk) ©THE BRITISH LIBRARY BOARD. ALL RIGHTS RESERVED

Western Morning News 17 Sep 1917. Image reproduced with kind permission of The British Newspaper Archive (www.britishnewspaperarchive.co.uk) ©THE BRITISH LIBRARY BOARD. ALL RIGHTS RESERVED

Recruitment of women became more and more prominent as the war progressed. The Women's Army Auxiliary Corps (WAAC) was established in 1917 to help with the war in France, mostly fulfilling the roles of cooks and waitresses to start with. An appeal for recruits to the WAAC was made in the Exeter and Plymouth Gazette of 16 May 1917, in which both married and single women were sought between the ages of 20 and 40. "Those women whose husbands are serving with the Army abroad are ineligible for service with the corps in France, though they may serve in England."

A visit to the Guildhall in Plymouth in November 1917 by Sir Auckland Geddes, Minister of National Service, attracted a packed audience and his rousing talk was also reported in detail in the Western Times of 13th November 1917. He set out the Government's plans to recruit more and more people over the coming months, so that the war could be brought to a conclusive end. He talked of needing more men, which the Government would achieve by 'combing out some men from civil occupations', who had so far obtained exemption. He also spoke of wanting 10,000 more women, by the end of the month, to come forward to join the WAAC; women with domestic experience, such as cooks and waitresses and those employed as servants in large households, were his particular target. They were to apply to their local employment exchange, which was acting as a government agency, from where they would be despatched to an appropriate centre with their rail fare paid. It has not proved possible to establish how many of Sampford Peverell's working women, if any, joined the WAAC, because records for them are sparse, but 22 single women were recorded with the occupation of domestic servant, waitress or cook in the 1911 census.

In the final year of the war the age limit for men was raised to 51, in an attempt to compensate for the enormous casualty rate. Our research has found that a further 32 Sampford Peverell men became eligible for military service as a consequence of the raised age limit and this resulted in a new spate of Tribunal hearings. The Western Times of 14th June 1918 reported that 45-year-old Robert Tambling of the New Inn, who was also a market gardener, and 46-year-old Walter Ridler, harness maker, were both referred to the War Agricultural Committee, whereas 45 year old Frederick Taudevin, grocer at 'Challis' in Lower Town, was given two months' exemption. The eventual result of Frederick's appeal is not known, but no military records for any of the 32 older men have been found, indicating that few, if any, actually took part.

During the War 4.8 million men from the UK had been recruited to join the Army, joining the 0.7 million force that was present at the outset. Approximately half of them were volunteers, the remainder having been conscripted under the Military Service Acts. Conscription was retained until 1920 to enable the army to deal with remaining trouble spots in Europe and the Empire.

The Volunteer Training Corps (VTC)

The VTC was established shortly after the beginning of the war as a volunteer home defence force. At this stage of the war, Britain relied entirely upon a voluntary system of enlistment to the armed services, and there were many men who - for family, age, health or other reasons - were unable to sign up. Despite the Government's initial disapproval of the VTC, seeing it as a means for some men to avoid enlistment, the VTC won popular support. Although the Central Association of the VTC gained recognition by the War Office in November 1914, local units were not formally recognised. These local units were set up around the country, but without any financial support. Consequently, the volunteers had to provide their own uniform (which could not be khaki) and a weapon, if they could afford one.

In the early months of 1915 a VTC unit was set up in Uffculme, under the leadership of Bertram Platt Faunthorpe. Born in 1872, he was the son of a clergyman and was brought up in Battersea, London, and then in Blackpool at Rossall School. This private boarding school was the first in the country to set up a cadet force, so it may have been here that Bertram acquired some military training. After leaving Rossall, he went to Keble College Oxford, and then became a schoolmaster in Bromley, Kent (according to the 1901 census). In 1912, still living in Bromley and now working as a tutor, he married Alice Wills. Shortly after the marriage, Alice gave birth to a daughter, Lorna Mary. Perhaps as a result of his changed circumstances, the family moved to Craddock Cottage, Uffculme.

Although the Uffculme detachment of the VTC may not have been recognised by the Government, the Rector of Sampford Peverell Church, Revd Rees, was keen to encourage them. He invited the men, under Commandant Faunthorpe and Police Sergeant Webb, to a Church Parade, as reported in the Devon and Somerset News of 1 April 1915:

> The St Boniface Home Boy Scouts, with their bugle band (under Scoutmaster Bradfield) marched to Uffculme to meet the detachment at their headquarters there. The church was crowded. In his address the Rector said he was proud to welcome the Uffculme Volunteers. There was a call at the present serious crisis for all to do something to show their manliness. That quality might be found among all classes. England wanted today men in whom the current of life was strong; men who would stand by a righteous cause come what might.

On another occasion, 55 men from the Uffculme Corps attended a parade at Cullompton Parish Church[22]. Their leader was now referred to as

---

[22] Western Times 7th June 1915

'Captain' Faunthorpe, and Police Sergeant Webb was described as an able drill instructor. The Vicar, Revd Phillips, conducted the service and exhorted more men to enlist, but acknowledged that the VTC members were unable to go to the front themselves; their role was to defend the Homeland.

A photograph of the Uffculme VTC featured in the Devon and Exeter Gazette on 11 June 1915 entitled "the members of the Uffculme Volunteer Corps at their church parade". It shows between 40 and 50 men, in four rather ragged ranks, dressed in dark suits and an assortment of hats, standing to attention, but with their heads turned and eyes gazing in sundry directions, standing in the middle of a road. At their head is a figure attired in what appears to be a light-coloured riding coat, plus fours, a trilby hat, holding a riding crop, with his head held high - presumably Captain Faunthorpe. In the front rank stands a moustached gentleman in policeman's uniform holding a cane or swagger stick - presumably Sergeant Webb. Perhaps this photo was taken at the Cullompton parade, held a few days earlier.

Photo courtesy of Tiverton Museum of Mid Devon Life

A month later there was another Church appearance by the men. 40 members of the Uffculme VTC went on a route march to Burlescombe Church, where they attended a service conducted by the Vicar, Revd Bramwell. On this occasion, the tone was rather different, as the Vicar gave a forceful address on the essence of Christian character, based on the scriptures.

Later in July 1915, 60 members of the Uffculme VTC underwent their first formal inspection at Bridwell Lawn, Uffculme, with Cullompton Town Band providing "strains of martial music"[23]. They were inspected by Colonel Dundonald Cochrane C B, who commented that they had been well instructed, and they were commended for their mobility and marching. The Colonel talked to them about the formation of a County Regiment, of which the Uffculme detachment would be a part, and said that in a short time, they would receive their brassards (*i.e. arm bands*). These were red and bore the initials GR for Georgius Rex (King George V) to show that they were soldiers of the King.

Given the size that the Uffculme VTC had grown to over the few months of its existence, it is very likely that, by the time of the inspection at Bridwell, its ranks included several Sampford Peverell men. A photograph taken at Bridwell in 1915, probably shortly after the inspection, shows 54 members of the Uffculme Volunteer Training Corps, which included 4 boys. All are smartly dressed in uniforms, with their new brassards proudly displayed on their arms. Judging by the names some of our Sampford Peverell men were amongst them.

The VTC at Bridwell,   *photo courtesy of the Blackdown Archives - www.blackdownarchives.org.uk*

The names attached to the photo are as follows, all Left to Right:
Back row: Hancock, Long, Webber, Cotterrell, Thorn, -, Brice, Crease, -, Alford, Prowse, New, -, -, Norrish, -, -, Hancock, Salter, Tolley.
Middle Row: Lemon, Helyer, Welland, Baker, Bass, Marshall, Williams, Sparkes, -, -, Williams snr, Stevens, White, L Thorn, J Drew.
Front Row: Westcott, -, Charlesworth, Rankmore, Pedlar, Webb, Faunthorpe, Salter, E Crease, Mesney, Laidlaw, D Drew, Ball, D Webber.
Those seated on the ground are not known.

[23] Western Times 28th July 1915

However, it is not until October 1915 that the extent of membership from this parish becomes evident. On the occasion of another inspection, this time by Colonel Kirkwood, officer commanding the Devon Regiment, there is the first mention of the Uffculme VTC including a contingent from Sampford Peverell[24]. In the following month, and copying Sampford Peverell's example, Culmstock was recruiting for volunteers to form its own contingent to come under the Uffculme VTC. The recruitment may have been unsuccessful, because there is no subsequent mention of a Culmstock contingent.

In November 1915 Lord Derby's scheme to recruit additional men to join up was being considered (*see Chapter on Recruitment*). It had now become apparent to the Government that the Volunteer Training Corps could actually assist in the war effort, rather than detract from the available pool of men for 'the front'. It was decided that men who volunteered to join the forces, but whose services were not required straight away, could undergo their initial training with the VTC. This would save money and, at the same time, would reduce the amount of training that the regular forces would have to provide.

Training provided by the VTC was primarily in drill and 'musketry' (*use of the rifle*). Beyond that, it would seem that the extent of training varied from place to place, depending upon the skills and knowledge of the commanding officer. Examples of additional training given were: digging a trench system; guard and escort duties, and preserving public order in the event of a Zeppelin raid. There was some interaction between the various VTC branches in Devon, for example in holding shooting competitions. By November 1915, there were nearby VTC branches at Exeter, Exmouth, Topsham, Crediton, Colyton and Budleigh Salterton, in addition to the Uffculme one (now described as D Company, Cullompton and Uffculme).

Formal recognition of the various Devon VTC branches came in 1916, when they became Volunteer battalions of the local regiment. This led to Government provision of uniforms and equipment, but not of suitable facilities, for which local fund-raising and initiatives were required.

In June 1916, Uffculme VTC was reported to have over 50 members including the small contingent from Sampford Peverell. The members met in a Drill-hall in Uffculme, which had been completed shortly before the war. There, they were trained in drill and indoor shooting, but the need for an outdoor shooting range was such that permission was sought from Tiverton

---

[24] Devon and Somerset News, 21st October 1915

Rural District Council to use a gravel-pit on Uffculme Down. Permission was granted, and the men gave up their free time to create a 100-yard range by clearing the land, in the process levelling an old refuse tip. The Hon. Mrs. Walrond of Bradfield was invited to open the range, and she "graciously officiated and fired the first shot, scoring a bull" (Devon and Somerset News, 13 June 1916). The official opening was followed by a shooting match, in which the Uffculme and Cullompton VTC beat the Uffculme Boy Scouts (narrowly!) and were also victorious over the Exeter A and B Companies. After tea, the Uffculme members and over 100 men of the Exeter Battalion, together with their band of 30 players, paraded and performed drill manoeuvres in Bridwell Park, "attracting numerous visitors from neighbouring places despite the demands of the hay field".

As more and more men were required for the Front, so some were taken from the ranks of the VTC to go on active service. However, membership of the VTC was constantly replenished, because Military Tribunals had the power to require men to join the Volunteer Force, if they could not be released immediately from their civil duties to join up. By the end of the War, it is estimated that more than one third of VTC members nationally had been directed to join by order of a Tribunal.

The VTC was not always regarded in such glowing terms as those found in contemporary newspaper reports. In Sampford Peverell, Denis Cluett, who would have been 11 years old in 1918, recalled (in later life) the VTC as follows: "Most of the men in Sampford belonged to this *[the VTC]* and once a week an ancient retired army captain used to totter out from Tiverton and supposedly teach them the rudiments of drill. Once a month on Sunday afternoons, weather permitting, they went for a route march. The village children did not take these activities very seriously and it was not unusual for them, after Sunday School, to gather on the route of the march where, first ensuring that their lines of escape were clear, they would sing to the hymn tune 'The Church's One Foundation':

We are the Sampford Army

We are the VTC

We cannot drill, we cannot fight

What bloody good are we?

And when we get to Berlin

The Kaiser he will say

Oh Gott! Gott! Gott!

What a bloody fine lot

Are the Sampford VTC

The VTC continued to fulfil its function until the end of the War, after which it was suspended in December 1918 and officially disbanded in 1920. However, the valuable role that volunteers had played was not forgotten, with the foundation of the Territorial Army and Volunteer Reserve coming about in 1920, which continues to this day as the Army Reserve.

4 Questions to the Women of England

1. **Y**OU have read what the Germans have done in Belgium. Have you thought what they would do if they invaded England?

2. Do you realise that the Safety of your Home and Children depends on our getting more men now?

3. Do you realise that the one word "Go" from you may send another man to fight for our King and Country?

4. When the War is over and your husband or your son is asked, "What did you do in the great War?"—is he to hang his head because you would not let him go?

Women of England do your duty! Send your men to-day to join our glorious Army.

God Save the King.

The women of the village in the war

A large part of this book concerns the men who served in the armed forces during the First World War, but in this chapter we want to focus on the women of the village. Women were not allowed to join the armed forces, but they were able to play an active role working as nurses or auxiliary helpers, while some worked in factories or on the land, and others helped keep the working life of the village running smoothly whilst at the same time looking after their families, young and old, and doing whatever they could to help with the war effort.

Women were also the target of a major advertising campaign urging them to allow, and encourage, their men folk to enlist.

This must have presented a terrible dilemma to women who did not want their husbands, sweethearts, brothers or sons to put themselves at risk, but who felt obliged to do their patriotic duty and help the war effort.

One active role which was open to women was that of nursing, and we know of a few women living in, or connected with, the village, who were either professional or volunteer nurses during the war.

Mary Pedler was born on 7th May 1868 in Sampford Peverell, the daughter of William Frederick Pedler, a farmer, and Elizabeth Garnsey Pedler, née Pocock. The Pedlers owned and lived in Sampford Barton. In 1881 the Pedlers had 8 children, 4 servants (housemaid, cook, nursemaid and indoor farm servant), owned 350 acres, and employed 7 men and 2 boys. They went on to have eleven children altogether: seven boys and four girls. Although the family were quite wealthy landowners, several of their children pursued medical careers: one of the boys became a doctor: two became dentists, and two of the girls, Alice and Mary, went into nursing. This was at a time when it was unusual for middle-class women to have careers.

Mary was educated at the Anglo-German college in Clifton, and then trained at University College Hospital in London from January 1892, staying there until January 1898. She then went to South Africa to work as a nurse during the Boer War. She joined the Queen Alexandra's Imperial Military Nursing Service in 1903, and in 1911 was a nursing sister in a barracks in Egypt.

During the first world war Mary worked as an acting matron, and a newspaper article in March 1917 reported that "Miss M Pedlar, acting matron of the Magdalen Camp Military Hospital, Winchester, is one of the nurses to whom the King has awarded the Royal Red Cross Decoration, in recognition of valuable services in connection with the war. Miss Pedlar already holds both the South African medals." She received her award from the King at Buckingham Palace on 31st March 1917. In 1918 she was awarded the 1914 Star, and in 1922, shortly after retiring, she received the Victory or British War Medal.

Mary Pedler's younger sister Alice Pedler was born in Sampford Peverell on 31st Aug 1873. Alice was a pupil at Fairfield college in Exmouth and then became a hospital nurse at the North Eastern Hospital in Tottenham, Middlesex and Guys in London. After a probationary period as a District Nurse in Bloomsbury she became a District Nurse in Cookham from 1904 to 1913, and then in Tamworth until July 1915. From July 1915 until January 1916 she worked as a Red Cross volunteer, giving her home address as Sampford Peverell. After this period, she continued working in Tamworth and then London, finally leaving nursing in 1921, when she was awarded a bronze leaving badge. The remarks in her record in all her placements are similar, saying that she was thorough, conscientious, kind, very interested in and attentive to her patients, and much liked by everyone. In later life Alice and Mary Pedler lived together in Rock House, near Halberton.

Lucy Wallington, née Harris, was born in Wales on 22nd March 1889. In 1909 she married William Claude Wallington, a bank cashier, in Cardiff. In the next year or two William Wallington's mother, Bright Wallington, a widow, moved to Sampford Peverell and set up a girls' school in Morrell's House, opposite the Globe Inn in Lower Town. Her daughters helped her with the

Magdalen Camp military hospital, Winchester

teaching. William and Lucy still lived in Cardiff, but in June 1915 William Wallington came to Sampford Peverell to give away his sister Florence at her wedding. From January to September 1915 Lucy Wallington was a part-time Red Cross volunteer at the Llwynarthern Auxiliary Hospital, Castleton, Cardiff, and was recorded as working for 73 days. She also assisted for a few days at the Dinas Powis Red Cross Hospital that year. Her Red Cross record gives her home address as "Morrell's, Sampford Peverell", so she must have felt that her mother-in-law's house was now her permanent home. Her husband, William, had enlisted in the army in late 1915, at the age of 39. Probably because of his clerical experience he worked in the War Office Records department and in the Pay Corps. Lucy's brother-in-law Charles Wallington was also in the army but he was on active service and died at Ypres in 1917. Lucy was probably living in Sampford then and would have attended his memorial service. In November and December 1918 she again worked as a Red Cross volunteer at the Beaufort War Hospital in Bristol, doing full time nursing work. Her husband William was discharged from the army in 1919, and they settled not far away in Teignmouth.

The nurses mentioned so far were helping the war effort away from the village, but nursing and midwifery skills were also needed in the village, and these were provided by Mrs Elizabeth Moon, née Candy. She was born in Sampford Peverell in 1855, and in 1877 married William Moon, a

Morrells, c1905

herdsman. Her background was very different from that of the Pedler girls, and at the time of her marriage she was unable to sign her own name as her marriage entry in the parish record has an X for her mark. She gave birth to twelve children, of whom only six were still alive in 1911. At least four had died in childhood – two of them, Emma aged 13 and William aged 10 months, within a few weeks of each other in 1894. Perhaps this was one of the reasons that she became a nurse and midwife when her remaining children had grown up. In 1911 they were living in a cottage in Lower Town, next to the Hare and Hounds, with two adult sons: Mark and Enos. Elizabeth is listed as a nurse in the 1909 trade directory, and as a registered midwife in the 1911 census. Registration of midwives was introduced in 1902, and as they had to comply with a long list of rules and regulations it is likely that by this time Elizabeth Moon had not only honed her nursing skills but had learned to read and write. Her sons both fought in the war, and both survived, but it must have been a worrying time for their family. Elizabeth worked throughout the war and was listed in trade directories as a registered midwife until 1923, just a few years before she died in 1927 at the age of 72.

Throughout the country the loss of young men to the war effort meant that businesses had to, reluctantly, start employing women. In Sampford Peverell the only factory was Norrish's Creamery in Chains Road, which produced and sold cream and cheese and supplied milk. Many of the workers had joined the armed services, and they were replaced by women, boys and old men.

In July 1916 a newspaper article[25] reported that:

> Owing to the depletion of the male staff at Messrs R T Norrish's creamery, Sampford Peverell, seven young ladies have been engaged in the butter and cheese departments. They are apparently well able to uphold the Devonshire girl's reputation for adaptability.

These adaptable girls helped to keep the business going through the war years. One of these young women was Alice Morrell, daughter of Mr J Morrell of Barton Cottage, Sampford Peverell. She married William Henry Osmond, a Royal Marine, in March 1919, and the newspaper report of the wedding says that their presents included "a handsome dinner cruet from Mr W Morrish [sic], where the bride has been employed for the past three years." After the war, adverts for workers specifically asked for men again; for instance, an advertisement for Norrish's in March 1919, perhaps needing a replacement for Alice, stated "Cheesemaker (male,

---

[25] Western Times 28th July 1916

good) wanted Lady-day. One with factory experience preferred." This preference for employing male workers was a common problem for women after the war, when returning servicemen needed work, and it was felt they should take back the jobs that women had been doing.

There were quite a few shops in the village during the first world war, and with so many men being away at war these were usually run by women and older men, with help from female relatives or

assistants. It was, in any case, often a male shopkeeper's wife who ran the administrative side of a business.

The main bakery in the village was Thomas's bakery in Higher Town, which was run by a brother and sister: Charles and Minnie Thomas. Holloways, the grocers and drapers in Higher Town, was run by Samuel Holloway, with help from his daughter Millford, until his death in 1916. His son, Samuel Cromwell Holloway, was on active service in the war, so was not able to help. The Holloway family continued to own the shop, but the running of it was taken over by Laura Chidgey, a grocer and draper, with bread supplied by her son William, a baker. The Jennings' grocery shop in Lower Town was largely run by Ellen Jennings, with her son Charles gradually taking on more of the responsibility. Mrs Caroline Taudevin, a widow, ran the very busy Taudevin's shop in Challis, Lower Town, with the help of her daughter Ethel, her son Frederick, and Frederick's wife Beatrice. Another son, Wilfred, was on active service and died in 1917.

The pubs in the village had male licensees, but in most, perhaps all, cases, the landlords were helped by their wives and families. The landlord of the Globe from 1916 onwards was William Parsons. As well as running the pub he and his wife, Miriam, had four children aged between five and eleven to look after. Miriam was probably under a lot of pressure and one evening, at 10.30 pm on 17th August, she vented her feelings in what she probably thought was the privacy of her own home. Unfortunately she was overheard by PC Blackmore who charged her with "using obscene language within hearing of the highway".

Meanwhile, at the Post Office, the sub-postmistress was getting into much more serious trouble. At the start of the war the Post Office was run by Rosa Jennings, the sub-postmistress, in London House, Higher Town. She had worked in the Post Office business all her life, and took over from her husband after his retirement in 1902. Rosa retired in 1915 when she reached the age of 60, and on 1st May 1915 Maud Taylor, an assistant for many years, was appointed sub-postmistress. Maud Taylor, born in Sampford Peverell in 1876, had moved away from the village for a while and in 1901 she lived in Torquay where she worked in the railway refreshment room. By 1911, now 35, she was back in Higher Town, Sampford Peverell, nursing her consumptive older brother who died that same year. She may have been appointed postmistress in 1915 due to the shortage of men in the village caused by the war, but she also had good practical experience. In his memoirs Dennis Cluett wrote that Miss Taylor was "a rather sweet but very dreamy middle-aged spinster". He also said that telegrams were assumed to bring bad news so there was never any hurry about delivering them:

> If one arrived for someone in one of the outlying farms Miss Taylor would wait until the end of school and then get one of the children going in that particular direction to deliver it. Telegrams for anyone in the village proper were delivered by Bert Cornish, and what with his one good leg and two crutches he was not a notably fast mover. In addition to this he was in the habit of stopping to discuss the contents of the telegram with everyone he happened to meet. Although this made for rather long delivery times, thanks to the astonishing efficiency of the village bush telegraph it usually happened that the person to whom the telegram was addressed knew all about it before the actual message arrived.

Unfortunately, it eventually became apparent that Maud Taylor was 'borrowing' money to pay for alcohol. She was found guilty of fraud and of falsifying accounts and was sentenced to 12 months in prison. Further details of the case can be found in the chapter on Public Services. Soon after this, on 6th December 1917, the Post Office business was taken over by Frederick Thomas Goffin, who moved the Post Office to Bridge Cottage where he ran it, without a hint of scandal, for many years.

Female staff were needed in schools and children's homes during the war. The headmaster of the Sampford Peverell village school was Mr John Smith, and he was assisted by his wife, Mary who also played an active role at the school. One of the teachers was a Miss Turner, who was given leave of absence on 15th June 1917 to meet her brother before his departure to the Front. The meeting had to be postponed as he failed to get leave but it eventually happened on 11th July. She may have been one of eight different teachers who were appointed to teach needlework during the war, most or all of whom would have been women.

A private girls' school was run at Morrell's by Mrs Wallington. They took in a number of girls as boarders and taught them more subjects than were covered at most primary schools. Mrs Wallington was helped by her daughters, especially Dorothy, who did most of the teaching.

The St Boniface Home for Waifs and Strays in Lower Town also employed a number of women. The Superintendent at the start of the war was William Keeley, and he was assisted by his wife, Lucy Keeley, as the Matron of the home. She continued to act as Matron after her husband joined the army in the early months of the war. The home also employed some local women to help with cooking, cleaning and laundry.

Many of the women of Sampford Peverell were involved in raising funds or supplying items or services to help the war effort. In the early months of the war a collection was made for the Devonshire Patriotic Fund. Five people went around the village asking for donations, and these included two women: Miss Pedler, who must have been Edith Pedler, a sister of the nurses Mary and Alice, and Mrs Taudevin, who ran the large shop in Lower Town. The sums donated ranged from pounds to a few pence, and all the donors are listed on the Sampford Peverell Society's website: https: //spsocresearch.weebly.com/ww1.html. They include the names of 49 women who contributed in their own right, even when some had husbands who were also contributing.

The chapter on fundraising describes the items that were made or donated to help the troops. These items were largely collected or produced by the women and children of the village, who wanted to help in whatever way they could. A whist drive to raise money for the Red Cross in 1917 was attended by over 200 people, and of the six prizewinners, five were women. Two of these ladies won men's prizes, as the shortage of men meant they had to play as men in their pairs. The work to help the Belgian refugees, described elsewhere in this book, was also largely done by the women of the village, such as Mrs Jennings, Mrs Heslop, and especially Maud Wood, who kept in touch with the refugee family after their eventual return to Belgium.

We know from the 1911 census that many women in the village already did paid agricultural work - for instance working on farms as dairymaids or general helpers - but more got involved with farming as the war progressed. During 1916, as more and more young men were being called up, the

Government decided that women should be encouraged to fill the jobs being vacated, wherever possible. In some parts of the country women were recruited as farm hands, but in Devon there seems to have been little appetite to do so. Reasons suggested for this reluctance were: that farmers did not trust women to do heavy work; the perceived difficulties that could arise by unrelated women living on the farm; and the need for additional labour at that time was not desperate[3]. In order to persuade the Devon farming community that there were benefits to employing women, the Under Secretary for Agriculture, Mr Francis Acland MP, enlisted the help of his uncle, Sir Thomas Acland. Sir Thomas was the owner of the Killerton estate, south of Cullompton, who arranged for a demonstration of farming by women to take place on his land in the summer of 1916[26].

The farming demonstration was in the form of a competition, with the majority of the competitors being single young ladies, many of them wearing 'different designs of semi-masculine attire'. They undertook such tasks as ploughing, sheep-shearing, manure-spreading and milking, and prizes were awarded at the end of the day. Land owners and farmers came from miles around, with the number of spectators reported to be over 1000. Perhaps some of Sampford Peverell's farmers were present on that day.

The newspaper report concluded that 'the consensus of opinion seemed to be that the demonstration proved women to be of greater and more varied service on the land than old and grudging prejudice had been willing to concede in the past'. In his speech to the assembled crowd, Francis Acland pressed farmers 'to do their bit' by employing women and paying them 'a reasonable, proper and liberal wage'.

There is limited evidence that farmers did actually change their employment practices in Sampford Peverell. Perhaps they did not need to as there was a good supply of teenage boys – too old for school, but too young to be called up – in the village. It was also the case that many women in local farming

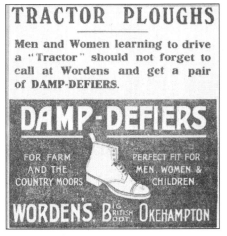

TRACTOR PLOUGHS

Men and Women learning to drive a "Tractor" should not forget to call at Wordens and get a pair of DAMP-DEFIERS.

DAMP-DEFIERS

FOR FARM AND THE COUNTRY MOORS
PERFECT FIT FOR MEN, WOMEN & CHILDREN.

WORDENS. BRITISH BOOT. OKEHAMPTON

Western Times 14 Jun 1918. Image reproduced with kind permission of The British Newspaper Archive (www.british newspaperarchive.co.uk) ©THE BRITISH LIBRARY BOARD. ALL RIGHTS RESERVED

---

[26] Western Times 2 June 1916

families were already working the land as a matter of course. Arthur Bass told his son that when he was called up in 1916 he appealed "as his father had a hernia and there was a lot to be done on the small farm which included an Uffculme milk round. But there were three sisters at home who were not afraid of hard work, so there was little hope of getting off." He added that "the pony and trap milk round was taken over by Minnie", his 14-year-old sister. Thomazine Ridler, wife of Walter Ridler, the harness-maker, told her grand-daughter that she used to work in the fields during the war, when help was needed with planting.

When two women did take up such employment, it was considered to be of sufficient interest to be reported upon in the local newspaper: "Miss B

A Real Necessity for

**WOMEN
WAR-WORKERS.**

WOMEN war-workers find that the grit and grime of the munition factories, exacting hospital work, and exposure to sudden weather changes are injurious to the skin.

Fortunately, they have in Ven-Yusa Cream a preparation which, by means of its special oxygen properties, revives the lustre of faded complexions and brings back the bloom of health and youth to pallid cheeks.

Thousands of women know from personal experience that no other toilet cream can be so invigorating, so agreeable, or so beneficial.

The regular use of Ven-Yusa will save you hours of discomfort, and banish for ever that tired, irritable feeling after a hard day's work.

To be had of all Chemists, Stores, Hairdressers, &c., or obtainable in post if any difficulty from the Proprietors, C. & I., London.

VEN-YUSA
The Oxygen Face Cream

Davey in the employ of Mr A Bowden of Providence House was the other day seen ploughing in a field and Mrs R Crook of Higher Town has assisted in the tilling of several gardens this season"[27].

Many women worked as servants, cooks and cleaners, either 'living in' or doing day work. Others did work which they could do at home, to fit in with looking after their family, such as needlework, dressmaking, or taking in laundry. Those with husbands at war were supposed to get some of their husband's pay sent to them, but it was not much and did not always get through (or disappeared if it went via Miss Taylor at the Post Office!)

Whether or not they had paid work, they would all have been doing their best to make ends meet and make the most of what little money they had, including growing vegetables or keeping livestock.

Western Times 1 May 1917. Image reproduced with kind permission of The British Newspaper Archive (www.british newspaperarchive.co.uk) ©THE BRITISH LIBRARY BOARD. ALL RIGHTS RESERVED

Edith Trevellyan's husband James was called up in 1916, leaving his wife and daughter, Ivy. The family lived in Wharf Cottage, (*2018: Fairview*

---

[27] Devon & Somerset News, 25th May 1916

Cottage), the cottage by Buckland Bridge in Whitnage Road. We know that Edith worked at Merriemeade House, which belonged to the Norrish family. In the cards and letters exchanged between Edith, Ivy and James, we get glimpses of their daily lives. In April 1917 Ivy says "Mam is busy mending rags this afternoon. Auntie came to tea yesterday and we all went to the concert. It was all right." In an undated postcard Edith wrote "Such a lovely day here today. Quite hot. Nearly finished gardening. The chicks are growing." Another time Ivy mentioned that "we heard an aeroplane yesterday but it was an English one." James wrote back asking if Edith was getting the money he was sending, and hoping she was able to make ends meet. James Trevellyan would never return home – there is more about him later in this book.

In his memoirs Denis Cluett recalls several interesting women in and around the village at this time, including the Honourable Mrs Lottie Walrond, about whom we have written an entire chapter in this book.

Denis and his friend used to play tricks on Mrs Church and Mrs Thomas, who were warring neighbours in Boobery. Elizabeth Thomas was particularly striking for Devon in this period:

> Mrs Thomas was a negress and weighed about 22 stone. Her arms were as thick as the average man's thighs and she was jet black. It appears that, as a young man, Thomas had fought in Africa during the Boer War and had brought her back as a souvenir.

We should bear in mind that Denis Cluett was a young boy at the time and although this souvenir theory made sense to him there was probably a lot more to the Thomas' relationship. In fact, she was born in St Helena in 1873 and we can't be sure what their back story was.

Another striking woman, in a more literal sense, was Emma Dunn, who lived in a cottage near the church. Denis Cluett wrote that

> She had no teeth and her jaws were continually working as if she were perpetually chewing gum. I believe her official job was that of church cleaner, but over the years she had managed to establish herself as a sort of general manager. She did everything from ringing the 'Passing bell' to decorating the altar.

He goes on to say that she would tell everyone where to sit in church, and would then sit at the back where she could watch the congregation

> and woe betide any child who was unduly restless or made too much noise by scuffing his hobnail boots along the front of the pew. On such occasions Emma would be out of her seat like a

flash and would fetch the offender a clout on the side of the head, which would leave the child in a complete daze for the rest of the service.

Denis Cluett's own mother played a role in the church. The usual church organist was the school headmaster, Mr Smith, but when he could not attend Mrs Cluett played the organ.

Denis recalled that it became increasingly common during the war years to see women riding bicycles, and to prevent their long skirts getting caught by the wind they would attach them to their shoes with pieces of elastic.

We get a glimpse of daily life in the village from this letter, written by Maud Wood to William Saunders, probably in 1916.

The women of the village would have been extremely busy during the war, whilst at the same time worrying about what was happening to their absent men folk. It was a small, closely woven, and often inter-related, community and everyone would have been affected by reports of those who died or were wounded as the war progressed. The end of the war brought its own problems for the women of the village. Some lost loved ones and had to face life without them. Some had loved ones return, damaged, physically or psychologically, by their experiences. The women had probably changed too, having

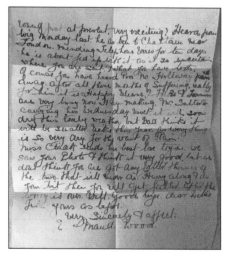

experienced more independence and self-reliance than ever before. In 1918 most women over 30 were given the right to vote in Parliamentary elections for the first time, new educational and career opportunities were opening up for women, and their lives would never be the same again.

Alexander Bassano's photograph of the Hon. Mrs Walrond, 1909, © National Portrait Gallery, London

Lottie Walrond

The name of Mrs or Lottie Walrond comes up in almost every chapter of this book, as she was clearly a major, and entertaining, influence in the life of the area during the First World War. At the start of the war her husband was the MP for Tiverton, and therefore also for Sampford Peverell.

She was born Charlotte Margaret Lothian Coats, the daughter of George Coats, a member of the Coats cotton family, and his wife Margaret Lothian Black. George Coats, who was given the title of Baron Glentanar in 1916, owned a number of properties including Bellisle, Ayr; Glentanar, Aberdeen; Burton Hall, Melton Mowbray, and 39 Park Lane, London.

On 18th June 1904 Charlotte, always referred to as Lottie, married William Lionel Walrond, known as Lionel to distinguish him from his father William, Lord Waleran. The Walrond family had owned and lived in Bradfield, Uffculme (near Willand), since the thirteenth century. Lionel was the third generation of his family to be MP for Tiverton, and at the time of his marriage he was also Chancellor of the Duchy of Lancaster. The marriage took place at St Margaret's Church, Westminster, which was filled with flowers and palms for the occasion. The 400 guests included the Prime Minister, Arthur Balfour, the Chancellor of the Exchequer, Austen Chamberlain, and representatives from most of the aristocratic families of Britain. When looking for an organist they clearly knew the answer to 'who ya gonna call' as it was Mr Reginald Goss-Bustard. A reception was held at 4 Buckingham Gate, and at the same time there was a huge celebration in Bradfield, Uffculme. A telegram of congratulations was sent from Bradfield to the reception in London, and a telegram of thanks was returned to Bradfield.

The couple moved to their new home: Tidcombe Hall, near Tiverton. Their son William George Hood Walrond was born in March 1905, and their second son John Humphrey Walrond was born in May 1908. They later moved to Bradfield when Lord and Lady Waleran moved to the South of France for their health.

This all sounds very conventional so far, but there was much more to Lottie than money and good looks. An article in August 1908 in The Sketch, a sort of upper-class gossip magazine which usually featured photographs of, and articles about, the aristocracy, said of the Hon Mrs Lionel Walrond:

> Among future Peeresses, there are few who can boast of better looks and better wits than Mrs Lionel Walrond, who, as Miss Lottie Coats, was equally popular in Ayrshire and London Society. Mrs Walrond is interested in politics, in sport, and in music, and immediately after her marriage, which occurred four years ago, she threw herself into the congenial task of winning the West-country constituency where her husband was already known and liked, and since he has been in Parliament she has thoroughly enjoyed the role of energetic political hostess. Mr and Mrs Walrond are now spending a few weeks at Glen Tanar, the lovely place on Deeside, where her parents entertain on so splendid a scale.

Lottie was very busy in Devon. In February 1909 the Exeter and Plymouth Gazette reported that Mrs Walrond "had presided at 37 meetings during the winter, and, besides making a speech, had sung three or four songs at each."

On 24th April 1909 the Western Times reported that Mrs Walrond arrived late to the opening of a bazaar for a Home in Exeter. She said:

> she wanted to apologize for being late, but she had done her best. The driving shaft (if they knew what that was) of her motor-car broke down three miles the other side of Broadclyst. "I walked" she added "for a mile and a half in this kit (with a sweep of the hand to draw attention to her attire), and then I held up a car driven by a man who travels with drapers' samples (laughter). The poor man was in a fix, but I insisted on his turning back and driving me here. You should have seen the people as I came down High street. I wish you could have seen their faces (laughter and applause).

She said how pleased she was to be there and congratulated them on their success. The reporter added that

> a propos of Mrs Lionel Walrond's reference to her walking 'kit' we may mention that she was attired in a trained Directoire costume of champagne colour, worn with handsome furs and a large picture hat.

Alexander Bassano's photograph of the Hon. Mrs Walrond, 1909, © National Portrait Gallery, London

The National Gallery has three photographic portraits of her in 1909, taken by society photographer Alexander Bassano. This is one of them:

There were two general elections in 1910, the first in January. The Walronds toured the constituency electioneering, and a visit to Sampford Peverell was reported in the Devon and Exeter Gazette on 12th January 1910:

> Mr J G Pedlar presided at a crowded meeting in the schoolroom at Sampford Peverell. Mr and Mrs Walrond were loudly cheered as they entered the room and were presented with a buttonhole and bouquet respectively by a little girl named Alice Jones. Mrs Walrond returned thanks briefly in a neat speech. ... Some amusement was caused by the questioning of Mr Walrond on women's suffrage by a lady, who said she was in favour of a vote being given to every man and woman over the age of 21. Mr Walrond explained that he voted in favour of a private Bill advocating female suffrage.

It is not surprising that Mr Walrond supported women's suffrage when he was being assisted by such a politically active and astute wife. The bill failed though, and no women were allowed to vote until 1918.

Lionel Walrond often suffered poor health, and on such occasions Lottie stood in for him. On 17th January 1910 the same paper reported that Mrs Walrond had attended four different meetings in one day in her husband's stead and spoke on such topics as tariff reform, unemployment, Home Rule, the Navy, unity with Ireland, and a closer commercial connection with the colonies. At one meeting she "admirably 'took off' one or two of the audience who had the boldness to interrupt her. Cheers were given as she left."

According to the 'Culm Valley Album' by Anthony Taylor "it was his wife, Lottie, who stole the limelight on the local political platforms – on occasions lifting her skirt to prove her drawers were the right colour!"

Two days later the election campaign was drawing to a close. According to the Devon and Exeter Gazette:

> The rival parties fired their last volleys in the fight in the Tiverton Division yesterday ... The Hon. Lionel Walrond was, unhappily, prevented from leaving Bradfield, owing to a cough, but Mrs Walrond, who has demonstrated over and over again how indispensable she is to the party, took her husband's place. She attended and addressed a continuous list of meetings from the early afternoon until late in the evening." ... Mrs Walrond was cheered again and again, and shouts of "Up Lionel" were raised.

On 21st January it was reported that the Conservatives had won Tiverton with an increased majority, despite a general swing to the Liberals elsewhere in the area. "The victory is due in the first place to the Conservative Candidate's own efforts and those of Mrs Walrond, who worked hard up to the last without thought of relaxation while there was still work to do." ... "When Mr and Mrs Walrond entered their motor car and drove to the Palmerston Hotel the crowd was wild with excitement." Lottie was described by one local newspaper as the finest electioneering agent her husband could ever have obtained, "not only giving speeches but also singing to the electors".

In February 1910 it was reported that at a concert and entertainment, which included a display of first aid work by the members of the Church Lads Brigade, she sang "'Our Farm', from 'Our Miss Gibbs'. She was encored. In the second part of the programme she sang 'The Flower Girl', and, in response to an encore, gave 'Yip milaidy'"

We know that Lottie knew the vet in Sampford Peverell, who lived in 'Pullens' in Lower Town. In 1912:

> A sheep dog belonging to Mr Jordon, of West Manley, was accidentally run over at Tiverton Junction on Monday morning by Mr L Walrond's motor car. Mrs Walrond, who was in the car, bandaged the dog's leg and had the animal taken in the car to Mr Down, veterinary surgeon, at Sampford Peverell. No blame was attached to the driver.

Mr and Mrs Walrond took a keen interest in the St Boniface Home in Sampford Peverell, of which Lionel was the chairman. In June 1914 the Exeter and Plymouth Gazette reported the visit of the Exeter Working-Men's

Conservative Union to Bradfield. They were photographed in front of the mansion and then:

dispersed to enjoy the beauties of the park and grounds. Some witnessed the cricket match between Bradfield and the Waifs and Strays of Sampford Peverell, in which the Hon Mrs Lionel Walrond was acting as umpire, while Master Billie Walrond was engaged in keeping a correct account of the scoring. The gardens were looking at the best, and later in the day Mrs Walrond kindly conducted a party to the kennels, where she keeps some fine black retrievers with which she has won several prizes, and is sanguine of still further success.

The following month, July 1914, The Sketch included this photo of Lottie and her sister, Lady Douro, later Duchess of Wellington, at an inter-regimental polo match at Hurlingham.

This was a happy day in the glorious Edwardian summer, just a few weeks before war was declared in August 1914, after which Lionel volunteered to join the army, and was made a Lieutenant in the Army

Lottie and her sister. The Sketch, 8 July 1914.
Image reproduced with kind permission of The British Newspaper Archive (www.britishnewspaperarchive.co.uk) ©THE BRITISH LIBRARY BOARD. ALL RIGHTS RESERVED

Service Corps. He arrived in France in December 1914 and was employed as a Railway Transport Officer, dealing with the transportation of supplies from Le Havre to the front, and the transport of the wounded and the belongings of the dead in the opposite direction.

According to the book 'Led by Lions' by Neil Thornton[28] his working conditions were difficult, and he witnessed a zeppelin attack on a railhead which killed 16 men, but he tried to stay upbeat in his letters home and wrote back to his constituency agent:

I often think how people would shriek with mirth to see me eating my lonely meal in a railway carriage – cold meat, biscuits, jam, sardines

---

[28] Neil Thornton, 'Led by Lions', (Fonthill Media, 2017) N. Thornton, Led by Lions: MPs and Sons Who Fell in the First World War (Fonthill Media, 2017).

and cheese all off one plate, one knife, and my palatial dining-room lit by one candle.

His health, never good, deteriorated, and in February 1915 he was sent home with acute laryngitis. He recovered enough to be able to return to France in April.

While her husband was away Lottie converted Bradfield into a convalescent home for wounded soldiers and personally superintended it. In June 1915 the Devon and Exeter Gazette reported that a wedding was held there for one of the soldiers, Private Joshua William Rigby (1st Gloucesters), who had served on the Front and had been invalided home with nerve trouble. He was expected to leave for the Front a few days later.[29] The account describes Mrs Walrond as the Matron, and says she had nine nurses working with her. Lottie accompanied the bride, Edith Priscilla Gardner from Gloucester, to the chapel in her VAD (Voluntary Aid Detachment) uniform. The bride wore a brown frock and white hat trimmed with yellow roses and carried a posy of 'roses and heuchera' made by the head gardener. Two of the nurses who acted as bridesmaids gave everyone present a buttonhole of a rose from the gardens, and as the couple left through the gathering of soldiers, nurses and others they were showered with rice. At the wedding breakfast in the house Lottie proposed the toast:

> It has given me very great pleasure to do what I could to make their marriage possible before the bridegroom returns to his regiment. I think a thing that makes life worth living is to have the affection of someone who can share the ups and downs of life, and be sympathetic and understand, and though they are going to separate tomorrow, I think each will be more contented and much happier, knowing that they have the right to call upon one another, to stand up and face together whatever life may have in store for them. With all our sympathy, and with our best wishes for a long life and a happy one. I ask you to drink their health.

Perhaps she was also thinking of her own marriage: a strong partnership but one which would not last much longer. Lionel's health deteriorated again and he was sent home in August with tubercular laryngitis, a dilated heart, and anaemia. Despite convalescence in Devon and at Lottie's family's home in Scotland, he never recovered, and died on 2nd November 1915 at Glen Tanar, aged 39. He is buried in the parish church at Bradfield.

---

[29] Joshua Rigby survived the war and in 1939 he and his wife Edith were living in Gloucester where he worked as a wholesale fish merchant.

Lottie continued to think of others, and a few days later she disposed of the kennel of retrievers she had established at Bradfield, giving the proceeds to the British Red Cross Society.

On 17th November this photo was published in the Tatler, with a caption describing her as "a strenuous worker for the Red Cross".

On 23rd November the Western Times published a letter which she had sent to Mr J Gould.

The Tatler 17 Nov 1915. Image reproduced with kind permission of The British Newspaper Archive (www.britishnewsp aperarchive.co.uk) ©THE BRITISH LIBRARY BOARD. ALL RIGHTS RESERVED

> Dear Mr Gould, Will you please thank the Unionist Party in the Tiverton Division for their resolution of sympathy with me and Lord Waleran in the death of my husband. We have been much touched by the love and friendship shewn for him, and by the universal kindness extended to us, and we will always have a deep interest in all that concerns the welfare of the Electors of the Division. Yours sincerely,
>
> Lottie Walrond.

Despite having two boys to raise and an estate to run, Lottie continued to work for charities and do all she could for the war effort.

One of her interests was encouraging women to join the Land Army. In June 1916 she attended a competition on Budlake Farm for women in agriculture: ploughing, harrowing, spreading farmyard manure, harnessing and driving horses, sheep-shearing and milking. The following month she attended the opening of a new range for the Uffculme VTC, which included a number of Sampford Peverell volunteers. "On Saturday the range was ready for opening, and the Hon Mrs Walrond, of Bradfield, graciously officiated and fired the first shot, scoring a bull." And talking of bulls, in August 1917 the Western Times reported: "A steer, given to the Exeter Rummage Sale in aid of local war hospitals by the Hon Mrs Walrond, was sold by Messrs Hussey and Sons to Mrs Willis, butcher, Magdalen Street, Exeter, for £40 5s. The animal was fed on the Bradfield Estate."

In May 1918 she attended a recruiting rally for women to join the Land Army, organized by the Devon Women's War Agricultural Committee. The Western Times reported that she "made a special appeal for part-time work, to those who were unable to give up their whole service to the cause. She mentioned that she was herself now managing the Bradfield estate, and she knew the hard task farmers had had to put in the crops. It would, she was afraid, be almost impossible to gather them unless the help of the women was forthcoming."

In his memoirs 'A village childhood' about growing up in Sampford Peverell, Denis Cluett recalls:

> I remember a terrific furore being caused in and around the village by a certain Lady Waldron [sic] who lived at a place called Willand about four miles away. She was a young woman and was on most of the fund-raising committees in the area. Towards the end of the war she attended one such committee at Sampford, and after the business of the meeting had finished she hitched her skirt to the top of her calves and perched on a corner of the table where she actually crossed her knees and lit a cigarette. The effect on the committee members was tremendous and the story of the fast and reckless behaviour swept through the village like a prairie fire. The women of the village spoke of the matter in horrified whispers while their menfolk fought like mad to try and get appointed to the committee.

Photos of her still appeared regularly in the press, including one on 2nd December 1918 in the Daily Mirror. Headlined 'Women on the Land' it said "Here is the Hon Mrs Walrond, who believes that women have a career as practical commercial farmers. To prove this, she is successfully farming four hundred acres in Devon. She thinks that women could be just as successful in estate management, given a chance, as men." In March 1919 the Tatler reported that she had sold part of her Bradfield estate. The local press suggested she had sold the land to help provide housing for returning servicemen.

In June 1920 Lottie married Henry William Allen Adams, a Commander in the Royal Navy, and went to live with him in Courtlands, Lympstone, but she still spent a lot of time running the estate at Bradfield as her boys were still teenagers.

On 1st July 1925 the Western Morning News and Mercury ran a full page spread on Bradfield and the Walrond family, as the Prime Minister, Stanley Baldwin, was visiting Bradfield to take part in a Unionist rally, hosted by Lottie. At the time her older son, William, was 20, so not 'of age', and was studying at Oxford, and his younger brother John was 17. The programme of events included speeches but also sports competitions for adults and children, and aquatic sports for men and women in the lake. Special arrangements were made with train and charabanc companies to provide transport for the thousands expected to attend, and the catering included a ton of cake and 6000 pounds of bread. The newspaper report includes a history of Bradfield and article on Stanley Baldwin, but there is also a long report on Mrs Adams. It talks about her efforts on behalf of her husband in the 1910 election and quotes a newspaper report afterwards which said:

> Since the last election Mrs Walrond has worked with increasing energy in perfecting the organization of the Primrose League in the constituency. Every little village can now boast of its Primrose League branch, and [it] is now one of the best organized divisions in the whole country.[30]

The article refers to the work she had done during the war:

> she converted Bradfield into a convalescent home for soldiers, and personally superintended it. Later she engaged in war hospital work in London. The vivacity and charm of her personality, which made such an impression upon her husband's constituency, have been carried into her private and social life, where her high spirits and good humour seem inexhaustible. Such qualities contribute to making her the ideal hostess for such an outstanding event as the visit of the Prime Minister, and at other functions in which Bradfield has played a prominent part. One of her favourite hobbies is amateur theatricals and tableaux vivant, in which she displays marked talent and originality. Several entertainments of this character have during the last two or three years been organized by her on behalf of the Conservative cause in the division.

By 1939 she and her husband were then living full-time at Bradfield, where Lottie was the estate manager. During the Second World War she again opened up Bradfield as an auxiliary hospital and acted as matron. Her younger son, John, died in Barnstaple in 1942, soon after the death of his wife following a car accident. Her older son married three times but had no male heirs so the family titles died out when he passed away in April 1966. Lottie died a few months later, on 30th October 1966. Bradfield was run as a residential school for boys with emotional and behavioural problems, until it closed in 1997. It was then converted into two private dwellings which is how it remains today.

---

[30] The Primrose League was an organization for spreading Conservative Party principles in Great Britain

State regulations during the war

As soon as war was declared on 4 August 1914 the government became very concerned about maintaining public order, maximizing work output, and potential espionage and/or invasion. It rapidly put together two acts which went through parliament and became law within days.

The Aliens Restriction Act 1914

The first act was the **Aliens Restriction Act** which was passed by parliament the day after war was declared. It required foreign nationals (aliens) to register with the police. Their movements were severely restricted; men of military age who were categorized as enemy aliens were arrested and interned, and restrictions were imposed on items and goods being brought into or taken out of the country. As far as we know this act did not affect anyone in Sampford Peverell.

The Defence of the Realm Act 1914

A few days later the **Defence of the Realm Act**, known as DORA, was passed by parliament. DORA was intended to prevent invasion and maximize the war effort by using social control. It gave the government wide-ranging powers and created new criminal offences. As the war progressed more and more regulations were added to it: it was amended and extended five times during the course of the war. DORA affected everyone in the country, adults and children alike, and must have had a big impact on the village.

The main points included these:

- Press censorship was introduced. Censorship of the reporting of British troop movements, their numbers, or any other operational information, prevented the enemy from finding out sensitive information, which potentially saved many lives. It was also an attempt to keep morale high. Many publications were banned.

- The government could take over any land or buildings that it needed.

Also, no civilian could:

- talk about naval or military matters in public places
- spread rumours about military matters
- buy binoculars

- trespass on railway lines or bridges
- melt down gold or silver
- light bonfires (in case they attracted zeppelins)
- set off fireworks (another zeppelin risk)
- fly a kite (again, in case of attracting zeppelins)
- give bread to horses or chickens (to prevent food wastage)
- use invisible ink when writing abroad
- ring church bells during periods when lighting restrictions were in force
- loiter near bridges or tunnels

Some other odd rules under DORA:

Whistling for a London taxi was banned, in case it could be mistaken for an air raid warning.

Possession of cocaine or opium, other than by authorized professionals such as doctors, was banned and became a criminal offence.

Private correspondence was censored. Military censors examined 300,000 private telegrams in 1916 alone.

Fines were issued for making white flour instead of wholewheat and for allowing rats to invade wheat stores (to prevent food wastage).

Pigeons played a vital role in communications in the First World War and an estimated 100,000 were used by the military to carry messages. Under Regulation 21 of DORA, anyone killing, wounding or molesting a homing pigeon could face up to 6 months' imprisonment or a £100 fine. A permit issued by the police was required to possess or transport homing or carrier pigeons, and publications about pigeons were censored.

If anyone broke these rules, they could be arrested and fined or sent to prison. It is estimated that almost a million arrests in the UK happened under DORA.

Alcohol regulations

The government was very worried about British drinking habits and numerous regulations under DORA were introduced to limit alcohol consumption, partly because of shortages of raw ingredients, but mainly to ensure that everyone was working as hard as possible.

In August 1914 powers to close public houses and to restrict pub opening hours were given to military and naval authorities. This power was extended to civil authorities shortly afterwards, and in October 1914 evening closing time in London became 10.00pm instead of 12.30am.

David Lloyd George, the Chancellor of the Exchequer, led a campaign to persuade people to drink less alcohol, but this had little effect so more stringent measures were introduced in 1915:

- Opening hours were more heavily restricted. Before the law was changed, public houses could open from 5 am, and could stay open for 16-17 hours a day (a little more in London), closing by 12.30 at night. The new rules meant pubs could only open for 5½ hours a day, and had to close by 9-9.30 pm. Public House opening times in cities and industrial areas were also restricted to 12.00 noon to 2.30 pm and 6.30 to 9.30 pm.

- Members of the public were prohibited from buying a drink for a member of the armed forces (in uniform).

- No member of the public could buy a round of drinks (known as the *No Treating Order*). Any drink ordered had to be paid for by the person drinking it. Breaking this rule could result in a penalty of up to six months in prison.

- Landlords were prohibited from selling drinks on credit.

- Alcohol could not be sold or consumed on public transport.

- The alcohol content of beer and spirits was reduced. Weak beer was later referred to as *Lloyd George's beer.*

The government also increased the tax on alcohol many times throughout the war, both to discourage drinking and to raise money. In 1918 a bottle of whisky cost £1 – five times what it had cost before the start of the war. Additionally, under the Output of Beer (Restriction) Act 1916, brewery output was significantly reduced.

All of this must have had a big impact on the alcohol trade and on the three pubs in Sampford Peverell, although the restrictions on hours may not have been so rigorously enforced in rural areas such as this one, especially once PC Blackmore left the area. Throughout the country arrests for offences involving drunkenness dropped dramatically, and we have found no reports of arrests for drunkenness in Sampford during the war, although reading the details of the case of Maud Taylor at the Post Office it seems alcohol was still readily available at a price.

The Globe Inn c1905

Food and rationing

At the start of the war about 60% of the country's food was imported from overseas, including most of the wheat used to make bread. Shipping losses and the need to feed both the civilian population and the troops abroad led to food shortages and the need to introduce rationing. Initially the government tried to control supplies and prevent panic buying and price rises by fixing maximum prices for basic items such as sugar, butter, cheese, tea, bread and bacon.

In 1916 the government created the role of 'Minister of Food Control' to organize the maintenance of food stocks, encourage efficiency and reduce waste. Initially a scheme of voluntary rationing was introduced under which people were encouraged to limit their consumption of key food items, including bread. There were rumours that the Minister, Viscount Davenport, delayed compulsory rationing to protect the interests of retailers.

The food situation became much worse in 1917, largely due to German submarine attacks on supply ships. The effects were devastating and basic supplies began to run short, prices soared and people had to queue for food. Britain was within weeks of running out of wheat. Further food regulations were introduced under DORA which included the introduction of government regulation bread (which contained a large potato content); restrictions on the sale of cake and bread sold in tea shops; restrictions on the feeding of corn to horses, and even the throwing of rice at weddings. Regulations also made it unlawful to feed or adopt stray dogs.

Coal was rationed from October 1916 and the allocation was linked to the number of rooms per house. In 1917, one of the coldest years on record, further restrictions were introduced to conserve fuel, including extensive restrictions on lighting and the early closure of shops.

Food rationing was introduced at the end of 1917 and a system of ration cards was introduced. Customers had to register with a retailer for each rationed item. Sugar was rationed from January 1918 and this was followed by meat, cheese, butter and margarine in April. This solved the rising prices and food queues, and actually led to an improvement in general health! Food-related offences created under DORA included obtaining meat in excess quantities; unlawfully obtaining and using a ration book, and retailers selling to unregistered customers. Advertisements such as this one encouraged people to reduce their meat intake.

The restrictions were gradually lifted at the end of the war, with sugar and butter rationing only ending in 1920.

We cannot tell whether or how much all this affected Sampford Peverell. Most probably many people here were able to produce, find, or catch, some food for themselves, but the grocers, butchers and bakers would have been hit by the regulations. Norrish's creamery in Chains Road probably benefitted from the high demand for its products, and it was sending its produce to London throughout the war.

Western Times 22 Nov 1917. Image reproduced with kind permission of The British Newspaper Archive (www.british newspaperarchive.co.uk) ©THE BRITISH LIBRARY BOARD. ALL RIGHTS RESERVED

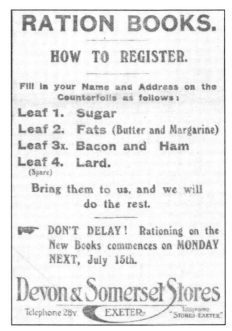

Exeter and Plymouth Gazette 9 Jul 1918. Image reproduced with kind permission of The British Newspaper Archive (www.britishnewspaperarchive.co.uk) ©THE BRITISH LIBRARY BOARD. ALL RIGHTS RESERVED

Summer Time Act 1916

One lasting legacy of the First World War was the introduction of British Summer Time (BST) in 1916. This advanced Greenwich Mean Time (GMT) by 1 hour, between 21st May and 1st October that year, to save fuel and increase the number of daylight hours available for getting work done. Under the terms of the Summer Time Act 1916, the provision for BST could be renewed each year by means of an Order in Council. The Time (Ireland) Act 1916 introduced similar provisions in Ireland in relation to Dublin Mean Time (DMT), which was 25 minutes behind GMT. DMT was abolished in August 1916. British Summer Time was later made permanent by the Summer Time Act 1925.

It seems that not all the residents of Sampford Peverell accepted the clock changes. A newspaper article in April 1919 reported that "There are two sets of times prevailing at Sampford Peverell, the old time and the new. The up-to-date are going by the new time"!

The 1916 Lights Order

This arose from the fear of attracting zeppelins, which were being used by the Germans for reconnaissance and for bombing raids. The Order stated:

1. All lights visible from the sea [to be] so obscured as to be invisible from outside.
2. All external lamps, flares, and fixed lights of all descriptions, and all aggregations of lights [to be] extinguished, except such public lights as the Chief Officer of Police directs for public safety. All lights not extinguished to be reduced to the minimum intensity and so shaded or obscured that direct light is cut off in all directions above the horizontal and no more than a diffused light is cast on the ground.
3. In dwelling houses, hotels, shops, factories, docks, shipbuilding yards, and other premises of all descriptions, all inside lights must be so reduced and shaded or the windows, roof lighting areas, skylights, glass doors etc so screened by shutters or dark blinds or dark curtains that no more than a dull subdued light is visible from any direction outside and no part of the pavement or roadway or any other building or other object is illuminated thereby,
4. Exemption may be granted to naval or military establishments or works of public utility subject to compliance with these orders.

5. These orders no not apply to working lights on railways (including lights in stations and in goods and marshalling yards) nor to navigation, riding or fishing lights, in accordance with Admiralty orders, nor to lights under [the] control of general or local lighthouse authority

6. Railway passengers are to lower blinds in railway carriages but are permitted to raise them as necessary when the train is standing still at a station.

7. In case of a sudden emergency, all instructions given by the competent naval or military authority or by the Commissioner of Police on the advice of the competent naval or military authority, as to the further reduction or extinction of lights, shall be immediately obeyed.

8. This order comes into effect from 7 August 1916.

These lighting restrictions had been expected for some months beforehand, and shops were, of course, quick to use the restrictions as a sales opportunity.

In Sampford Peverell the Parish Council took the decision not to use street lamps until the war was over. Street lighting was normally used during the winter months, so the roads would have been very dark without no street lamps. An article about Sampford Peverell in the Western Times on 10th October 1919, following the lifting of lighting regulations, included the happy news that "The lighting of the village lamps commences tonight."

Exeter and Plymouth Gazette 21 Feb 1916. Image reproduced with kind permission of The British Newspaper Archive (www.britishnewspaperarchive.co. uk) ©THE BRITISH LIBRARY BOARD. ALL RIGHTS RESERVED

Farming and food production

At the outbreak of the War, Great Britain was not self-sufficient in food. Over the previous 40 or so years, cheap American grain had poured into the country, so much so that Devon farmers had given their cornfields over to grass and clover. Similarly, increasing quantities of cheese, butter, bacon and beef had been imported from overseas. In 1914, Britain imported 80% of its wheat, 70% of its cheese and bacon, about 66% of its butter and 33% of its beef[1]. In addition, Sodium Nitrate fertiliser was imported from Chile and Potash from Germany, the latter supply ceasing upon the declaration of war.

As long as merchant shipping remained largely unaffected by the hostilities, food imports continued to arrive, and the population was fed. In the early months of the war, the Government's efforts were directed elsewhere - towards recruitment of manpower, manufacture of armaments and military logistics. With an expectation that the war would be brief, no priority was given to food production in the first two years of the war. During this time the main difficulty facing farmers was the growing shortage of manpower, as more and more young men joined the armed forces. This was addressed mainly by an increased input from the family members of farmers: their wives, children and other relatives who had not been called up. At harvest time, when the workload peaked, additional help was sought from schoolboys - at least 13 years old – who could be exempted from their studies with the consent of the Local Authorities.

At the beginning of the War, in the parish of Sampford Peverell[4], there were 1,863 acres of farmland divided between 31 farms, all but one of which were run by tenant farmers. Most of the land, some 73.6%, was given over to grass and clover, with 16.4% being cereal crops (mainly oats and barley); 8.0% fodder crops (swedes, turnips and mangolds); 0.3% potatoes, and the rest being orchards, soft fruit and other crops. As most of the farms were tenanted, it is likely that each comprised a patchwork of fields spread around the parish and beyond, the composition of which could change from one year to the next. The proportions of crops remained almost the same over the first few years of the war, showing just a small reduction in cereals (0.6%) and fodder crops (1.0%) with a consequent increase in grassland. This is probably because growing crops was more labour-intensive.

As for livestock, the numbers did not vary a great deal in the early years of the war. If any horses had been commandeered for the War they had been replaced, as the numbers stayed much the same throughout the war. Although suffering a reduction in manpower, farmers were benefitting financially from the effect that dwindling supplies had on market prices. At Sampford Fair, which was primarily a cattle fair, held annually in April, 'record demand and prices' were reported in 1915[31] and similar results occurred in 1916.

In this book, the names of all the Sampford Peverell farm workers who took part in the War are listed, but it would seem that, in the early stages at least, other workers were found to take their place. When an application was made to the Local Authorities to close the village school for the 1915 hay harvest, so that the children could help with it, that application was

Arthur Bass, home on leave at Leonard Moor Farm

[31] Devon & Somerset News, 29 April 1915

rejected because '... shortage of agricultural labour was not deemed to be exceptional in this parish'[5]. Perhaps this is because Sampford Peverell had one very useful source of young male labour, with the presence in the village of 'St Boniface Home', one of many homes run by 'The Waifs and Strays Society' (see the chapter on St Boniface Home). Housing boys up to the age of 14 (and older, when no employment could be found for them), it became the Society's national policy in 1915 for the older boys not to go to a camp during the summer holidays, but to be available to help on local farms instead. It seems likely that boys deemed suitable for such holiday help would have been kept on by some local farmers once they reached school-leaving age.

During 1916 the Government decided to encourage women to help on farms or become 'land girls', and some Sampford Peverell women did indeed work the land. There is more on this in the chapter on women. By the end of 1916, nationally, retail prices of food had risen by 60% over those of two years earlier. Merchant shipping had been affected by a U-boat campaign and the Government realised that food shortages would soon follow. A new policy was put in place from early in 1917 to address what was rapidly becoming an urgent need.

A new Ministry of Food was established early in 1917 and a department for Food Production was created to increase home production. Agricultural Executive Committees were set up in each county, whose main role was to increase the arable area and, in particular, the output of cereals and potatoes[2]. Devon was divided into 4 'vice-counties', each chaired by a prominent local patriot and landowner: men of power and influence. The Tiverton district (within which Sampford Peverell fell) already had a War Agricultural Committee, which, until this time, had been concerned with such matters as military tribunals for farm workers and canvassing for more women to help on the land. This committee was given a new role and powers, with Sir Ian Amory (otherwise, Heathcoat-Amory) appointed as its Chairman. Sir Ian had inherited the Knightshayes estate from his father in 1914, and was the managing partner for Heathcoat and Son, Tiverton.

The initial steps taken by the Tiverton War Agricultural Committee (TWAC) in January 1917[32] were: to arrange to conduct a farm census; to employ German prisoners as farm workers, where they were available (Sir Ian Amory suggested they could be used at Knightshayes); to emphasise the need to increase production of potatoes and oats, rather than wheat,

---

[32] Exeter & Plymouth Gazette (18 and 19 January 1917)

for which the risk of a poor harvest was greater; and to appoint farming representatives for each parish in the District. To begin with, Edward Pearce, farmer of Boehill, and John Garnsey Pedler of Sampford Barton, both Parish Councillors, were appointed, and later in the year, Tom White of West Pitt was added to their number. Their role was to establish whether all farms in the parish were producing the maximum possible, and to find out if the smaller farms needed any assistance. It was stated that, although the TWAC had compulsory powers to intervene in farms, it did not wish to use them.

In order to provide some incentive for farmers to produce more cereals, a Corn Production Act was passed, which provided farmers with a guaranteed minimum price for wheat and oats for four years. Barley was excluded in deference to the temperance movement - it could be used in alcohol production. The TWAC also offered to supply temporary labour to assist with ploughing up some of the grassland, with its source being from among the military men who had not yet been posted to the front or were at home for other reasons. Central Government was also attempting to acquire tractors (the tractor was a very recent invention), and other machinery, to ease the problem of manual labour shortages, and heavy horses for farm work were also being sought where needed. In return, farmers were expected to do their patriotic duty by ploughing more of their land for oats, wheat and potatoes. They were also expected to raise employees' pay so that available labour was not channelled into better-paid work elsewhere. In April, an

THE MOLINE UNIVERSAL
ONE-MAN MOTOR PLOUGH
For Ploughing, Harrowing, Cultivating, Haying, Harvesting.
Either 2 or 3-Furrow Ploughs may be fitted.
AS POWERFUL AS 5 HORSES—AS ENDURING AS 7 HORSES—COSTS LESS THAN A
HORSES—REQUIRES LESS CARE THAN 1 HORSE—EATS ONLY WHEN IT WORKS.
MAY BE SEEN WORKING IN EXETER DISTRICT ANY TIME BY APPOINTMENT
SOLE AGENTS FOR DEVONSHIRE:
PARKER'S GARAGE, Ltd.,
150a, SIDWELL STREET, EXETER.

Agricultural Bill was introduced to set the minimum pay for a labourer at 25s a week, with workers' cottage rents also being fixed[33] . This wage rate was about 50% greater than the national average rate

[33] Devon & Somerset News, 26 April 1917

before the war but was more or less matched by increases in prices over the same period.

In the early months of 1917, there is little evidence of change in farming practice. Very few farmers applied to have temporary labourers, and the census carried out showed that over a quarter of farms in the Tiverton District needed to be inspected as they appeared to be under-productive. Sampford Fair took place as usual in April, with most of the livestock selling at good prices, although it was reported that 'prices had dropped somewhat'[34]. The Agricultural Returns for Sampford Peverell showed that cattle and sheep numbers dropped a little during the year, whilst pigs were down 48%.

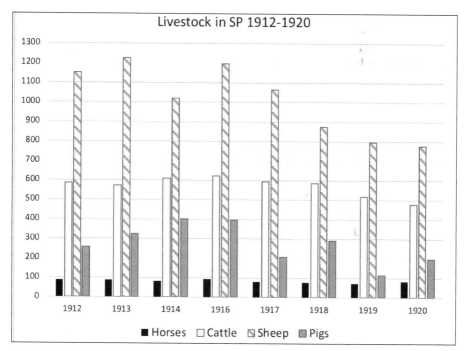

Livestock in Sampford Peverell 1912-1920

As the year progressed, so the pressure was ramped up on farmers. Production quotas were set, and although the changes were still said to be voluntary, there was the underlying message of enforcement and a request for compliant farmers to inform on their more reluctant neighbours[35].

---

[34] Western Times, 15th June 1917
[35] Exeter & Plymouth Gazette, 17th Sept 1919

In May 1917 the Minister of Food warned that feeding the country from September would be a difficult problem and started to introduce Control Orders to regulate food production methods. For example, the Bread Order of 1917 made it illegal to sell bread until it had been baked for at least 12 hours, with the expected result of reducing consumption. This particular Order remained in force after the War, which resulted in Sampford's baker, William Chidgey, being fined for selling freshly baked bread in September 1919[36].

Towards the end of 1917, it became apparent that the quota set for land to be ploughed for corn would not be met, and so additional pressure was put on farmers. Sir Ian Amory told the TWAC that 'there is a real danger of shortage of food in this country...' and 'Farmers were the only people to save the country [*from it*]'.[37] We do not know what the quota set for Sampford Peverell was in that year, but the agricultural returns suggest that the target was missed. For wheat, barley and oats combined, there was only a slight increase in acreage over the previous year, but there had been a significant shift away from wheat towards oats. An increase in land given over to oat production had been the original aim of the TWAC, but not at the expense of wheat! The TWAC emphasised that it was the duty of the parish representatives in future to follow through the promises made.

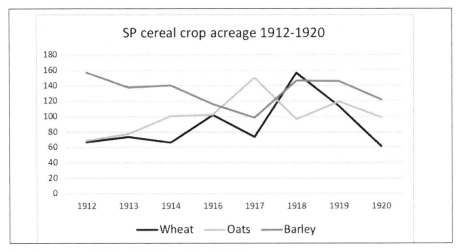

Cereal crop acreage in Sampford Peverell 1912-1920

[36] Exeter & Plymouth Gazette, 17th Sept 1917
[37] Exeter & Plymouth Gazette, 17th October 1917

Reports about the 1917 harvest in newspapers were mixed. Favourable weather in late summer meant that most crops did well, but heavy rain set in after that, resulting in poor yields for the late harvests. Unfortunately, no statistics for crop yields in Sampford Peverell for that year have been found.

As the year progressed towards winter, so more regulations were passed to control prices and restrict demand. The Tiverton Butchers Association fixed prices for various cuts of meat and a scheme was being devised to compel shop customers to register at one shop for butter and margarine[38]. The TWAC, probably reflecting the public mood, noted: 'We in this country have too long been the victims both of profiteers and of hoarders'[39]. Meanwhile alternatives for meat were being advertised, such as Baked Beans:

Exeter and Plymouth Gazette 6 Nov 1917. Image reproduced with kind permission of The British Newspaper Archive (www.britishnewspaperarchive.co.uk) ©THE BRITISH LIBRARY BOARD. ALL RIGHTS RESERVED

Sir Ian Amory's message about the seriousness of the situation, and the role of farmers in easing it, did get through in 1918. More farm labour was found by the TWAC in the form of 'Roumanians', who were coming to work the land; German POWs who started arriving in Devon in February 1918, and 16-year-old public schoolboys, who were placed in camps around the district to help during their summer holidays. Tractors and other machinery remained in short supply, but some farmers found them unsuitable for their fields and preferred to use horse-power anyway.

During 1918, yet more orders were introduced to limit use of scarce resources. A Government Order was made that 'no corn that could possibly be used for human consumption could be used for beast or bird' (Western Times 22 February 1918). A Rural Food Order for Tiverton imposed a number of new restrictions relating to offal, pickling pork, other cuts of meat and the preserving of eggs. Anyone wishing to buy sugar for jam-making had to apply for permission. Across the Tiverton District, 1,587

---

[38] Western Times, 14th September 1917
[39] Western Times, 20th December 1917

such applications had been received and it was decided that, where the request was for over 10 lb of sugar, the request should only be granted if the jam was being made for the Government (Devon & Somerset News 2 May 1918).

The use of cream for anything other than cheese-making was prohibited, and milk, which was plentiful locally, was sold at fixed prices. At Norrish's Creamery production of cheese was said to be 3 tons per week in May 1918, 25% of which was sold in the district and the remainder sent elsewhere in the country by train. Mr Norrish intended to double his factory's cheese production within two weeks, thus providing his reason for maintaining exemption from war service[40].

By August 1918, the TWAC was able to report that the acreage for ploughed land had been exceeded by the district, and by almost every parish therein, including Sampford Peverell[41]. Sir Ian Amory congratulated farmers for doing their patriotic duty without compulsion. Now, farmers needed to look ahead to the next two years or more, when the demands upon them were not expected to ease.

When comparing the proportion of the acreage under crops, it is apparent that the parish's farmers had made a substantial change over the preceding year. The earlier graph shows that an additional 6.3% was sown with cereal crops. Compared to 1914, almost the same acreage was devoted to barley and oats, but that for wheat had increased by 136%.

In addition, over the four-year period, the acreage of potatoes, although still relatively small at 20 acres, had more than tripled. The increase in land under wheat and potatoes had been achieved at the expense of fodder crops and grass.

After the war ended in November 1918, the work of the TWAC was not over. Farmers started to press for a relaxation to the food production requirements, in order to give the land a rest. However, Sir Ian Amory told them that the regulations were expected to remain in place until at least 1921, as would the minimum prices for corn, which benefitted farmers[42]

After the exceptional effort made by Sampford's farmers in 1918 to grow the crops that were demanded of them, over the course of the following two years they reverted to using their land in much the same way as they had

---

[40] Devon & Somerset News 2 May 1918
[41] Exeter & Plymouth Gazette, 28th August 1918
[42] Western Times 27 November 1918

before the war. With imports of wheat restored, the pressure on them to grow more of this crop was relieved, and they were able to turn more land over to root crops as they had previously.

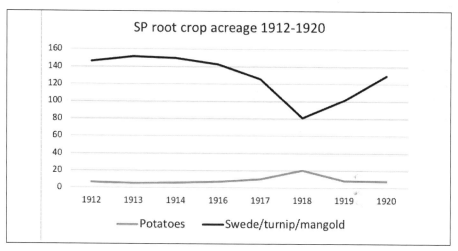

Root crop acreage in Sampford Peverell 1912-1920

World War 1 had forced a change upon farming practices, which continued long after the war was over, and the echoes of which can still be heard today: a reduction of manual labour; higher, regulated, wages for those that remained; the employment of women; the introduction of the tractor and other machinery to replace the horse; support for crop prices; the drive to increase the productivity of the land; and the consolidation of small farms into larger ones.

Sources:

1. British Agriculture in the First World War, P Dewey, published by Routledge, London, 1989.

2. The Agrarian History of England and Wales vol V111, 1914-39, by E Whetham, published by Cambridge University Press, 1978.

3. The people of Devon in the First World War by David Parker, published by The History Press, 2013.

4. MAF68 Agricultural Returns: Parish Summaries for Devon, held at the National Archives. These were produced annually in June, although the summary for 1915 is missing.

5. Sampford Peverell School Log Book, 25 June 1915.

Belgian refugees in Sampford Peverell

A couple of months after the start of the war, on 13th October 1914, the Western Times carried an article about the War Refugees Committee and the urgent need to help Belgian refugees. It said:

> The Government have undertaken to receive the refugees en bloc upon arrival and give them hospitality until they can be allocated by the Committee to places in the country where hospitality is offered. But, owing to events in Belgium, the number of refugees arriving in England is increasing daily. In addition to the allocation work yesterday, the Committee had themselves to find beds for seven or eight hundred people. More are expected today. Offers from Local Committees in the country to receive large parties at once are urgently wanted. Offers from private hosts to receive families are now practically exhausted, and that form of hospitality is essential for the allocation work.

The article goes on to say "Many thousands of refugees are expected today from Ostend and Flushing" and "There are whole families of both the tradesmen class and the better class among the refugees". The paper also describes the arrival of twenty to thirty refugees in Exeter that day, all 'well-dressed' but with few possessions, and says a further hundred are expected the next day.

So who were these people? Germany invaded Belgium in 1914, forcing many of its residents to flee, and from August onwards Belgian refugees arrived in the UK almost daily. Exeter was the first provincial city to receive Belgian refugees, within weeks of the start of the war, and throughout the war 8,000 Belgians were housed in Devon, all arriving by train to Exeter and being distributed from there. Agatha Christie based her character Hercule Poirot on Belgian refugees and soldiers that she met in her home town of Torquay during the First World War when she was a volunteer nurse. In her first detective novel, The Mysterious Affair at Styles, written in 1916, Poirot explains that it is due to a lady's charity that he is there: "She had kindly extended hospitality to seven of my countrypeople who, alas, were refugees from their native land. We Belgians will always remember her with gratitude."

A letter to the editor of the North Devon Journal in November 1914, from the resident of a Presbytery in Barnstaple, suggests that in some cases there was either ignorance of the refugees, or condescension towards them:

> Sir, As the Belgium refugees are quite unaccustomed to intoxicated liquors, it takes very little to upset them, and the Local Government Board and the War Refugees Committee earnestly hope that the British public will refrain from offering them any such drink.

In some areas the initial enthusiasm with which they were greeted began to turn to resentment as the war went on longer than expected, and they were seen as being treated better than some of the poorer residents, but the refugees were also able to contribute to the war effort by working in agriculture and industry, filling vacancies left by those serving in the war. This was the case at Coldharbour Mill in Uffculme, where Belgian spinners and weavers were employed to replace the men who had been called up.

The first mention we have of Belgian refugees in Sampford Peverell comes in the Devon and Somerset News of 26th November 1914:

> Quite a good number of parishioners of Sampford Peverell attended a meeting in the schoolroom on Monday evening to consider the question of affording hospitality to Belgian refugees. In the absence of the rector Mr J G Pedlar C.C. presided. It was unanimously decided to provide for a family of five or six people. Mr Sterling Marshall kindly offered his cottage, the free loan of which was gratefully accepted. Mrs J Jennings and Mrs Heslop offered their services as hon. secretary and head of the furnishing department respectively, and a few others volunteered to assist them in the work generally.

Soon after this meeting the Mahieu family arrived in Sampford Peverell and were offered the use of Boobery Cottage *(2018: the site of 1/1a Boobery).*

On 8th January 1915, the following was written in the log of the village school "Admitted a Belgian girl of eleven, Julia Mahieu, Flemish in her native tongue, but as she has some knowledge of French, the language difficulty is not great, and she promises to pick up English rapidly." A week later, on 15 January 1915, this was added to the school log: "Am allowing Julia's brother, Jules (16) to sit in one of the spare desks for the purpose of improving his English. He does not conform to the school timetable, nor, of course, does his name appear on the books."

Mrs Jennings, the secretary of the committee helping the Belgian family, retired from Post Office work in 1915 and moved away, so was replaced as secretary by Ellen Maud Wood, known as Maud. She was one of the two daughters of Henry Wood, the saddler and harness maker, and clerk to the Parish Council.

Unfortunately, we do not have any information on what the family did while they lived in the village, but it is likely that Jules found work here. The next we hear of them is when they were about to leave. When the war ended the government wanted to get its soldiers back, and it was keen for the refugees to return to Belgium as soon as possible. Employment contracts were terminated to force the issue, and they were offered free one-way tickets home for a short period only. Belgium, as well, wanted to get its people back into the country to help rebuild it. More than 90% of the Belgian refugees returned home within 12 months of the end of the war[43].

According to the Tiverton Gazette of 18 Mar 1919:

> At a meeting held at the Sampford Peverell School on Tuesday, presided over by Mr J G Pedlar, to make arrangements for the departure of Belgians, it was reported they had been self-supporting since August 1918. They are leaving on the 18th and go to Exeter for a week in an hostel preparatory to returning to their own country. The Hon Secretary (Miss Wood) was heartily thanked for the untiring effort she had made on their behalf. It was decided to hand over to the refugees part of the £9 in hand, and to return the furniture to people who had kindly lent it. It was reported that Mr Pearce, of Boehill, in whose house they resided, had offered to hand back part of the rent.

On 21st March the Western Times reported that on the 18th the Mahieu family had gone to Exeter for the first stage of their journey home:

> They desire to return grateful thanks to all those whose kindness made their sojourn in a strange land endurable if not pleasurable, more especially to Mr Mathews [this should probably say Mr Marshall] (who has paid the rent of their cottage for several years) and Miss

---

[43] Ibid

Wood, the hon secretary to the local Committee, who has never spared herself when the welfare of the refugees was in question. In making the final arrangements the hon secretary has received valuable help from several well-wishers, especially Mr Stam, whose knowledge of French and Dutch has been of great assistance. Owing to Miss Wood's indefatigable labours, additional subscriptions in cash and kind were forthcoming form many sympathisers, enabling her to hand over £13 in cash and many articles of domestic utility, which will be of great value in the reconstruction of their devastated home. Letters from Belgium show that Belgium prices are three or four times those prevailing here.

The last we hear of the family is on 6th May 1919 in a Tiverton Gazette article which reports that:

Miss Julia Mahieu, daughter of the Belgian refugees, who recently left here, has written to Miss Wood, the local secretary of the Refugees Committee, saying that they had arrived safely in Belgium. After relating events during their journey home, she describes the havoc the war has wrought. Their house and two others they possessed are almost past recognition, one being beyond repair. The shells had burrowed great holes in the earth. They are glad, however, to get back to their old country and among their own people, many of whom are constructing wooden houses to live in. Miss Mahieu says prices there are very high. On behalf of her people she thanks all the inhabitants of Sampford Peverell who helped to make their sojourn here so comfortable, mentioning quite a number of names of persons who showed extra kindness, and to whom she wishes Miss Wood to convey her special thanks and gratitude.

Fund raising

The first world war was a very expensive operation fraught with logistical difficulties, and the government and armed services needed financial and practical support from the civilian population. Britain declared war on Germany on 4th August 1914, and on 7th August the Lord Lieutenant of the County of Devon held a public meeting at Exeter Castle at which resolutions were passed including these, as reported in the Western Times on 10th August:

> That this Meeting assures His Majesty of the loyalty and devotion of his subjects in the County of Devon, and of their desire to assist his Government in every possible way in carrying out whatever is considered necessary for the safety and welfare of the Empire.
>
> That public subscriptions be invited to provide a Fund to be called 'The Devonshire Patriotic Fund' to be used for the benefit of the wives and families of the Regulars of both Services, the Reservists, and the Territorials, belonging to the County of Devon, and of the sick and wounded.
>
> That the amounts be received by a Representative Committee, and be applied by them for the above objects in connection with the existing organization of the Soldiers and Sailors Families Association, and any necessary development thereof, and so as to ensure the proper disposition of all funds available. That all Mayors and Chairmen of Urban, Rural District, and Parish Councils and Parish Meetings be requested to form Local Committees in their various Towns and Parishes to canvass and collect for the Fund, and to provide clothing, linen and other necessaries for Hospital use.

The Association mentioned above, the SSFA, was renamed the SSAFA in 1919 when Airmen were added. It collected more than one million pounds in the first five months of the war. Sampford Peverell appointed five people to collect subscriptions for this fund, and in October the Parish Council decided that the names of all the subscribers should be recorded in the minutes. The collectors were Mr W H Pedler, Miss Pedler, Mrs Taudevin, Mr Disney and Mr Hart. The subscriptions ranged from three pence to three guineas, and totalled £51. 7s. The full list of names can be seen on the Sampford Peverell Society website: https://spsocresearch.weebly.com/ww1.html

Another fund to which Sampford Peverell contributed was the 'Devon Linen League', of which Countess Fortescue was President. The Western Times, 1 Sep 1914 reported that 597 articles had been received for group

1 (hospitals) and had been distributed to hospitals and headquarters. The report adds that "the following articles are very urgently required: slippers, house flannels, lavatory cloths, table cloths (4 yds x 50in), dressing gowns, games, and magazines. Patterns and information to be obtained at the Linen League." 1561 articles had been received for group 2 (Soldiers and Sailors) including some from Sampford Peverell and had been distributed to various military units.

Sampford Peverell also contributed to the 'Devon and Exeter Association for Supplying Comforts to our Sailors and Soldiers'. This group sent parcels to men on the front, and also provided hospitality to all the men on troop ships which passed through Exeter. On 10th November 1915 the Western Times reported that the Mayoress of Exeter had received 1,162 articles, including some from Sampford Peverell schoolchildren. It adds that "Bootlaces, note paper, postcards, candles, soap, shirts, scarves, mittens, socks, and sandbags are urgently required if the supply of comforts are to be kept up for the troops. During the week parcels of comforts and clothing and vegetables have been despatched" to various military units. The article includes a letter sent to the Mayoress of Exeter's depot from the wife of a Dulwich soldier, saying "Will you accept the heartfelt thanks of myself and my children for Exeter's thought for our dear one to whom we were unable ourselves to say good-bye". She enclosed a letter from her husband which said:

> When we arrived at Exeter from –– at 4am we had bags handed to us by ladies, containing ham sandwiches and apples. We also went on to the platform and were given hot tea, and the ladies then filled our water-bottles with good hot tea. When the train steamed out they waved their handkerchiefs to us, and the men raised rousing cheers for them. I was so cut up at this display of ladies' sympathy for a body of unknown soldiers that I could not raise even a murmur. The tears were rolling down my cheeks, and I am pleased to say I was only one among dozens who showed their tears. If only those ladies could have seen dozens of men in khaki with tears rolling down their faces, touched by such a simple action, they would have felt repaid a thousand-fold for their kindness. It does one good to meet ladies of this kind, and I shall always have a warm corner in my heart for Exeter. [44]

---

[44] The Red Cross website redcross.org.uk gives a lot of information on what the Red Cross did during WW1.

Another charity for which money was raised in the village was the British Red Cross. On 21st December 1917 the Western Times reported that:

A whist drive, held at St Boniface Home, Sampford Peverill [sic], on Thursday of last week, in aid of the British Red Cross Society, resulted in a sum of £25 being sent to the Society. There were over 200 present. The drive was organized by Mr W H Norrish (Chairman), Mrs W H Norrish, and Mrs W M Browne (Hon Secretary). Mr J G Pedlar and Dr W M Browne were the MCs. The refreshments were in [the] charge of Mrs Brooking, Mrs Salter and Mrs Mansfield, assisted by a large General Committee.

The prize winners were Miss F M Merry, Miss E J Bailey, Miss B Gay, Miss K Hancock, Mr C W Baker, and Miss W Smith, and a competition to guess the top score was tied between Miss M Wood and Mrs Howe. The Red Cross's work during WW1 included the provision of Voluntary Aid Detachments, auxiliary hospitals, working parties to supply clothing and equipment for soldiers and hospitals, transport for the wounded and rest stations. Fundraising was vitally important and by the end of the war the amount raised nationally was £21,885,035 of which over £20m had been spent on hospitals, medicine, clothing, grants and aftercare for the sick and wounded.

In his memoirs Denis Cluett remembered that during the war, when he was a young boy, "Mother and Father spent a great deal of their time organizing concerts, dances, whist drives etc. for various causes concerned with comforts for the troops. Most of these functions were held in the big assembly hall at the St Boniface Home." Denis Cluett also remembered the impact caused by Lottie Walrond's attendance at a fund-raising committee meeting, generating increased enthusiasm amongst male villagers to get more involved in these meetings, as we have seen in the chapter about her.

The children of the village were encouraged to contribute to the efforts to raise money, and to send items in to the charities. On the 20th November 1914 the school log reports that "With the permission of the Education Committee, the first half of the Sewing Time is being devoted to work for the soldiers engaged on the continent." This sort of sewing work, probably involving making the garments listed above for a charity, would have continued regularly throughout the war.

The school log and the Western Times both reported in January 1918 that the teachers and children of the school had donated £1 12s 6d to the Christmas Fund for the Children of Blinded Soldiers. This was a fund set up by Sir Arthur Pearson, a newspaper magnate and founder of the Daily Express, who lost his own sight due to glaucoma. He founded The Blinded Soldiers and Sailors Care Committee, later renamed St Dunstan's, for soldiers blinded by gas attack or trauma during the First World War. His goal, radical for the time, was to provide vocational training rather than charity for invalided servicemen, and to help them and their families live as normal a life as possible. In a letter to "The Spectator" he explained that although the government made a weekly allowance for children born before, or within nine months of, a soldier's discharge, there was no additional help for any children born later, so he set up the Blind Soldiers' Children's Fund to allow them to pay 5s per week until the age of sixteen for each of these children. Five shillings a week was far more than Sampford Peverell children would have received, so although their donation may seem small, it was a considerable sum to them during such hard times.

By the end of the war there were so many charities asking for money, from so many people struggling to make ends meet, that people were overwhelmed by it all. And it didn't stop there – following the war there were more appeals to help those who returned from the war and to set up memorials and peace funds – of which there is more in another chapter.

Collecting from the wild

During the First World War a number of government initiatives urged everyone in the country to help the war effort by foraging for particular items from the countryside. In this chapter we'll look at what was collected in this area, and why.

The role of conkers in helping to win the war

In the autumn of 1917 children were asked to collect conkers, the nuts of the horse-chestnut tree, for "invaluable and urgent war work" or for "munitions purposes". The precise reason was not explained at the time, but a highly enthusiastic response was achieved, probably due to the War Office paying 7s 6d for each hundredweight collected. The conkers were initially stored at, and collected from, local railway stations, so Tiverton Junction would have been Sampford Peverell's local depot. The conkers were collected across the whole country but many rotted before they could be transported. Around 3,000 tons did finally reach their destination. Some boys in Exeter, perhaps misinterpreting the reference to 'munitions purposes', were fined for throwing chestnuts and husks at house windows!

It later transpired that the conkers were used to produce acetone, a solvent used in the production of cordite, a propellant needed for firing bullets and artillery shells. Military strategy had changed by the start of WW1 and there was a much heavier use of artillery in determining the outcome of battles, both on land and at sea. This resulted in a well-publicised shortage of artillery shells in the early part of 1915, despite denials by Lord Kitchener. The eventual outcome was the collapse of the UK government later in the same year and the appointment of a new Prime Minister, David Lloyd George.

The propellant "cordite" (originally called cord powder) was developed and patented in 1889, and consisted of a mixture of nitro-glycerine, guncotton (Nitro cellulose) and petroleum jelly. Using acetone as a solvent, cordite could be shaped into spaghetti-like strands: thin strands for rifle bullets, and much thicker strands for artillery shells. When the cordite was ignited it produced a large quantity of hot gases which expanded rapidly and pushed the bullet at great speed down the barrel of the gun. The First Lord of the Admiralty, one Winston Churchill, had always insisted that the Royal Navy should have an independent factory for the production of the cordite required for their shells. He learned with extreme interest that a new process had been invented for the production of acetone, which was the limiting factor in producing sufficient cordite and, therefore, enough shells to win the war.

The new process involved bacterial fermentation and had been developed by a biochemist, Dr Weizmann, at the University of Manchester. The process he developed required the isolation of bacteria which were able to break down starch and produce Acetone, Butanol and Ethanol at the same time. This was called the ABE process and was the forerunner of all industrial fermentation.

The "laboratory" process for acetone production was developed into a full pilot study late in 1915 using the fermentation equipment of a commandeered gin factory in London! Once the process was proven, a brand-new factory was constructed at Holton Heath, just outside Poole in Dorset. The factory was built well away from any other residential buildings due to the explosive nature of the products. The factory became operational late in 1916 and initially used maize and potatoes as the raw material containing starch. It soon became apparent that there was insufficient maize available and, more importantly, it was also needed for animal feed. Importing additional maize from the USA and Canada was impractical so an alternative natural source of starch was sought. Dr Weizmann was approached in 1917 and he modified the fermentation method so that acetone could be produced from conkers – a product with no nutritional value to animals due to poisonous toxins within the nut. A Government statement was printed in the Times in July 1917: "Chestnut seeds, not the green husks, are required by the Government for the Ministry of Munitions. The nuts will replace cereals which have been necessary for the production of an article of great importance in the prosecution of the War".

Six huge storage silos were constructed to hold all the conkers. The formulation of the cordite was changed slightly, and it was used extensively by the Royal Navy. School children and boy scouts were urged to collect conkers and hand them in, rather than destroying them as they usually did in their playground games. With a good supply of horse chestnut trees in this area the children of Sampford Peverell probably made a good contribution to the collection.

Fruit stones and nut shells

In July 1918 an appeal for fruit stones and nut shells was published in newspapers, including the Western Times on 29th July 1918, as follows:

Fruit stones and hard nutshells are urgently demanded by the Government for conversion into charcoal, which is to be used in the British respirator for the protection of our troops against poison gas. The urgency of the need will be seen from the fact that at present no other substance is known to give equal protection. The charcoal thus produced has a power of absorption many times that of charcoal obtained from other materials. The appeal of the National Salvage Council is designed to meet an emergency which will be particularly acute during the next few months.

During this period the public are invited to meet the need. It is recognised that owing to the scarcity of fruit, the quantities available are not very large. But stones and shells must be secured at the rate of hundreds of tons a week, and it is hoped that every town and village in the kingdom will at once take steps to organize collections. Hotels, clubs and institutions have already been invited to save every available stone and shell. In addition to stones from fresh fruit, dates and prunes provide a source of supply. Cocoanu [s shells are also quite suitable for this purpose.

In Sampford Peverell the Parish Council offered prizes to the school children who collected the largest quantity of fruit stones and hard nut shells. The children willingly helped the war effort in this way, and in October 1918 the Parish Council awarded prizes as follows:

1st   Minnie Hayward   5 shillings
2nd   Phyllis Lovell   4 shillings
3rd   John Collings   3 shillings
4th   Eileen Jennings   2 shillings
5th   Frank Williams   1 shilling

Herbs

In May 1918 the Sampford Peverell school log reported that children were out collecting herbs "in response to a request from Tiverton - dandelion (root), coltsfoot (whole) celandine (leaves)".

This followed a national call for medicinal herbs. Before the war many herbs including, surprisingly, dandelions and stinging nettles, were imported from continental Europe and parts of the Empire, and obviously these sources were no longer available. Additionally, the Western Morning News on 12th July 1917 reported that before the war "Drugs from herbs were even exported from England to Germany, but of late years we have allowed the Germans to filch almost the whole of the drug-making industry from us." It suggests that

Boy Scouts, and boys and girls of other organizations who have country rambles, disabled soldiers and many others, might find the work of collection pleasant and profitable. It is required, however, that the herbs when collected should be quickly and effectually dried, and it is for this purpose that some central association is specially needed.

For this reason, the National Herb Growing Association was set up. Sir Charles Thomas Dyke Acland, of Killerton House, wrote a letter to a local newspaper on June 21st 1917 on this subject:

> Sir, I am informed by the National Herb Growing Association that there is a great need for the collecting of Foxglove and Sanicle leaves and I believe this is also true of Dandelion roots. In many parts of the country they are being collected for this Association by school children under the leadership of their teachers. May I ask you to draw attention to this in your paper, as Devon, Somerset and Cornwall ought to give a good supply. The National Herb Growing Association will be glad to send advice and instructions to anyone who cares to write to them.

Of course a lot of effort was wasted when plants were incorrectly identified, or were not dried quickly and properly, but many useful collections were made. The biggest success story was the collection of sphagnum moss. This followed the publication of a medical article pointing out that sphagnum moss could absorb over 20 times its own weight of water (or blood) before dripping, was at least twice as absorptive as cotton wool, and had excellent antiseptic properties. The Prince of Wales enabled a 'moss depot' to be set up in Princetown, where large quantities of sphagnum moss were being collected from 'the surrounding boggy wastes'. The moss was dried, treated, and sewn into 2oz bags by the women working there. By the end of WW1 up to a million moss dressings per month were being sent to military hospitals, and they helped save the limbs, or lives, of countless soldiers[45].

Blackberries

Food was in short supply throughout the war, and this item appeared in Sampford's Parish Council minutes in July 1918: "Devon Fruit and Vegetable Society - after discussing the scheme of the Devon Fruit and Vegetable Society the Chairman said it was the duty of the Council to do their share, in helping to collect surplus fruit and vegetables, so that there should not be any waste in our parish during the war. "

---

[45] Peter Ayres, Britain's Green Allies: Medicinal Plants in Wartime, (Matador, 2015)

The Devon Fruit and Vegetable Society was founded in May 1918 as a cooperative for growers, and they worked on projects initiated by the Government to help the war effort. For example, in August 1918 a letter appeared in most local newspapers from the 'Devon War Agricultural Executive Committee' saying:

> Sir, - the Ministry of Food is anxious that none of the blackberry crop should be wasted, that everything should be done to harvest the crop, and that as large a part as possible should go to licensed factories to be made into jam for Army and civilian needs.

> With this object in view an organized collection of blackberries will be made throughout the county, and the County of Devon Fruit and Vegetable Society, of this address, will act as agents to the Ministry of Food in paying the pickers and handling the crop.

> The Food Production Department is cooperating with the Ministry of Food in the carrying out of the scheme, and my Committee asks that landowners and farmers will assist to their utmost in this matter (1) By giving reasonable facilities for the gathering of blackberries from the hedges surrounding their fields, and (2) By not clipping the hedges until the blackberries have been gathered.

A few days later another article stated that the Devon Education Committee had "circulated a letter to headmasters and teachers requesting them to arrange parties of school children for blackberry picking." It added that "Three half-holidays a week for this purpose will be sanctioned" and that they would be paid 3d per pound. The Sampford Peverell school children would certainly have helped with this too. A report given in Exeter in October 1918 said that "Although hindered by the bad weather the blackberry gathering resulted in 100 tons of the fruit being obtained" and now they were appealing for help in "gathering sloes, enormous quantities of which were required for the jam factories". Note, the sloes were for jam, not gin, allegedly!

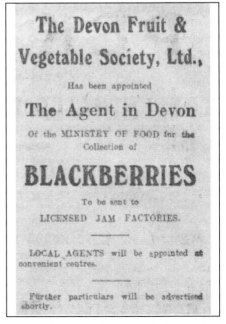

The Devon Fruit &
Vegetable Society, Ltd.,

Has been appointed

The Agent in Devon

Of the MINISTRY OF FOOD for the
Collection of

BLACKBERRIES

To be sent to

LICENSED JAM FACTORIES.

LOCAL AGENTS will be appointed at convenient centres.

Further particulars will be advertised shortly.

Exeter and Plymouth Gazette 30 Aug 1918. Image reproduced with kind permission of The British Newspaper Archive (www.britishnewspaperarchive.co.uk) ©THE BRITISH LIBRARY BOARD. ALL RIGHTS RESERVED

Public services

The Parish Council

Sampford Peverell Parish Council met every few months throughout the war years, under the chairmanship of John Garnsey Pedler, who farmed Sampford Barton farm. Henry Wood the saddler, and captain of the fire brigade, was the Parish Clerk. The most regular council member was William Dunn, the shoemaker, who attended every meeting from October 1914 until April 1919. Regular members of the council included W H Norrish, who ran the Creamery, and Edward Pearce, who farmed Boehill Barton. Other members at different times were W Cluett, A J Down, R Gater, James Salter, C Radford, W H Saunders, W H Warner, T White, W J Williams, and E A Williams.

Members of the Parish Council, especially the Chairman and Vice-Chairman, were very involved in the recruiting effort and in fund-raising. In October 1914 the council instigated the collection for the Devonshire Patriotic Fund, which is referred to elsewhere in this book. The minutes recorded the names of all the collectors and contributors, and this list can be seen on our website: https://spsocresearch.weebly.com/ww1.html

In January 1917 the Parish Council received a letter from the County Council respecting the supply of seed potatoes to cottagers, allotment holders, and small holders, asking how many would be required. This was because, due to the food shortage, everyone was encouraged to grow their own vegetables. Devon County Council supplied seed potatoes to people via their local council at a favourable price of 16s per cwt. (though Seaton urban council complained that the potatoes contained an unusually large quantity of earth!). Another agricultural task for the council was to make sure enough corn was tilled, and in July 1918 they were contacted by the Devon Fruit and Vegetable Society to help collect surplus fruit and vegetables to avoid waste. The council also encouraged children to collect fruit stones and hard nut shells and rewarded them for their efforts, as described in the last chapter.

Although it is not recorded in the meeting minutes, the Parish Council played a part after the war in planning how to commemorate the war and celebrate the peace; topics which are covered elsewhere in this book.

Besides matters relating to the war, much of their time was spent discussing drains and sanitation: putting tenders out for the creating of new sewers or repairs to the existing sewers and road gullies. In September 1917 they also had to get the parish pump repaired – this and much of the other building work was completed by Mr Frederick Goffin. The Parish Council also paid for street lighting, which included repairs to street lamps, buying oil for them, placing out the lamps in the winter, and cleaning and storing them in the summer. Frederick Vickery was paid 1s 3d per night to go round lighting the lamps. In August 1916 they agreed that following the government order to ban street lights, they would not use them again until further notice. The lights were not re-lit until October 1919.

Fire service

During the First World War the village continued to have a need for fire, police and medical services, but we have the impression that the providers of these services were not called upon as much as they were during peacetime.

Sampford Peverell had its own fire brigade, under the captaincy of Harry Wood, the saddler, who lived on Turnpike. He always had horses on his premises and kept the fire pump in one of his barns. In his memoirs Denis Cluett described the pump as follows

> The fire pump consisted of a long rectangular box affair which had to be filled with water, usually by buckets from the nearest pump. Beams were mounted, one on each side of the container, and these were pumped up and down by a couple of men to each. In theory this pumped the water through the hoses on to the fire.

If Henry Wood heard of a fire he would have to round up his volunteers, assemble his equipment, and fill the fire pump with water using buckets and a water pump, before being able to do anything. Denis Cluett casts aspersions on the Sampford brigade's ability to tackle fires promptly, but we have examples from outside this period of their doing a very good job. Thankfully, as far as we know, they were not called upon to deal with any fires during the war period.

Police and court cases

At the start of the war Sampford Peverell had its own village policeman: PC Alfred John Blackmore, who lived in the police house in Lower Town (*2018: 21 Lower Town*) with his wife and family. He had been the local policeman since PC Fewings left in 1909 after more than ten years' service in the village. PC Blackmore was quoted in a few court cases during early years of the war. The cases did not concern major crimes, but they give a glimpse of life at the time.

The Hare and Hounds

On 13th October 1914 the Western Times reported that Frederick Payne, a contractor, and William Coppin, an insurance agent were summoned for blowing the whistle of a steam engine on the road on September 29th. PC Blackmore gave evidence that a traction engine was standing outside the Hare and Hounds in Lower Town when Coppin climbed onto it and blew the whistle, contrary to the bylaw. Payne was also summoned as he owned the engine, but the case against him was dismissed. Coppin was fined 10s. Frederick Payne junior, the driver of the engine, was summoned for leaving the engine unattended outside the public house for two hours, and for using obscene language to PC Blackmore. He was fined 10s on each count.

In January 1915 William Williams, a GWR platelayer, was summoned for using obscene language in Lower Town. "PC Blackmore said at 10.15 pm he saw defendant outside the Globe Inn. When reproached for swearing he replied, sneeringly, 'It's a long way to Tipperary.' He was under the influence of drink." He was fined 8s 6d. William Williams enlisted in the army later that year and is in our list of surviving participants in the war.

In May 1915 Ida Goffin and Theresa Trevellyan, both married women, were found guilty, on PC Blackmore's evidence, of stealing a quantity of wood, valued at 6d, from Stanley Williams, a butcher in Sampford Peverell.

PC Blackmore stated that he noticed defendants going towards a wood-rick. Having received a complaint, he followed and found them taking wood from the rick. The prosecutor said he had not given the defendants permission to take wood. He had been missing wood for some time.

They were fined 10s each. Stanley Williams joined the army later that year and is in our list of surviving participants.

In October 1915 three of PC Blackmore's cases came to court. According to the Western Times:

> Thomas Cornish, 18, carter, of Sampford Peverell, pleaded guilty to using bad language, and was fined 10s. The Chairman gave the defendant some good advice as to his future conduct, and commented on the spectacle of a fine young fellow like the defendant being in the dock on such a charge.

> John Norman, 55, dairyman, of Sampford Peverell, who according to PC Blackmore some years ago underwent an operation to the head, was fined 7s 6d for being drunk whilst riding a horse. Defendant pleaded guilty and expressed contrition for the offence.

> For not burying the carcase of a sheep, James Wright, of Sampford Peverell, was fined 10s. PC Blackmore proved the case.

We have more detail of the Cornish and Wright cases in the report from the Exeter and Plymouth Gazette. In relation to Thomas Cornish, of Higher Town:

> PC Blackmore proved the case. Superintendent Joplin said the police had a great deal of trouble with youths at Sampford using obscene language. The defendant was cautioned about twelve months ago for his conduct. The language used by the defendant was disgusting, especially when said to passing females.

There is more about Thomas Cornish in our section on casualties, as he enlisted in 1916 and was killed in action. On the Wright case:

> PC Blackmore said that, in consequence of information, he went to Ridge Farm. On the way he met the defendant and his wife going to Tiverton Market. Witness asked defendant if he had the carcases of three sheep unburied, to which he replied, "No, only one." Witness then proceeded to the field, and, in a ditch at the end, saw the carcase of one, but not of three sheep, as had been alleged. A fine of 10s was imposed.

We do not know what PC Blackmore looked like, but may be able to hazard a guess from a case heard in Tiverton in August 1916. Revd William Frank Lamplugh of Clayhanger, his wife, Gertrude, and his sister, Beatrice, were summoned for riding bicycles without showing red rear lights, in contradiction of the Defence of the Realm Act. The facts were given by PC Blackmore of Sampford Peverell. The Western Times reported that "Rev.W.F.Lamplugh suggested that this was one of the instances where the police, who might be corporally large but mentally deficient, were trying to get cases." Mrs Lamplugh said she did not know the regulations and thought they were all right if walking. Nevertheless the bench fined the defendants 7s 6d each, and said that they considered the criticism of the police was entirely uncalled for.

In August 1916, Miriam Parson, the wife of the Globe's landlord and mother of four young children, was in the newspaper. She pleaded "guilty with an explanation" to using obscene language within hearing of the highway at 10.30 pm on 17th August. "PC Blackmore said defendant was in the kitchen of the inn, and the window was wide open, so that the objectionable language was audible to passers-by." Mrs Parsons said that she had nothing to say against the constable, for whom she had the greatest respect, but she was highly upset by some family affairs. The Superintendent said the brewery company had been communicated with and she was fined 10s.

PC Blackmore and his family left Sampford and moved to Buckfastleigh later that year, leaving the village without a policeman. This was probably due to the shortage of manpower caused by the war, with many policemen signing up for military duty, with those who remained being reassigned. Another factor may have been that many of the troublesome youths of the village had gone to war. A later newspaper article did report, however, that PC Searle from Halberton was a frequent visitor while Sampford did not have its own policeman.

Coincidentally, it was during the village's unpoliced spell that its biggest crime came to light. In August 1917 Miss Maud Taylor, the sub-postmistress who ran the Post Office in London House, was found guilty of fraud and of falsifying accounts after a visit from the postmaster in Tiverton who found discrepancies in the accounts: £132 6s 5d was missing, plus £14 3s owed to Mrs L Davey of Sampford Peverell, the wife of a naval petty officer. Mrs Davey had handed that sum to Miss Taylor to be paid into the Savings Bank account for Mrs Davey's son. She also presented signed vouchers and orders for £26 12s 9d for her husband's pay and pension. The money did not appear, and after a number of letters and telegrams Miss Taylor said she did, a month later, pay in the £14 3s to the savings account, but 'forgot' to make a return to the Savings Bank in London as she should have, so Mrs Davey received no acknowledgement of the money and the GPO never received it. A search revealed a falsified statement concerning the payment. Miss Taylor did eventually pay Mrs Davey the pay and pension money but in instalments over a period of time. Various witnesses testified that Miss Taylor often appeared "stupefied or ill". Charles Ponsford, who worked as her assistant for two years, said

> it often happened when people came to cash vouchers they were unable to be paid as there was not sufficient money in the till. On these occasions defendant would send him out into the village to borrow money, and if he was unable to get it the customers were told it would be forwarded to them. He sometimes, at defendant's instructions, took money from the till to do 'shopping' for her.

The prosecutor told the jury they would hear that

> almost daily the defendant would send out two or three times for a noggin [a quarter of a pint], or a noggin and a half, of spirit, and when they remembered that this would cost about 5s or 6s they would easily understand where the money had gone.

During the court case Miss Taylor, when asked if she wanted to say anything, replied "I have been tempted from my commencement of postal duties to do all manner of things, that have not been right." She was found guilty and sent to jail.

Other offences in Sampford Peverell during the war years were relatively minor. In April 1917 WH Norrish and Sons of Sampford Peverell were summoned under the Food and Drugs Act for adulterating milk after some samples were tested and showed that they contained too much water. In their defence the representative for Norrish and Co said it was difficult to get feeding stuffs so the quality of milk would vary, and in any case according to his samples the public were getting much more cream in the separated milk than they should. They were fined £2.

The following month a Halberton man, Walter Doble, was fined 10s for stealing a piece of larch board and a chopping hook worth 1s from Thomas Ponsford of Sampford Peverell. Another Halberton man, Walter Philips, was fined in October 1917 for not having a rear light on his motor tractor at Sampford Peverell. Rear lights were also the issue in another case that month: Miss Florrie Salter of Sampford Peverell was fined 5s for riding a bicycle in Tiverton without a rear light. It should be borne in mind that street lights were not turned on during the war, so lighting on vehicles was all the more important.

A new policeman, PC Bertram Beavis, arrived in the village a few months after the end of the war, and the Tiverton Gazette reported on 15th April 1919 that "Sampford Peverell is to have a police constable after being without one for about two years." At about the same time a previous policeman, Thomas Fewings, who had retired in 1918 but still owned property in the village, moved back to Sampford and "intends to spend the residue of his days in our peaceful village among friends." His son, Herbert Fewings, had been killed in action in May 1918. The article adds that Thomas Fewings "retires with an exemplary character, and has the distinction of never having been cautioned by the police chief." An interesting comment suggesting that perhaps another policeman had been so cautioned!

Medical matters and accidents

The village doctor during the war years was Dr William Mitchell Browne, who then lived with his family in Turberfield House, Lower Town. He was described in Kelly's 1914 trade directory as "physician and surgeon, and medical officer and public vaccinator for the districts of Halberton and Uplowman of Tiverton Union". He was also a Captain in the Royal Army Medical Corps.

We don't have any record of how busy or otherwise he was with village illnesses, though his work as medical officer for other areas, for St Boniface Home, and for the Tiverton Union (the workhouse) would have kept him busy. We do know, though, from a newspaper report, that there were several cases of scarlet fever in the area, including one in Sampford Peverell, in the period leading up to 4th August 1915. Dr Browne may also have been called to any difficult cases of childbirth, but this was mainly seen as the province of midwives in those days, and the village had its own resident midwife throughout the war in Elizabeth Moon.

Dr William Mitchell Browne

Dr Browne would have been called to most of the accidents in the area, and these again give glimpses of everyday life in the village during the war years. Some of the incidents also show the increasing number of accidents on roads as the result of bicycles and cars joining what used to be exclusively the domain of horses.

On 19th November 1914 the Western Times reported that Tom Disney, farmer, of Landside, Sampford Peverell, sued A S Western, motor engineer of Uffculme,

> for £70 damages sustained to himself and horse owing to the alleged negligent driving of a motor car by defendant's servant. There was a counter claim for damages to the car and consequent loss for £23 16s. " ... "It was alleged that defendant did not exercise proper caution when driving around a bend in the Uffculme Road and failing to blow his horn with the result that a collision occurred between plaintiff's horse and the car, the plaintiff being thrown. The horse that plaintiff was riding was injured to such an extent that it had to be killed. " ... "John Richardson, motor engineer, Wellington, stated that to go around the corner at a speed of 15 miles an hour was dangerous. It should be taken at a crawl."

It's interesting that to us 15 mph would now seem like a crawl! The driver, Frank Graves, said he did sound the horn, was on the correct side of the road, and was going at about a walking pace. He said the plaintiff was cutting the corner and going at a sharp canter on the wrong side of the road. The judge decided neither side had proved their claim, so he gave judgement and costs to both for their claim and counterclaim.

A very different type of accident happened in November 1915 when it was reported that "Whilst at a ringing practice at Sampford Peverell on Friday, Mr Bert Cornish fell and broke his leg. He is progressing favourably". In his memoirs Denis Cluett recalled that Bert Cornish used to go around the village on crutches, doing odd jobs, so he may not have recovered fully. A broken limb was also sustained by a St Boniface boy on Connigar Hill in October 1916, reported by the Western Times as follows:

> What might have been a very serious accident occurred on Saturday last. An inmate of the St. Boniface Home named Arthur Pearce, was flying a kite on the top of Comgear [sic] Hill, and not noticing that he was near the edge of the cliff fell headlong down. The Superintendent of the Home (Mr Mansfield) was called to the scene of the accident, and being a certificated ambulance man, rendered first aid, and removed the lad to the Home, and Dr W M Browne, medical officer to the Home, was called in, and found that the boy had sustained a fractured wrist. The

injured limb was set, and the lad is going on comfortably. All who know the place where the lad fell wonder that he was not killed.

If PC Blackmore had been around he might have also have pointed out that the Defence Of the Realm Act had made it illegal for civilians to fly kites, but the village was unpoliced at this time!

In January 1917 there was a terrible incident at Merriemeade House in Lower Town, then occupied by Mr and Mrs W H Norrish (Mr Norrish was the manager of the creamery) and their family. Two of the children were playing upstairs in the morning while their parents were out. Mrs Edith Trevellyan, a day servant (and wife of casualty James Trevellyan) saw the older child come downstairs but then she heard screams. A servant (it is not clear if this was Edith or someone else) rushed upstairs to the nursery and found that the younger child, Grace, aged 3½ was on fire. They wrapped the child in a blanket to extinguish the flames and sent for Dr Browne. The doctor was there within minutes and did all he could, but the child died the next day from shock. Some burnt matches and a box of matches had been found on a chair in the nursery, so it is thought the child was playing with them and accidentally set fire to her clothes.

A newspaper report from September 1917 describes another road accident:

> Mrs. Hurford, Higher Town, Sampford Peverell, narrowly escaped a serious accident whilst cycling towards Tiverton Junction on Tuesday. As she reached the four cross roads a motor car travelling at a furious pace and without the slightest warning, came on from the direction of Tiverton. Mrs. Hurford threw herself from her cycle, and thus escaped with a severe shaking and a torn coat.

A series of accidents occurred in mid 1918, as reported by the Western Times on 5th July:

> SAMPFORD PEVERILL. A chapter of accidents occurred here this week. Mr R Trevellyan, of Lower [Town], whilst working at the Quarries, had the misfortune to let the trolley run over his foot.
>
> Mrs Hine, Lower Town, fell downstairs, bruising herself rather badly and dislocating her wrist.
>
> During haymaking operations a horse bolted, throwing Mr J Gale off the top of the load. Mr Gale sustained a shaking and considerable bruises.
>
> Whilst driving a horse and lorry in the direction of Uplowman, Pte. W Creedy, a soldier substitute, in the employ of Mr Leaman, of Uplowman,

negotiated the corner too sharply, with the result that the lorry overturned, throwing both horse and driver to the ground. Happily help was forthcoming, and in this case no one was any the worse.

Thankfully 1918 seems to have continued without any further mishaps occurring to the residents of the village, at least to those who were not on active service in the war.

The St Boniface Home for Waifs and Strays

The year 1907 marked a significant change for Sampford Peverell. The East Devon County School, which had been functioning in Lower Town for over 40 years, closed upon the retirement of its owner and master. The three buildings which comprised the School were taken over by the 'Church of England Society for Waifs and Strays' for use as a boys' home (*2018: the site of 1-3 Court Way*). This Society provided places in their homes, which were situated all over the country, for boys and girls in desperate circumstances, such as being orphaned, in extreme poverty, or from broken homes. There being no State social security system at the time, the Society would step in where no other support from relatives, or from the local Board of Guardians of the Poor, was available. The Society obtained its funds from its supporters, who were encouraged to make regular donations in order to pay for the running costs.

Within a matter of a few months of the East Devon County School's closure, about 60 boys became the new residents at 'St Boniface Home' under the supervision of a resident master. Most of the initial intake of boys had been transferred from another of the Society's homes in Bognor Regis, which was closed as it was too small for the boys' needs. The youngest boys to be admitted to the Home were aged 7, and 'inmates' (as they were sometimes referred to) could be accommodated there until at least the age of 14. Many had a shorter stay, arriving at the Home after having been in care elsewhere, and then sometimes being moved again before they reached 14, either to another home or to foster parents.

During their time at St Boniface Home, they were educated at the National School in Higher Town (which is now the Primary School) alongside the local children who lived with their families in the village. Out of school hours, the boys' activities were strictly controlled at the Home. They had to do all the cleaning, as well as some of the food preparation, and they were given lessons in carpentry and gardening, the latter partly to provide food for the Home and partly to prepare them for later life. There was also a Scout troupe, a band and a gymnastics team for them to join, in addition to other sporting activities such as swimming and football. [The Sampford Peverell Society intends to make St Boniface Home the subject of a future publication, in which a much fuller account will be given].

Once a boy reached the age of 14, the master of the home made every effort to find him gainful employment through the network of the Society's supporters and also through the Diocesan Offices of the Church of England. As these networks extended throughout England and Wales, boys could be found work far away, often as farm hands, gardeners and servants. The employer would remain in contact with the home from which the boy came

Boys arriving at St Boniface in 1907.   *Photo courtesy of The Children's Society*

to let the master know about his suitability for the work. For some boys, several changes of employment followed in quick succession, resulting in the continued involvement of the Waifs and Strays Society with the boy's welfare throughout his teenage years. The alternative option was for the boy to be sent overseas, subject to parental consent *(if available)*, usually to Canada, but occasionally to New Zealand or Australia. The Society ran a boys' home in Quebec, Canada, called Gibb's Home, which acted as a receiving home for new arrivals from England. After a short stay in Gibb's Home, boys were moved on into jobs, there being plentiful employment opportunities there at that time.

By July 1913[1], after St Boniface Home had been open for 6 years, 173 boys had lived in, and then left, the Home. Of the leavers, 41 had become farm workers, 44 had emigrated, 33 had become indoor servants or gardeners and 7 had joined the Army or Navy. The remainder had either been moved to other homes or contact with them had been lost. 60 boys were resident in the Home at that time, of which number 51 attended the National School.

At the outbreak of the War St Boniface Home was under the supervision of Boer War veteran and army reservist William Keeley and his wife Lucy, whose role was matron. Mr Keeley had only been the superintendent at St Boniface Home for a year when he was recalled to serve in the Army in August 1914. The gardener, John Thomas, was also a reservist and was called up at the same time.

St Boniface Home remained open throughout the War, with the number of boys accommodated reaching the home's capacity of 66 by 1917. The Society of Waifs and Strays, through its monthly magazine called 'Waifs and Strays' was keen to show support for the war effort, by including articles and letters from the many 'Home Boys' who fought in the War. A new policy was introduced throughout its homes to admit children whose fathers were called up and who had nobody to care for them, wherever possible. Consequently, as the War progressed, a growing proportion of the inmates fell into this category; when, and if, their fathers returned, they were able to go back to their family homes.

There was a local committee appointed to oversee the running of each of the Society's homes. In Sampford Peverell, this was chaired by the Hon

St. Boniface, Sampford Peverell.

Staff and Emigrant Party, 1912.

Staff and Emigrant party 1912   *Photo courtesy of The Children's Society*

Lionel Walrond MP, ably supported by his wife Lottie (see the chapter on Lottie Walrond). The couple were strong supporters of the Society's work and, before the War they held a fête and a cricket match in the grounds of their home (Bradfield near Willand), to raise funds for St Boniface Home. Day-to-day management of the Society's homes was delegated to the master at each establishment. Both William Keeley and his assistant Percy Bradfield (who took charge of the home when Keeley was called up) were able to use their positions to assist with army recruitment. It was probably they who arranged for the grounds of St Boniface Home to be used for the first army recruitment drive in Sampford Peverell, which took place on 9 September 1914 (see the chapter on Recruitment). The boys' camping trip was next to be affected in the late summer of 1914[2], when it was cut short so that the 40 strong Scout troop attached to the Home, under the leadership of Percy Bradfield, could help with the War effort by guarding bridges and railway lines.

Thereafter, the Scouts and the bugle band were to be seen and heard on several weekends, marching around the countryside in support of army recruitment, often attending church services in the parishes that they visited. The bugle band would also use these occasions for raising money for the Home. Each of the Society's homes held annual 'Pound Days'

The St Boniface bugle band   *Photo courtesy of The Children's Society*

during which they collected supplies for use in the home. Local people gave generously to these days, and donations of either cash or in kind were gratefully accepted. A perambulation of the parishes within about a ten-mile radius of Sampford Peverell raised £44 5s in April 1915[3], with the boys walking between 16 and 20 miles a day. The cash was supplemented by donations of provisions from residents of Sampford Peverell and surrounding villages. The grand total donated at the April 1915 Pound Day was £51 17s 5d and 984 lbs of goods in kind[4]. These were sometimes itemised in the local newspaper, with the donor's name attributed to each, for example "Mrs Chave, Uplowman, quantity of cauliflowers; Mrs Sanders, 1lb butter", and at Christmas time, "Miss D Wallington, a bag of oranges, and Major Marshall, Halberton, 130 buns for the boys' tea"[5]. The thought that one's generosity, or lack of it, would be published in the local newspaper for all one's neighbours to see must have encouraged the residents to be especially charitable towards the Home!

Apart from money and provisions for the household, the residents of Sampford Peverell acted in a kindly manner towards the boys of St Boniface Home in many other ways. For example, they provided transport for occasional trips, usually for the scouts and bugle band; they attended fund-raising events such as lectures at the Home and garden parties organised by some of the wealthier residents; they organised parcels of clothing to be sent to the Home; and they provided musical instruments and games for the boys. The Home even managed to obtain sufficient donations to fund the purchase of an 'American Organ' for their chapel. In return, the Home allowed its facilities to be used by the local community. In his memoirs, Denis Cluett mentions that his father and mother organised dances during the War, which were held at St Boniface Home.

Another proposal made by the Society, through the medium of the Waifs and Strays magazine[6], was that Homes should cease taking their boys on summer camps. Instead, they should stay and work on the land, helping with the harvest to compensate for the men who had joined up. Although we do not know for sure that this happened at St Boniface Home, it would seem likely that it did and may account for there apparently being no critical shortage of farm labour (see chapter on farming and food).

Despite the generosity of the local community, the Home remained dependant financially on its benefactors around the country. As the War progressed, many of them found it more difficult to maintain their contributions. The problem was compounded by rising prices meaning that the average annual cost of maintaining one child at one of the Society's homes rose from £16 to £18 between 1914 and 1916[7].There was some financial relief for the Society, because they received an allowance from the War Office for each child in their care who was the son or daughter of a serving soldier. This allowance ceased, however, as soon as the father was discharged or died.

A new superintendent and matron, Mr and Mrs Mansfield, were appointed in April 1916 in the continuing absence of William Keeley and the impending departure of Percy Bradfield, who had received notice that he would be called up later in the year. Neither William nor Percy returned to St Boniface Home. William Keeley survived the War and went on to become master of another boys' home. Percy Bradfield was not so fortunate, having been killed at the third battle of Ypres in October 1917. The news of his death must have been a terrible shock for the boys, as many would have known him since they arrived at St Boniface Home.

The new Master, Mr Mansfield, made a special plea for people to be even more generous at the next Pound Day, although the success or otherwise of this action is not recorded. As the War continued through 1917 and into 1918, the problem of food shortages became more apparent (see the chapter on farming and food). St Boniface Home was fortunate in having a large garden, and it is probable that every inch of it was now turned over to growing vegetables for the Home. The boys were quite resourceful, 'scrumping'[8] apples from nearby orchards to supplement their diet!

By 1918 regulations about hoarding food had been introduced, and the Society was becoming concerned that the concept of Pound Days could infringe the regulations, because their homes could suddenly come into possession of large quantities of provisions. They were eager to keep Pound Days going, not least because central funds had been almost exhausted, and lobbied Government to that effect. They even advocated the idea of 'Amnesty Days' whereby any member of the public who had inadvertently infringed the regulations could hand in their surplus foodstuffs at their local Society home[9]! Fortunately, the War came to an end before any serious hardship affected the running of the Home. Gradually, things returned to normal, and those boys who had been accommodated there because their fathers had joined up were able to return to their own homes.

St Boniface Boys

Due to the policy of confidentiality maintained over the individual files on the boys of St Boniface Home, now held by The Children's Society (successor to The Church of England Waifs and Strays Society) a comprehensive list of those who lived in the Home is not publicly available. Research into which boys from the Home fought in the War has, therefore, been restricted to published sources, principally a 'roll of honour' published (up until 1916) in the Society's monthly magazine 'Waifs and Strays' and the 1911 Census which records details of the boys residing at the Home at that time.

Our Waifs and Strays.

OUR ROLL OF HONOUR.

THE time has come to publish a first instalment —and it is one of which to be proud—of those among our own "Old Boys" who are serving their country during this momentous period of its history. We know that the following list is a most imperfect one, but the very fact of its publication will make the authorities of those Homes who have been hitherto somewhat "slack" in answering the request issued some while ago "hurry up" their returns. There is included in the list those also of whom the Society is justly proud, members of the Head Office staff and masters in charge of Homes, who are setting such an excellent example of loyalty to a younger generation.

Any information which will add to the value and interest of the list will be gratefully received at the Head Office.

The heading of the roll of honour
Photo courtesy of The Children's Society

Neither source provides the basis for a comprehensive list, and the details available are not generally enough to establish the identity of any one person with certainty. However, we do know the full names of three men who had been St Boniface boys, and who died in the War. They were Matthew Richardson Bell, Frank Gordon Ensor and Walter George Brown. A full account of each of them is to be found in this book, drawing on information kindly provided by the Children's Society.

The list of other former St Boniface boys known to have served, taken from the Society's Roll of Honour as at 1916, is reproduced below, but there may well have been others later. Where we have more information on them it can be found on our website.

Boyce P — Canadian Contingent
Brown, Fred — 4th Devon Territorials
Burgess A J J
Byers, Chas. — Canadian Contingent
Chandler, Albert — Canadian Contingent (wounded)
Cooper T — R.N.
Eaton J W
Edgar C — Canadian Contingent
Edwards W — K.K.L.R.

Freeman W G	HMS Cochrane
Fuller H	T.S. Mount Edgcumbe
Garnsey, Ernest G	Canadian Contingent
Girdlestone T	Canadian Contingent
Guest, Richard	R.N.
Hawes P	Canadian Contingent
Hawkins C	Canadian Contingent
Haynes H	Canadian Contingent
Hicks, H G	HMS Collingwood
Holland W	R.W.R.
Hollingsworth H	HMS City of London
Holloway, A C	R.N.
Johnson, Alfred	A.S.C.
Kemp N	A.S.C.
Lane, Geo. T	Canadian Contingent
Lawrence, Wm	Canadian Contingent
Manners S Arthur	South Wales Borderers
Mansfield, Fredk.	Army
Martin W	Canadian Contingent
Mitchell H	Somerset Yeomanry
Murray, Robert	R.N. Training Home, Liscard
Murthea F	R.N.
Nunns W	Australian Force
Osborne W M	
Page A	Army
Peter W	HMS Impregnable
Pick A	HMS Impregnable
Read Fred	D.C.L.I.
Rowe, Wm F	R. West Surreys
Russell C	Gloucester Regiment
Russell G	Canadian Contingent
Shelmerdine, Josiah	Army
Sheppard Wm	3rd Devons
Stamp, Horton G	Wessex Regiment
Tate, Allen	West Kent Regiment
Thompson R	A.S.C.
Weedon E	Canadian Contingent
West, Albert	Canadian Contingent
West W H	Canadian Contingent
Westcott F	3rd Devons

Wheeler J H	Canadian Contingent
Wilson J	K.S.L.I.
Woodcock, Wm Ernest	Lancashire Fusiliers
Woolsey J J	
Young Sydney M	Army (wounded)

Notes:

1. Devon & Somerset News 24 July 1913.

2. Waifs and Strays Magazine, November 1914.

3. Devon & Somerset News 22 April 1915.

4. Devon & Somerset News 13 May 1915.

5. Devon & Somerset News 3 January 1913.

6. Waifs and Strays magazine, May 1915.

7. Waifs and Strays magazine, May 1916.

8. 'Scrumping' is the process of trespassing into orchards and stealing fruit from the trees!

9. Waifs and Strays magazine, March 1918

I wish my dear, that you
were here,
And not so far away
I'm sending you a good
big kiss,
With all my love to-day !

Hearty Greetings from
SOUTHAMPTON.

A postcard sent from James Trevellyan to his family before leaving for France

Those who died in the war

We have tried to find out as much as possible about the Sampford Peverell men who died during the war. Defining who to include as being 'from the parish' has proved difficult, but we have decided to include anyone with a close connection to Sampford Peverell. They had to fall into at least one of these categories:

- they were born here
- they lived here at some point
- they enlisted from here
- they had close family here during the war

Any of these criteria would mean that they were likely to have been known in the parish, and their fate would affect those living in the parish. All of them are commemorated in St John the Baptist church in Sampford Peverell.

The information we have found is probably not complete, and we are always happy to hear from anyone who knows more about them. You can contact us via our website http://www.sampevsoc.co.uk/contact-us.html

For this and the following section on participants in the war, we have used a number of sources including:

Ancestry.co.uk
Britishnewspaperarchive.co.uk
Cwgc.org (The Commonwealth War Graves Commission)
Findmypast.co.uk
Iwm.org.uk (The Imperial War Museum)
Livesofthefirstworldwar.org
Longlongtrail.co.uk
Nationalarchives.gov.uk (The National Archives)
Sampevsoc.co.uk (the Sampford Peverell Society website)
The Children's Society - for information on St Boniface Home boys
Thegazette.co.uk (The London Gazette)
Thegenealogist.co.uk
The National Archives in Kew
Tiverton Museum of Mid Devon Life

And some descendants of those listed below, to whom we are particularly grateful.

Matthew Bell

Matthew Richardson Bell was born in Denmark Street, Westoe, South Shields, on 1st December 1895. His sister Miriam was born two years earlier in April 1893. They were the children of William Bell (born in 1859, the son of a coalminer, in Mickley, Northumberland) and his wife Margaret (née Hicks). Matthew was probably named after a relation of the family named Matthew Richardson, an innkeeper and licensed victualler.

On the 1901 census the Bell family were still living in Denmark Street, South Shields, where William was described as a barman; Miriam was aged seven and Matthew was five. They had Margaret's relative Septimus Hicks, a 24-year-old joiner, living with them as a boarder.

Two years later, in 1903, tragedy struck the family: Matthew's father William died when Matthew was just 7 and his sister 9 or 10. Much of the following information was kindly provided to us by the Children's Society (formerly known as the Church of England Children's Society, and before that as the Waifs and Strays Society) either by letter or via their web site: http://www.hiddenlives.org.uk

According to this information Matthew's mother fell into debt and was in increasingly ill health; because of this she was unable to work and she had no relatives able to help (they had children of their own to look after). As a result of these circumstances, an application was made for Matthew to be looked after by the Waifs and Strays Society. Matthew was initially sent to the Bersted Home for Boys in Bognor, which housed boys aged 8 to 14, but

St Boniface residents c 1908, probably including those mentioned here. Many of these boys would have taken part in the war.   *Photo courtesy of Peter Higginbotham*

it closed down in August 1907 and all the boys were transferred to the newly opened St Boniface Home for boys in Sampford Peverell, which also took boys up to the age of 14. Frank Ensor, another casualty, was also transferred from Bognor to St Boniface at the same time. In that same year, on 6th May 1907, Matthew's mother, Margaret, passed away and by 1911 his sister Miriam was at the All Saints Home for Girls, Hawley, Blackwater, Hampshire, run by the Sisters of Mercy, where she was in training to be a kitchen-maid. Matthew was at St Boniface Home from 21st August 1907 until 19th November 1909. From there he was found a place as a domestic gardener with the Reverend William Whittley at Towednack Vicarage, St Ives, Cornwall, where he was working in 1911. We know from his naval service record that he joined the Royal Navy in May 1912 as a 16-year-old boy on the training ship HMS "Impregnable".

Matthew's training continued for the next two years on other ships or shore-based training establishments – "Ganges". "Donegal" and "Victory" – before his naval service proper began on his 18th birthday, 1st December 1913 on HMS "Dreadnought". According to his service record he had grown two inches in those two years, and was now 5' 10½", with brown hair, grey eyes, and a fresh complexion. He was still on the "Dreadnought"

HMS Dreadnought in 1914, when Matthew Bell was a crew member.   *Photo courtesy of the Imperial War Museum*

when war was declared in 1914 and remained with her as an Able Seaman until April 1915. Thereafter he served on "Excellent" (April to August 1915) and "Attentive II" (September 1915 to February 1916), an Adventure-class scout cruiser which mainly operated with the Dover Patrol. The Dover Patrol had a wide variety of jobs in the Southern North Sea and the Dover Straits including carrying out anti-submarine patrols, escorting merchantmen, hospital and troop ships, laying sea-mines, constructing mine barrages, sweeping up German mines, bombarding German military positions on the Belgian coast and sinking U-boats. Finally, on 1st March 1916 he transferred to HMS M25, a 'Monitor' (M15) class vessel.

After the outbreak of war in 1914 the magazine of the Waifs and Strays Society started issuing a periodical Roll of Honour naming former residents of Homes (those they heard about) who were then serving in the armed forces. M.R.Bell was named in December 1914 and January 1915, as being on HMS Impregnable. In 1915 he was just listed as being in the Royal Navy, and in the last list we have, issued in December 1916, he is listed as "HMS Monitor (killed)". From his service record we know he was actually on M25, a 'monitor' class ship.

The Waifs & Strays Magazine for February 1917 included an item headed 'Sampford Peverell' recording that

> Matthew B is on the ever-growing list of those on our Roll of Honour who have laid down their lives for King and country. He met his death in rather an unusual way. While serving on HMS M- he was assisting to load a cargo of gas cylinders for France, when by some accident an escape took place, and Matthew got the full force of it. He was treated in hospital, then discharged and died at his sister's house.

Matthew died in a house in Stanley, Durham, occupied by a coalminer named John Plews - maybe Matthew's sister also lived there, or was in service nearby. His service record on findmypast.co.uk indicates that he had been invalided out of the Royal Navy on March 11th 1916 with tuberculosis, a detail confirmed by the certificate relating to his death six months later which recorded that he died of phthisis pulmonalis (TB) and exhaustion. TB was prevalent in the Navy and even in the 1920s and 1930s, despite efforts to improve conditions on ships, the death rate from TB was twice as high as for civilians. It was difficult to diagnose until it had reached a late stage, and it is likely that Matthew's illness was only diagnosed when he was treated in hospital for the effects of gas inhalation from the accident. Matthew Bell died on 9th September 1916, aged just 20.

The Ships & Shore Establishments on Matthew Bell's Service Record (from findmypast)

HMS Impregnable   Training ship for boy seamen at Devonport: 16Jun12 –31May12

HMS Ganges   Training establishment at Shotley, Suffolk: 1Jun12 – 02Oct12

HMS Donegal   Monmouth Class armoured cruiser: 03Oct12 – 9 Jan13

HMS Victory 1   Portsmouth Naval Barracks: 10Jan13 – 30Jun13

HMS Dreadnought   Battleship: 01Jul13 – 16Apr15 (inc promotion to AB in Dec 1914

HMS Excellent   Shore Establishment, Whale Island, Portsmouth: 17Apr15 – 31Aug15

HMS Attentive 11   Base Station, Dover: 7Sep15 – 29Feb16

HMS Victory I M25   Portsmouth: 1Mar16 – 11Mar16, invalided (tuberculosis)

Matthew Bell is part of this family tree which can be seen by subscribers to ancestry.co.uk:
https://www.ancestry.co.uk/family-tree/tree/154479014/family

Percy Bradfield

Percy Charles Bradfield was born in Autumn 1891 in Wokingham and baptized on 11th October 1891. He was the son of George Bradfield and his second wife Louisa. George was a domestic servant – a "gardener" in Reading in 1881 and a "groom" in Sonning in 1891 – and married his first wife Sarah Lewendon, a gardener's daughter, in 1880. They had two daughters, Agnes and Annie – before Sarah died in 1883. He married Sarah's younger sister Louisa in 1885, and they had six children together – Elsie, George, **Percy**, Florence, Ernest and Alfred.

Following the death of his father George in 1900, his mother Louisa, not in the best of health and finding it impossible to keep the family together, sent Percy and his brother George to the "Reading & Wokingham School District" School in Wargrave, Berkshire, where they are recorded on the 1901 Census as being two of 114 "pauper scholars". Later the same year Louisa entrusted Percy to the care of the Church of England Waifs and Strays Society, where he clearly prospered and at the age of only 16 became an assistant master when the Society opened St Boniface Home for Boys in Sampford Peverell in 1907. In addition he became the Home's "Carpenting Instructor "*(1911 Census),* Assistant Scoutmaster of the Scout Troop and Director of their Bugle Band. In the latter capacity he appears to have been a great asset to St Boniface's: providing the boys with a morale-boosting interest and taking the band on concert tours of local towns and villages, raising much-needed funds for the Home and helping to inspire young men at Recruiting Meetings. By all accounts they were "cordially received" wherever they went. *(Exeter and Plymouth Gazette, 24.7.1915)*

In February 1916 the Home Committee applied to the Military Tribunal in Tiverton for postponement of Percy Bradfield's military service, on the grounds that the then Master (Mr Keeley), a "reserve man" had been wounded at the Front. The Tribunal officer, Mr New, "...thought the proper course would be for the master to come back when he had recovered, and take charge of the Home, so that the younger man Bradfield could go."[46]). The Tribunal "thought the Committee should endeavour to get a man over military age [to take charge of the Home], and meanwhile postponed Bradfield from group 7 to group 15."

Percy Bradfield enlisted at Exeter later in 1916, joining the 1st/5th Battalion of the Royal Warwickshire Regiment. He saw action in France and Flanders and was killed during the third battle of Ypres on 5th October 1917. The Western Times of 9th November 1917 reported that:

---

[46] Devon and Somerset News, 10 Feb 1916

he was held in the greatest respect by everybody, and the news of his death was received with profound regret. In a letter...it states that Lance-Corpl. Bradfield...was in command of a Lewis Gun team, which was held up by a Hun sniper. In endeavouring to push on he became a target for the sniper, and was shot through the chest, dying two or three days later. He was [ie had been] recommended for a commission, and was promoted corporal to give him further experience in commanding men. The letter concludes: 'His life and death was an example to all. He died a hero's death and was a credit to his country.

The Magazine of the Waifs & Strays Society in November 1917 commented:

Percy Bradfield was taken into the Society's family in 1901 owing to the inability of a delicate widowed mother to keep the large family together. He bore a blameless character and eventually became assistant master at Sampford Peverell in 1907. There, till his time came for joining the army, he served faithfully, and many friends will regret to hear that he died of wounds on October 5th. He seems in a double sense one of the Society's devoted sons

Following this item the Waifs and Strays magazine must have received letters about Percy Bradfield, but unfortunately were unable to publish any of them due to the paper shortage. They just printed this in December 1917:

More than one touching testimony has been received of the personal power and singleness of heart which characterised Percy Bradfield, of whose record, first as a boy and then as a faithful officer of the Society, a short summary was given last month. But our space will not allow even the insertion of one specially valuable appreciation by a fellow-worker.

Battle of Broodseinde 4 October 1917: A battery of 1st Division Pioneers being hauled through the mud and watery shell craters near Sans Souci. Photo courtesy of the Imperial War Museum

Percy Bradfield was in the 1st/5th Royal Warwicks, a territorial battalion. He was killed during the 3rd battle of Ypres on 5th October 1917. There were 3 battles during 3rd Ypres, and the Royal Warwicks took part in the battles of Langemarck on 31st July till 28th August, during which 10,266 British lost their lives. Then they took part in the battle of Polygon Wood, which lasted from the 26th of September till the 3rd October, during which 1215 British were killed. On 4th October 1917, the battle of Broodseinde started, which was recorded as a "black day for the German Army". On the 5th October Percy Bradfield was killed.

According to the Soldiers' Effects list on ancestry.co.uk his outstanding pay of £8 11s 6d was paid in August 1918 to his sister and legatee Elsie Louisa Simmonds, and in December 1919 she was sent a further £5 10s 0d war gratuity.

Like fellow Sampford Peverell men Walter Brown, Robert Hine, Wilfred Taudevin, and Charles Wallington, Percy Bradfield is commemorated at the Tyne Cot Memorial in Zonnebeke, Belgium, where his name is on stone 24. The Commonwealth War Graves Commission website records that "The Tyne Cot Memorial is one of four memorials to the missing in Belgian Flanders which cover the area known as the Ypres Salient... It bears the names of almost 35,000 officers and men whose graves are not known."

Percy Bradfield is part of this family tree which can be seen by subscribers to ancestry.co.uk:
https://www.ancestry.co.uk/family-tree/tree/79099585/family

Tyne Cot Memorial, Zonnebeke, Belgium.   *Photo courtesy of Commonwealth War Graves Commission*

Walter George Brown

Walter George Brown was born in March 1899 in Cruwys Morchard, Devon, the youngest of five children of Elizabeth Ellen Brown. His mother, known as Ellen, was one of twins born in Willand in October 1858, to farmers John and Eliza Brown. In 1882 Ellen's twin sister Susanna married Henry Gibbons, born in 1860 in Oakford, Stoodleigh, Tiverton. He was a farmer and they had three children over the next few years. Susanna died in 1888, shortly before her thirtieth birthday. The unmarried twin sister, Elizabeth Ellen Brown, then moved in with Henry Gibbons and in January 1891 a child was born – also called Elizabeth Ellen. On the 1891 census in Butterleigh she is recorded as Ellen Brown, niece, aged 2 months and her mother is shown as a servant working for Henry. Interestingly her daughter's birth is recorded in Tiverton as Ellen Gibbons. During the 1890s a further four children were born: Eva, William, Frederick, and Walter George, the youngest.

By 1901 Henry Gibbons had moved from Butterleigh, via Cruwys Morchard, to Higher Combe Farm in Cadeleigh, on the other side of the Exe Valley. His three teenage children, Ethel, Henry and Susanna, were still living with him, as was his sister in law/partner Elizabeth Ellen Brown (described as his housekeeper) and her five children. In the census the surnames for all these children, including Walter George, is not recorded as Brown, but as Gibbons. We have learned from the Children's Society records for Walter that soon after this the family split up, with Ellen and two of her boys having to move to the Tiverton Union, ie the workhouse, due to neglect by the father. On her application form to the Waifs and Strays society Ellen reported that Henry Gibbons discovered that Ellen had left him to go out and work, so he drove the two boys, Frederick and Walter, aged just 4 and 2, to the farm where she was employed, and left them in the road. They and their mother had nowhere to live, so had to enter the Tiverton workhouse, where they stayed for nine years – most of Walter's childhood. On the form the boys were described as "good characters, and are promising lads", and it reported that Ellen "is anxious to earn enough to make a little home for the boys." Walter and his brother Frederick were admitted to St Boniface Home in Sampford Peverell in August 1910.

The 1911 census shows that Walter's mother, Ellen, was working in Cullompton as a servant, on a farm run by a younger single woman. Frederick had recently turned 14 so had left St Boniface Home, but Walter was still there. In July 1912 he became an apprentice weaver at the Devon Arts and Crafts Guild, but he was readmitted to St Boniface Home in March 1914. He left again later that year to work on a farm in Devon where his eldest sister worked as a housekeeper. His brother Frederick later joined the 4th Devonshire regiment, probably in 1915 when he reached 18, and is recorded on the 1916 St Boniface Roll of Honour. Frederick survived the war and by 1921 had moved to Fulham, London.

On 9th May 1915, aged 16, Walter decided to increase his age by 3 years to 19 years 2 months and enlisted at Exeter in the 3rd Battalion, H Company of the Devonshire Regiment, service number 17833, giving his occupation as a labourer and his address as Loxbeare, where his mother was living. His service record tells us he was 5' 5½", with hazel eyes and dark brown hair. After nearly a year of training his true age was revealed and he was discharged from the army on 3 Apr 1916 at Devonport, aged 17 years 1 month, "in consequence of having made a mis-statement as to age on enlistment." However his character was described as "sober, honest and industrious".

He left Devon and moved to Gletsdale, Monmouth with his older sister Elizabeth Ellen. On 19th April 1917 in Cardiff he re-enlisted in the army, declaring his previous 11 months under-age service with the 3rd Devons. This time he joined the 72nd training reserve for the 52nd Battalion of the Manchester Regiment, service number 38917. He correctly gave his age as 18 years and 1 month and described his occupation as motor driver. He seems to have grown three inches – his height was now 5' 8½"!

On 1st Aug 1917 he was transferred to the 74th reserve then on 31st August transferred again to 229th Infantry Battalion with the Manchester Regiment as service number 63621. Four months later, just after Christmas 1917, he was promoted to acting Lance Corporal. On 1st Apr 1918 he was transferred to the British Expeditionary Force as a private. He left Folkestone the next day and sailed to Boulogne in France. He was then transported to Étaples and on 5th April joined the 20th Battalion of the Durham Light Infantry with yet another regimental number: 82203. There is an interesting disciplinary note in his military record: on 8th July 1918 he was found guilty of not complying with an order and being "deficient of socks"! He was confined to barracks for five days and then immediately posted to the Durham Light Infantry Battle Rallying Station on 13 July 1918. His battalion became part of the 124th Brigade of the 41st Division, which took part in the 'Advance in Flanders' from 18th August to 6th September 1918, recapturing ground lost in April 1918.

On 4th September 1918, just two months before the end of the war, and at the age of 20, Walter was killed in action. He is remembered on panel 129

Soldiers in the 'Advance in Flanders' on 1st Sept 1918.   *Photo courtesy of the Imperial War Museum*

of the Tyne Cot Memorial, near Ypres in Belgium – a memorial to 35,000 UK and New Zealand men who lost their lives in Flanders from August 1917 to November 1918 and have no known grave. Those commemorated there include fellow Sampford Peverell men Percy Bradfield, Robert Hine, Wilfred Taudevin, and Charles Wallington. There is a picture of the memorial in the section on Percy Bradfield. At the end of January 1919 Walter's few personal effects were found and sent back to his sister, Elizabeth Ellen, in

Orchard View, Tiverton, where she lived with her sister Eva. These effects were two memo books, a wallet and a photo. Elizabeth sent a touching letter of thanks for the receipt of these few mementos. Their mother, Ellen, died later in 1919.

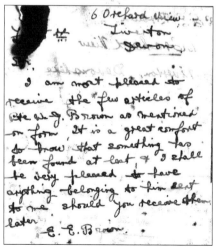

Walter Brown is part of this family tree which we have created on ancestry.co.uk and which subscribers to the site can see here: https://www.ancestry.co.uk/family-tree/tree/119246233/family

Thomas Cornish

Thomas Cornish was born early in 1897 in Hillfarrance, Somerset, the son of Eli Cornish (1860-1940) and his wife Elizabeth Maria, née Rossiter (1871-1938). In the 1901 census his father Eli was a "platelayer and railway worker", (a platelayer was someone who repaired and replaced railway track), living in Hillfarrance with his wife and children: Albert James (9), Edith Mary (7), William Henry (5) and Thomas (4).

To judge by the birth dates of the later children, they must have moved to Devon in the next three years and by 1911 the family was living in Higher Town, Sampford Peverell (*2018: in part of 30 Higher Town*) where they spent the rest of their lives (both parents were buried in the village). The father, Eli, was then a canal labourer; Albert was a shoemaker's apprentice, and William was a labourer for a builder. Two more sons had been born and were baptized in Sampford Peverell: Herbert Charles, born 30th October 1903, and Wilfred Eli, born 20th June 1906. Another son, Clifford, was born in 1914.

In the 1911 census Thomas Cornish was listed as a "servant (boots, cleaning, garden, etc.)", living at Ivy Grove, Sampford Peverell (*2018: 2 and 2a Chains Road*), working for William Henry Norrish, the butter manufacturer. His sister Edith was a live-in servant in Willand for Thomas

An 18-pounder battery of the Royal Field Artillery in action in the open, a tank, and cavalry horselines, April 1917. Notice "bivvys" with corrugated iron roofs and waterproof-sheet ends in the abandoned communication trench in foreground.   *Photo courtesy of the Imperial War Museum*

Mills, a butter factory manager, and his family. A later newspaper report said that he "before joining up had worked at Messrs. Norrish and Son's Creamery, Sampford Peverill (sic), from the time he left school."

Thomas was only 17 at the start of the war so was too young to enlist but his brother William was in the Navy by late 1915. We know Thomas was still in Sampford Peverell and working as a carter in October 1915 because his name appeared in a local newspaper, reporting on a court case in which he pleaded guilty to the charge of using bad language, and was fined 10s. The Chairman of the court "gave the defendant some good advice as to his future conduct, and commented on the spectacle of a fine young fellow like the defendant being in the dock on such a charge".

Perhaps these words encouraged him to sign up, or perhaps he was caught up in the 1916 conscription. He enlisted in Tiverton and became a gunner in the Royal Field Artillery A Battery 50th brigade. Thomas was killed in action near Arras in France on 30th March 1917. We don't know the exact circumstances but according to the CWGC "The experience of the Somme caused the Germans to reconsider their strategy on the Western Front. They constructed a formidably strong defensive position many miles in the rear and withdrew to it in early 1917. The British called the part that they face the Hindenburg Line. A large French offensive, supported by a British attack at Arras, withered against the new German defence".

The Faubourg d'Amiens cemetery, Arras.

Photo courtesy of the Commonwealth War Graves Commission

Thomas Cornish is buried in the Faubourg d'Amiens cemetery, Arras, France. The inscription on his grave, 'Rest in Peace', was chosen by his mother. As his sole legatee she was sent his outstanding pay of £7 1s 0d in June 1917, and in 1919 she was sent a further £3 war gratuity (according to the Soldiers' Effects list on ancestry.co.uk).

The newspaper report of his death recorded that "This makes the second Sampford Peverill boy to make the Supreme Sacrifice".

In the 1920s his brother Albert Cornish was a newsagent and shoemaker; William, who had served in the Royal Navy during the war, became an engine driver; and Herbert was a labourer and later a miller. His parents continued to live in Higher Town, as did Wilfred and his family until they had to vacate their cottage, which was opposite the school, when it burnt down in 1939. There may still be relations of Thomas in the village today.

Thomas Cornish is part of this family tree which we have created on ancestry.co.uk and which subscribers to the site can see here: https://www.ancestry.co.uk/family-tree/tree/75458494/family

Thomas Cornish's grave.   *Photo courtesy of*
                              the Royal British Legion

Frederic V Coupland-Smith

Frederic Vyvyan Coupland Smith was born early in 1897 in Steyning, Sussex. He was the only child of Frederic Geoffrey Coupland Smith (1871-1924), and Ida Mary Ruffell (1870-1951), who married in 1895. Frederic Smith senior was the son of a surgeon, also called Frederic Smith, who came from a wealthy farming family, and his wife Harriett (née Coupland). Frederic senior later adjusted his and his family's surname by connecting his middle name, Coupland, to the surname, Smith, to form Coupland-Smith.

The Coupland-Smith parents were well to do and did a lot of travelling, though not necessarily together. In the 1901 census the father, Frederic G Smith, was visiting his widowed mother in Nottinghamshire, and his wife, Ida Mary Smith, was having a spa break at the Smedleys Hydropathic Company in Matlock. We're not sure where 4-year-old Frederic V was staying at the time. In October 1903 Mrs F G Coupland-Smith was on the passenger list of a Bibby Line ship travelling from Liverpool to Marseilles.

An article in the Cheltenham Chronicle in July 1917 records that Frederic was educated at Ayshford School in Uffculme and Blundell's, a public school in Tiverton. He attended Blundell's from September 1909 to summer 1913. Their website:

http://www.blundells.org/archive/in-memoriam/coupland-smith_fv.html

has a page about Frederic which records that:

> He entered "Old House" when he first came to the school at the age of 13 years. He boarded at various times in his school life; 1909 to 1910 and again in 1912 and in 1913; at the other times he was a "Day Boy". He was, most of the time, a member of the Choir. He studied the Classical side and intended to take [Holy] Orders but left rather prematurely to accompany his parents to the Holy Land and Egypt in the summer of 1913.

The period when he was a day boy covers the period when his parents were based in Sampford Peverell. A newspaper article published on 3rd November 1910 lists Mr and Mrs Coupland-Smith among the mourners at the funeral of the local vicar, Rev P C Rossiter. In the 1911 census Frederic Geoffrey Coupland-Smith, 39, and his son, Frederic Vivian, were living in High Cross House in Sampford Peverell (there is a photo of it in the first section of this book). Frederic G had private means and they had a cook/servant and a groom. Frederic V's mother was not there at the time. We know from the Land Tax Returns that Frederick Coupland-Smith senior rented High Cross House from Mrs Rossiter until 1914. Shipping passenger lists show that Frederic Coupland-Smith senior travelled, unaccompanied, to Cape Town, South Africa, in December 1911, to Lima in Peru in December 1912 (when he's described as a 'merchant'), and from Chile to London in May 1913.

As we have seen, Frederic left Blundell's in the summer of 1913, and the Cheltenham Chronicle article reported:

> At an early age he showed a desire to enter the Church, and on leaving Blundell's was coached by Mr Butler, of Cheltenham, and in the ordinary course would have gone up to Merton College, Oxford, in October 1914. But on the declaration of war he joined up, serving in the ranks for a month and then receiving a commission in the RFA. Afterwards he was sent to the Dardanelles, Egypt, Serbia, and finally to another front.

Frederic's medal card shows that he initially joined the 54th brigade of the Royal Field Artillery, and the first theatre of war he served in was Egypt, in July 1915. He was made a temporary Second Lieutenant on 29th September 1914 (London Gazette).

The Long Long Trail website tells us that

> this brigade sailed from Devonport on 7th July 1915 for operations in the Mediterranean and arrived at Alexandria in Egypt two weeks later. It moved to Mudros, the forwards base for operations at Gallipoli, arriving on 11 September 1915 but did not proceed into that theatre of war. It left Mudros on 5 October 1915 and arrived at Salonika 10 October (the ammunition column followed a little later).

Meanwhile Frederic's father became an orderly with the British Red Cross Society, at the age of 44, serving initially in France from 10th August 1915, and later in Greece where he served until 19th August 1917. Given his age and background this was an extraordinary thing for him to do. He was in Salonika when his son died.

At some point Frederic V joined 173rd brigade RFA. He was promoted to Lieutenant on 2nd July 1917, but the relevant announcement in the London Gazette in December recorded that he had since been killed in action. He is buried at the Lone Tree Cemetery, Heuvelland, West-Vlaanderen, in Belgium. Lone Tree Cemetery is close to the Lone Tree Crater, one of the nineteen bomb craters which were made immediately before the infantry attack at the Batle of Messines in early June 1917. The crater is now designated a 'Pool of Peace'. Nearly all the graves in the cemetery are those of soldiers who fell on the first day of the battle on 7th June but there are also a few men who died between 30th June and 5th July, including Frederic V Coupland-Smith.

Village of Wytschaete, near Lone Tree cemetery, captured on 7th June 1917.   *Photo courtesy of the Imperial War Museum*

Frederic was just 20 when he died. The inscription on his headstone was chosen by his father: "Blessed are the pure in heart, for they shall see God. Matt. V 8". According to the list of Soldiers' Effects on ancestry.co.uk his outstanding pay of £93 1s 6d was sent to his father in August 1917, as was a further £12 8s in 1918, and a war gratuity of £5 in 1919.

As well as his headstone in France, his name is engraved on the war memorial at Blundell's school in Tiverton, and on a memorial stone in Retford, Nottinghamshire, at the foot of the grave of his grandparents.

Frederic Coupland-Smith is part of this family tree which we have created on ancestry.co.uk and which subscribers to the site can see here: https://www.ancestry.co.uk/family-tree/tree/73887918/family

Frederic V Coupland-Smith's grave in Lone Tree Cemetery.   *Photo courtesy of Wikipedia*

127

Richard Crook

Richard Crook was born in Loxbeare in 1882, the son of Richard Crook, a "casual labourer", of Cruwys Morchard, and his wife Anne. He was baptized in Loxbeare on 11th June 1882. He married Elizabeth Mary May in 1904 and they had 4 children: Harold, Albert, Victoria and Reginald.

Richard Crook's address in Sampford Peverell is not easy to establish. Although his home address is shown on his Army enlistment record (1917) as "Higher Town, Sampford Peverell", the exact property he occupied is not known. On the 1911 Census (for Burlescombe Parish) he was recorded as living at "Ayshford Hamlet, Burlescombe" but in the same year he appears on the Electoral Roll for Sampford Peverell, living at "Landside Cottage". Later Electoral Rolls show him at, "Landside and Ayshford", or "Ayshford".

On the 1911 census he was a farm worker and "Stationary Engine Driver", probably operating an early threshing machine or similar, and as such, it is likely that he was employed as a 'casual' labourer on a number of farms, moving frequently – with his family – to 'tied' cottages in neighbouring

Troops of the Royal Engineers, Inland Water Transport Unit on barges passing through a lock.
Photo courtesy of the Imperial War Museum

parishes. He was probably working for a Sampford Peverell farmer with a cottage in the village at the time of his enlistment.

After call-up he enlisted on 19th January 1917 in the Inland Water Transport division of the Royal Engineers. His military record on the findmypast website shows his occupation on enlistment as "Stationary Engine Driver", and his rank as "Pioneer" (aka Sapper) with the regimental number 23307, sometimes written as 233307.

The Royal Engineers Inland Water Transport division was based in Richborough on the Kent coast, near Sandwich. Ships and barges were built there, as was the first roll-on roll-off ferry, and men were sent to France to handle canal transport.

Richard Crook's war service was very brief indeed, as he contracted German Measles which led to pneumonia, and he died in the Military Hospital Canterbury on March 8th, 1917. His lungs had become very blocked and his medical notes say that in addition to expectorants, brandy and hypodermic strychnine were administered to him but his breathing was "sterterous" and his pulse gradually weakened until he died at 10.10 am on 8th March.

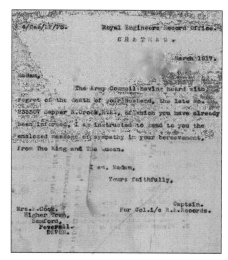

The numerous documents making up his military record on the findmypast website include:

A letter from the army to Mrs Crook in Higher Town. From findmypast.co.uk, copyright National Archives

1. A detailed record of his progress in hospital – both hand-written and transcribed.
2. A hand-written letter by Elizabeth Mary Crook (widow), dated 18th February 1918, giving her address as "Uplowman Cross".
3. A declaration by the widow (as above) dated 11th November 1919, giving her address as "19 Little Silver, Tiverton".
4. A reference to a "Memorial Plaque and Scroll".
5. A letter dated June 1917 from R.E. Record Office, Chatham to War Pensions Committee in Tiverton requesting confirmation that Richard

Crook was father of Harold George and was supporting him prior to enlistment. [this was required because the child was born out of wedlock – i.e.in 1904, before his parents' marriage]

6. A letter confirming the above.

7. A document authorising payment of pension of 28/9 per week from 10th September 1917.

It seems his widow moved to Uplowman after his death; hence his inclusion on the War Memorial Roll of Honour in St Peter's Church Uplowman, but Richard Crook was certainly thought of as a Sampford man at the time of his death, as shown by an article in the Western Times of March 16, 1917 under the Sampford Peverell heading:

> Quite a gloom was cast over the village on Friday when it became known that Sapper Richard Crook, R.E., formerly of Sampford Peverill [sic], had died of pneumonia at the military hospital at Canterbury. The funeral took place on Wednesday at Uplowman, the Rev. G. German officiating.

The article goes on to list the mourners, coffin bearers and senders of wreaths.

Elizabeth Crook seems not to have remarried and died in 1943, aged 70.

Richard Crook is part of this family tree which we have created on ancestry.co.uk and which subscribers to the site can see here:

https://www.ancestry.co.uk/family-tree/tree/153814349/family

Image above reproduced with kind permission of The British Newspaper Archive (www.britishnewspaperarchive.co.uk) '. Image © THE BRITISH LIBRARY BOARD. ALL RIGHTS RESERVED.

Sidney Dunn

Sidney Dunn was born on 3rd January 1884, the son of Frederick John Dunn (born 9th July 1843 in Halberton, son of John and Anne) and his wife Fanny Eliza, née Gosling (baptized 25th January 1846 in Sampford Peverell, daughter of Isaac and Harriet). Sidney was baptized in Sampford Peverell church on 22nd January 1884, and at that time his father was described as a 'coal merchant', but from the mid 1880s he was also the licensee of the Hare and Hounds public house in Lower Town *(2018: Coronation Cottages)*. Judging by a case mentioned in the local newspaper it seems Frederick was not always strict about closing hours in the pub, claiming his clock must have been wrong, by half an hour ...

In the 1891 census the family, who lived in the Hare and Hounds, consisted of Frederick, Fanny, and their children: Mary, 14, Harriett, 12, Sidney, 7, and Theresa, 5, all born in Sampford Peverell.

Frederick Dunn died, aged 56, in 1900, and was buried in the churchyard on 18th October that year, when Sidney was 16 years old. Sidney's mother,

Sidney Dunn, on the right, with his sisters and (probably) his mother, outside the Hare and Hounds, c 1897.

Fanny, continued to run the pub, helped by her daughter Theresa who, aged 15, was described as a 'licensed victualler's assistant' in the 1901 census. Sidney now also had a nine-year-old sister, Annie. Sidney himself worked as a "grocer's assistant".

In April 1906 Sidney's younger sister Theresa married Robert Trevelyan, a quarryman, from Burlescombe, and in 1907 Sidney himself married Caroline Trevelyan, daughter of George Trevelyan, carpenter, of Always Cottage, Sampford Peverell and his wife Caroline. Theresa's husband Robert and Sidney's wife Caroline were second cousins to each other and also to James Trevellyan, another local war casualty. In 1881 Caroline's family had been living next door to the Hare and Hounds where Sidney's family lived, so the children of the two families would have known each other well. Caroline's nephew, Stanley Trevelyan, was another casualty in the war.

In October 1908, according to the Western Times, Sidney was fined 6s for "using bad language towards his wife". Nevertheless by 1911 they had two children, Frederick, 2, and Leslie, 1, and were living in Kings Cottages Lower Town *(2018: the site of 5-7 Lower Town)*, in a 4-roomed house near Morrells. Sidney was now a builder's labourer, and by this time his mother Fanny had retired and was living in another house in Lower Town with her daughter Annie, a laundress. The Hare and Hounds had been taken over by Allan Gunn.

Sidney and Caroline went on to have another son, William, born in August 1911, a daughter Daisy, born in August 1912, and another daughter, Violet, born in July 1915. In the parish register for Violet's christening Sidney's occupation is 'soldier', so he must have enlisted by then. Sidney's mother Fanny Dunn died in 1916 aged 69, and was buried in the churchyard on 13th May.

In September 1917 Sidney's sister Annie married Rifleman Thomas Drew who was home on leave, having been wounded in France. According to the Western Times Annie was given away by her brother-in-law, Robert Trevellyan, and her sister Therese Trevellyan was her bridesmaid.

On 7th December 1917 the Western Times reported that Caroline, now living in Higher Town, had "received intimation from her husband, Pte. Sydney Dunn, Dorsets, that he is now convalescent from his recent severe illness and has returned to India from Mesopotamia". Her address was then Royal Oak cottages *(2018: the space next to the school).* In the early 1900s the "Charity Lands of Sampford Peverell" had money left over from an insurance claim and used it to buy "a piece of land with the two cottages thereon known as Royal Oak, containing 2.5 perches or thereabouts, situate in Higher Town". The charity rented out this and other properties and used the money raised to help the poor and needy of the village.

Sidney was in Mesopotamia (largely modern-day Iraq) because he had been transferred from the Devonshire Regiment to the 2nd Dorsetshire Regiment. From January 1917 to April 1918 the 2nd Dorsets came under the 9th Indian Brigade, 3rd Indian Division. This division, largely comprised of troops from India, arrived in Mesopotamia in April 1916 to fight the Turks, who were allies of Germany, and the action there continued until the end of the war. The following comes from the Long Long Trail website:

> Like Gallipoli, conditions in Mesopotamia defy description. Extremes of temperature (120 degrees F was common); arid desert and regular flooding; flies, mosquitoes and other vermin: all led to appalling levels of sickness and death through disease. Under these incredible conditions, units fell short of officers and men, and all too often the reinforcements were half-trained and ill-equipped. Medical arrangements were quite shocking, with wounded men spending up to two weeks on boats before reaching any kind of hospital. These factors, plus of course the unexpectedly determined Turkish resistance, contributed to high casualty rates.
>
> 11012 killed, 3985 died of wounds, 12678 died of sickness, 13492 missing and prisoners (9000 at Kut), 51836 wounded - data from "Statistics of the Military Effort of the British Empire" (London: HMSO, 1920)."

The Wandilla

Sidney was suffering from malaria and having earlier been sent to India, he was now sent back to Alexandria on the 'Wandilla', an Australian naval ship that had been converted into a hospital ship. Alexandria was an important hospital centre during both World Wars and was much used by hospital ships and troop transports carrying the sick and wounded out of the theatres of war.

On 10th May 1918 the Western Times carried this report: "Mrs Sydney Dunn, of Higher Town, Sampford Peverell, was officially informed on Tuesday that her husband, Pte. S Dunn, Dorset Regt., had died from heart failure on April 10th while on his way home from India on sick leave. Much sympathy is felt for the widow and five young children. A memorial service was held in the Parish Church on Sunday, and muffled peals were rung."

Sidney died in Egypt on 10th April 1918 and is buried in the Alexandria (Hadra) War Memorial Cemetery in Egypt. The wording chosen for his headstone by his wife Caroline is "Thou wilt keep him in perfect peace whose mind is stayed on thee". According to the list of Soldiers' Effects on ancestry.cu.uk his outstanding pay was just five shillings, which was sent to his widow, Caroline, in October 1919.

A year after his death, on 11th April 1919, Caroline Dunn placed this In Memoriam article in the Western Times.

Sidney Dunn's photo in the Western Times on 24th May 1918, under the heading 'Others Who Have Laid Down Their Lives For Their Country'.

Sidney Dunn is part of this family tree which we have created on ancestry.co.uk and which subscribers to the site can see here: https://www.ancestry.co.uk/family-tree/tree/75095161/family

IN LOVING MEMORY
Of my dear husband, Pte. S. Dunn, of the 2nd Battn. Dorset Regt, who died in Alexandria, Egypt, on H.M.S. "Wandilla," on the voyage from India on the 10th April, 1918, aged 34 years. Peace, perfect peace.—
Royal Oak Cottage, Sampford Peverell.

From the Western Times 11 Apr 1919.

The Alexandria (Hadra) War Memorial Cemetery. Photo courtesy of the Commonwealth War Graves Commission

Frank Ensor

Frank Gordon Ensor was the son of William Ensor and his wife Anna Maria, known as Annie. Annie was born Anna Maria Hook and was baptized at St Anne's Siston, Gloucestershire in 1857. She married Edmund Denning, a widower with two sons, Edmund and Gilbert, at Barton Regis in 1880. In the 1881 census they were all living in Kingswood Road, Bitton, (between Bath and Bristol). The Dennings had five more children together between 1882 and 1889: Mary (Pollie), Alice (later 'Annie'), Christopher, Stanley and Wilfred. Edmund Denning died, at the age of 38, in 1889 - the same year that Wilfred was born.

The 1891 census shows that Anna Maria, now widowed and calling herself 'Annie', was living in Kingswood and working as a 'Boot Machinist' to support her large

Frank G Ensor, photo courtesy of the family tree on ancestry.co.uk

family - taking to the same trade as her late husband. Her step-son Gilbert, now 15, was also working as a shoemaker, and they had two teenaged lodgers, also shoemakers, helping to pay the rent. Nearly all their neighbours were also working in the shoe trade. Annie Denning then married William Ensor in the second quarter of 1894 in Keynsham, Somerset, and Frank Gordon Ensor was born there towards the end of 1895. He was baptized in Kingswood on 13th October 1895. By the time of the 1901 census William and Annie had another son, Roydon, born in Q2 1899, but William was not listed in the census. Annie was living in Bristol, described as 'married', with no occupation listed, and with seven children living with her. Four of the older Denning children were working as chocolate packers or chocolate makers. Frank and Roydon Ensor were aged 5 and 2 respectively.

The Children's Society who hold the records of the former Waifs and Strays Society, kindly passed this information on to us about what happened next:

Frank's mother had been left a widow since 1902. She had been in bad health for some years and almost completely dependent on what her elder son and daughter were able to earn. There were no relations able to help Mrs Ensor and as a result of this, an application was made for Frank to be looked after by the Waifs and Strays Society.

The Children's Society also told us that Frank initially went to the Bersted Home for Boys in Bognor, but when it closed in 1907 he was transferred (as was Matthew Bell, another casualty) to the St Boniface Home for Waifs and Strays in Sampford Peverell. He was there from 21 Aug 1907 until 19 Nov 1909 (boys left when they reached the age of 14).

Frank must have returned to his family because in the 1911 census his mother Annie was living in Redfields, Bristol with some of her children: Annie Denning (now 27 and working as a 'Packer' for a Chocolate Manufacturer); Christopher Denning (25, a Labourer at an "Oil & Colour Works"); Frank Ensor (aged 15 and a plumber's labourer) and Roydon (11 and still at school).

Frank probably enlisted in 1915 because we know from his medal record that he was in France from 14th July that year, as a Bombardier with the Royal Field Artillery. He was later promoted to Corporal, still with the RFA.

Royal Field Artillery officers firing a captured German field gun at the German lines. South edge of Mametz Wood, August 1916.   *Photo courtesy of the Imperial War Museum*

Frank served with B Battery, 80th Brigade, which became part of the 17th Ammunition Division. In July to August 1916 they were involved in a number of engagements including the battles of Albert and Delville Wood, which were part of the Battles of the Somme. These battles included the taking of Mametz Wood followed by successive attacks and counter attacks around Delville Wood and Pozieres. Frank was wounded in one of these battles and died of his wounds.

According to a family tree on ancestry.co.uk "Frank was mortally wounded in France. His mother Anna Maria crossed the Channel to see him. She went with Polly (family memory from Anna's step granddaughter Louie)." Polly was Annie's oldest daughter. Frank was taken to the 13th Station Hospital Boulogne. Boulogne was one of the two main hospital areas throughout the war. He died on 25th Aug 1916, aged 21, and he is buried in Boulogne Eastern Cemetery in France. According to the list of Soldiers' Effects on ancestry.co.uk his outstanding pay of £9 9s 2d was sent to his mother and sole legatee, Anna Maria, in January 1917, and in 1919 she was sent his £10 war gratuity.

Frank Ensor's older half-brother, Christopher Denning, also joined the army early in WW1 and survived, but Frank's younger brother, Roydon Ensor, was killed in action on the 24th April 1918 aged just 19.

Frank Ensor is part of this family tree which we have created on ancestry.co.uk and which subscribers to the site can see here: https://www.ancestry.co.uk/family-tree/tree/61000046/family

Boulogne East cemetery, France.   *Photo courtesy of the Commonwealth War Graves Commission*

Herbert Fewings

Herbert Reginald Fewings was born on 9th October 1898 in Sampford Peverell and baptized the next day at St John the Baptist Church. He was the third of five children of William Thomas Fewings (1867-1950) and Catherine Jane Stoneman (1867-1947) from North Tawton. Catherine left home shortly after the 1881 census, aged 14 and became a domestic servant. In the 1891 census she was working in Tormoham, now part of Torquay. Herbert's father, William Thomas Fewings, was born into a farming family in Rose Ash, five miles south-east from South Molton in West Devon. He assisted his father on the 108-acre farm until just after the 1891 census when William had a career change and left farming to join the police force. He served in the North Tawton area until early 1898. William and Catherine were married in 1894, and their first two children Lily and Percy were born in North Tawton. In 1898 William, known as Thomas, took up the position as police constable for Sampford Peverell where later that year Herbert Reginald was born.

In the 1901 census the Fewings family, now with four children less than 5 years of age, were living in the police house in Sampford Peverell *(2018: 21 Lower Town)*. Herbert spent his childhood in Sampford Peverell and

A modern photo showing the police house where the Fewings family lived - the middle cottage of the three.

would have gone to the village school, until 1909 when the family moved to Stoke Canon, 10 miles south down the Exe Valley road from Tiverton towards Exeter. The father, Tom Fewings, was now police constable for Stoke Canon, and by the 1911 census had 5 children. The eldest, Lily Gwendoline, had left school and was an apprentice dressmaker. The other 4 children were all still at Stoke Canon school. Herbert's father continued to own several properties in Sampford Peverell, such as Coombe Cottage, in Higher Town. After his eventual retirement in 1918 Tom Fewings moved back to Sampford Peverell to spend "the residue of his days in our peaceful village among friends."

Herbert left Stoke Cannon school in April 1912 (just before his 14th birthday) and started at Exeter National school. He stayed there for 16 months and his school record shows that he "left and goes to work" August 1913 and joined the GWR (Great Western Railway). One year after the war started, Herbert's elder brother, Percy Victor Fewings, who had previously been working for the GWR, enlisted as a private in the Army Service Corps (later called the RASC) and served there for the duration of the war. His service record is in the list of Sampford Peverell surviving men (and women) who served during the war. There is a record on findmypast.co.uk showing that Herbert joined the NUR (National Union of Railwaymen) on 9th November 1915. His occupation at that time was a Motor Condr (presumably conductor) working in Paignton. On 23rd August 1916 he transferred to branch 974 (location unknown) and less than 3 months later, on 9th November 1916 he transferred to branch 1714 for a short period before enlisting. He was serving as a porter at Churston, Brixham, according to his war enlistment record in Exeter.

Herbert initially joined the Royal North Devon Yeomanry Company as Private #4031 at the end of 1916. This regiment was originally formed in 1798 and was a volunteer infantry regiment based in Barnstaple. It had been a cavalry regiment and by 1893 was divided up into 4 squadrons. It saw service in the Boer War and on 1 Apr 1908 was renamed the Royal Devon Yeomanry and trained and equipped as Hussars. The regiment was mobilised when the UK joined WW1 on 4th August 1914. It moved to the Colchester area in Essex, but in September 1915 the regiment was dismounted (ie was no longer cavalry), transported to Liverpool and sailed to arrive at Gallipoli (now part of Turkey) on 9th October 1915. The regiment were initially used to dig trenches, but by November were in the firing line, then on 19 December they were evacuated and sailed to Egypt, landing in Alexandria on 30th December 1915. They served on the Suez canal defences and were part of the Western Frontier force.

Prince Arthur, Duke of Connaught, inspecting the Guard of Honour of the Devonshire Regiment, 16th Battalion, at the GHQ of the Egyptian Expeditionary Force, at railhead near El Ramle, March 1918. Photo courtesy of the Imperial War Museum

Herbert must have joined the regiment (maybe not in action in Egypt though) at the end of 1916, as on 4th January 1917 the regiment was amalgamated with another regiment to form the 16th Battalion Devonshire Regiment - where he was given a new service number #71971.

This regiment took part with the 74th Division in the invasion of Palestine throughout 1917. In the early part of 1918 the regiment was involved with the capture and defence of Jerusalem. On 3rd April 1918 the 74th Division was advised that it would be posted to France. Disembarkation from Alexandria was completed by 30th April 1918 and they landed at Marseilles a week later on 7th May 1918. The Battalion served in France and Flanders for the remainder of the war.

Herbert transferred into the 10th Battalion of the Cheshire Regiment #72279 where he served until his death near Reims on 27th May 1918. There are detailed Cheshire Regimental diaries for the 10th Battalion which record day by day and in some cases hour by hour what the regiment were doing. Copies of the diary entries for the days leading up to his death are held on www.ancestry.co.uk

It seems that there was an apparent breach in the German line and the Battalion advanced the ¾ mile into this perceived breach. The German forces countered attacked with gas, heavy bombardment, machine gun fire and gunfire from low flying aircraft. The 10th Battalion retreated towards Pevy, some 8 miles West of Reims, where they had started from, but sustained considerable losses, with some companies being totally devastated. The deaths of non-ranking soldiers are not recorded by name, but Herbert's death is almost certainly part of the "200 OR (Ordinary Rank) casualties" mentioned in the diary entry for the day following his death.

Herbert's death is recorded on the Soissons Memorial on the banks of the river Aisne, Reims – 60 miles NE of Paris. The location is very close to where he lost his life and the memorial records the names of nearly 4,000 men who suffered the same fate.

His death is also recorded on the GWR Memorial List in Paddington Station, London and on platform 5 at Exeter St David's station.

Herbert Fewings is part of this family tree which we have created on ancestry.co.uk and which subscribers to the site can see here: https://www.ancestry.co.uk/family-tree/tree/116827186/family

Exeter station memorial

Soissons War Memorial, Reims, France.

Photo courtesy of the Commonwealth War Graves Commission

Walter Gale

Walter John Gale was born in Bampton, Devon in the first quarter of 1894, and was baptized there on 4th March, the son of George Robert Gale, a "general labourer" and his wife Blanche (née Banbury) both born in Bampton.

In the 1901 census the family was living in Lower Town, Sampford Peverell, in one of a group of eight cottages *(2018: the site of 16 Court Way)*. The family had probably not been there long as Lewis, 9, and Beatrice, 2, had been born in Bampton, and Florence, 1 month old, was born in Huntsham. Baby Florence was buried in Sampford Peverell on 20th September 1901 aged just 5 months.

In the 1911 Census Walter was listed (aged 17) as a "general labourer" for a builder, and was living with his parents, two brothers (Lewis, 19, a blacksmith, and William, 7) and two sisters (Beatrice, 12, and Hilda Mary, aged 1). They lived in a four-roomed house in Lower Town, Sampford Peverell. We know from the log of the village school that Walter Gale was an attendee at the school, but his parents were summoned by the County Education Committee a couple of times for not sending William to school often enough. In 1912 the Gales were fined 2s 6d because William only made 96 out of a possible 112 attendances. Mrs. Gale said he was often ill but had no medical certificate. In 1913 they recorded that "Mrs. Gale persisted in keeping her son home from school once a week", and he only attended 101 out of 114 times. Mrs. Gale said he suffered from an abscess in the ear, and she was told to procure a medical certificate. There are no further reports of this nature in the papers so hopefully things were settled amicably.

Immediately before the war Walter Gale was working for the GWR as a "canal man" in the Engineering Department, based at Burlescombe.

Walter Gale Article from the Western Times 29 Sep 1916: Image reproduced with kind permission of The British Newspaper Archive (www.britishnewspaperarchive.co .uk) '. Image © THE BRITISH LIBRARY BOARD. ALL RIGHTS RESERVED.

This newspaper article published on 11th September 1914 describes a recruitment meeting held in the courtyard of the St Boniface home in the village, and reports that the recruiting sergeant returned the next day and took nearly twenty recruits to Tiverton, including Walter and Lewis Gale.

Like many of the men from this area Walter and Lewis Gale joined the 8th Devonshire Regiment. They were both sent to France on 25th July 1915. The 8th Devonshires were part of 20th Brigade, 7th Division.

A newspaper article from 21st Jan 1916 has a report on Walter and Lewis, whose parents were still living in Lower Town. It records that Walter "has been in France since July of last year and was gassed in the attack made on the Germans on Sept 25th. His brother Pte L Gale, being with the same regiment, also took part in the above engagement, but he, fortunately, escaped being gassed." There is another photo of Walter Gale with his brother in the section on Lewis Gale later in this book.

SAMPFORD PEVERELL

An open-air meeting was held on Wednesday evening in the Court-yard of the St. Boniface Home, Sampford Peverell. The Mayor of Tiverton and Mr. W. H. Martin, who came from Tiverton to address the meeting, were met on Canal Bridge, in the centre of the village, by the Boy Scouts from St. Boniface Home with their bugle band under Assistant Scoutmaster P. Bradfield, the Scoutmaster (Mr. Keeley) having joined the Army. Mr. J. G. Pedler, C.C., presided, supported by Mr. Marshall and Captain Lyat. The Mayor, who spoke with great feeling, exhorted the men to wake up to the danger of the position and do their duty as patriots and men. Mr. Martin spoke in a similar strain. Mr. J. Jones (Halberton) gave a stirring speech. A resolution pledging the meeting to do all in its power to promote recruiting for Lord Kitchener's Army was then carried by acclamation. The National Anthem was sung, and cheers given for our soldiers and sailors and the Mayor, after which several recruits gave in their names to Sergt. Beer and Mr. Lovett (Halberton). Sergt. Beer visited Sampford Peverell next day and took nearly twenty recruits to Tiverton, amongst whom were C. Kirkman, H. Ponsford, W. Heals, A. Scorce, J. Sweet, B. Hine, W. and Le Gale, D. Moon, W. Parker, J. Hicks, and others.

Western Times 11 Sep 1914: Image reproduced with kind permission of The British Newspaper Archive (www.britishnewspaperarchive.co.uk) '. Image © THE BRITISH LIBRARY BOARD. ALL RIGHTS RESERVED.

25th September 2015 was the first day of the Battle of Loos, when the British used poisonous gas for the first time, during which the British suffered badly from this gas cloud which did not move towards the Germans as expected due to the lack of wind. An account on 1914-18.net reads:

The right-hand 7th Division found that the gas cloud generally moved well in this sector, but local wind variations meant that not all cylinders were turned on here. Many men struggled to breathe in their gas helmets as they advanced into the cloud and removed them, consequently suffering from gas themselves. Heavy losses were incurred by the lead units of 20th Brigade in No Man's Land from German shelling, which had been opened up to try to dispel the gas and smoke cloud. The 8/ Devonshire suffered heavy machine-gun casualties, the wire in front of their sector having been only partially cleared.

Battle of Guillemont 3-6 September 1916. British infantry waiting their turn to advance. A tank moving in distance. *Photo courtesy of the Imperial War Museum*

However Walter survived the gas and either remained in, or returned to, France. In 1916 the 7th Division was involved in the battles of Albert, Bazentin, Delville Wood, and Guillemont (3-6 Sep), all battles of the Somme. Walter Gale was killed in action on 4th September 1916, during this last battle, aged 22, and is remembered at the Thiepval Memorial in France. There is more information about the Thiepval memorial and the Somme on cwgc.org as follows:

On 1 July 1916, supported by a French attack to the south, thirteen divisions of Commonwealth forces launched an offensive on a line from north of Gommecourt to Maricourt. Despite a preliminary bombardment lasting seven days, the German defences were barely touched and the attack met unexpectedly fierce resistance. Losses were catastrophic and with only minimal advances on the southern flank, the initial attack was a failure. In the following weeks, huge resources of manpower and equipment were deployed in an attempt to exploit the modest successes of the first day. However, the German Army resisted tenaciously and repeated attacks and counter attacks meant a major battle for every village, copse and farmhouse gained. At the end of September, Thiepval was finally captured. The Thiepval Memorial, the Memorial to the Missing of the Somme, bears the names of more than

72,000 officers and men of the United Kingdom and South African forces who died in the Somme sector before 20 March 1918 and have no known grave. Over 90% of those commemorated died between July and November 1916.

Walter was the first man from a Sampford Peverell family to die in the war. A newspaper report of his death, published on 22nd September 1916, recorded that

Quite a gloom was cast over the village when news came of the death in action, on the Somme front, of Pte. W. Gale, of the Devons, son of Mr and Mrs G Gale of Sampford Peverell. Deceased joined up at the beginning of the war, and had been in France about 18 months. He is the first from Sampford Peverill to make the supreme sacrifice. Deceased was spoken highly of in a letter from his commanding officer to the parents: "He has always done his work splendidly," he writes "and has shown great courage on all occasions. At the time he was killed he was taking up a stretcher party to remove wounded from the front line. All my bearers suffered heavily at this action, as the German artillery fire was very severe."

Sampford Peverill Lad Killed in the Somme Battle

Quite a gloom was cast over the village when news came of the death in action, on the Somme front, of Pte. W. Gale, of the Devons, son of Mr. and Mrs. G. Gale, of Sampford Peverill. Deceased joined up at the beginning of the war, and had been in France about 18 months. He is the first from Sampford Peverill to make the supreme sacrifice. Deceased was spoken highly of in a letter from his commanding officer to the parents. "He has always done his work splendidly," he writes, "and has shown great courage on all occasions. At the time he was killed he was taking up a stretcher party to remove wounded from the front line. All my bearers suffered heavily at this action, as the German artillery fire was very severe."

Western Times 19 Sep 1916: Image reproduced with kind permission of The British Newspaper Archive (www.britishnewspapearchive.co.uk) '. Image © THE BRITISH LIBRARY BOARD. ALL RIGHTS RESERVED.

According to the list of soldiers' effects on ancestry.co.uk, Walter's outstanding pay of £9 17s 1d was sent to his father, George, in January 1917, as was his £8 10s war gratuity in August 1919.

By the time the information about him was put together after the war, his father must have died and his mother had moved to Uffculme, as he is described as "the son of Blanche Gale, of Selgar's cottage, Uffculme, and the late George Robert Gale".

Walter Gale is remembered on the war memorial plaque in Sampford Peverell parish church. His brother Lewis survived the war, and there is more information about him later. GWR employees who died in WW1, including Walter Gale, are commemorated on plaques at major GWR stations such as Exeter St David's.

Walter Gale is part of this family tree which we have created on ancestry.co.uk and which subscribers to the site can see here: https://www.ancestry.co.uk/family-tree/tree/76011902/family

The Thiepval memorial in France.

Henry Heyward

Henry Thomas Heyward (written as Hayward in some documents) was born on 21st December 1890 in Burlescombe and was the 6th of 10 children (2 boys, 8 girls) of Thomas Heyward (1859-1947) from Bampton, an agricultural labourer who eventually became a cowman, and his wife Louisa Holley (1859-1936) from Butterleigh. Henry Heyward's grandparents and great-grandparents all came from the Bampton area.

Henry's parents, Thomas and Louisa, married in 1880 and their first 5 children were born in Somerset, in and around Wiveliscombe. The family then moved in around 1890 to the first of the row of five terraced cottages at Ayshford, Burlescombe, right next to the canal. We believe that Thomas Heyward worked at Pugham farm which is half a mile to the east of Ayshford. Henry was baptized in Sampford Peverell church on 18th January 1891.

In 1896, the family moved half a mile north-west across the canal to Landside Cottage, in the parish of Sampford Peverell. They were still living at Landside Cottage in the 1901 census, by which time they had 9 children. In 1901 Henry's older sister Emma Louise was a servant to the Pearce family at Boehill Barton, and Henry's elder (and only) brother, William James Hayward, born 1883, was an apprentice blacksmith working for Leon Arthurs at the Smithy, Lower Town, Sampford Peverell. The 10th and last child, Ida Minnie, was born in 1904.

1907 saw the marriage of Henry's brother William to a Somerset girl called Bessie. They had a daughter, Ethel May, in 1910, and by the time of the 1911 census he was living in Canington, Bridgwater, Somerset working as a Blacksmith. 1907 was also the year that Henry's sister Emma died at the age of 22. She was buried in Uplowman on 25th October 1907.

By 1911 the family had moved to Mill House *(2018: 23 Higher Town)* in Sampford Peverell. The father, Thomas, was a cowman, while his son Henry Thomas, then aged 20, was single, lived with his parents and was an agricultural labourer. Henry's sister Harriet married Ernest Kerslake that year and they went on to have four children, all born in Sampford Peverell. Another sister, Lily, emigrated to Canada that same year with Wilfred Pillar who was also from Sampford Peverell. They married and settled there.

A newspaper report tells us that on Boxing Day 1914 Henry, referred to as "Harry", was best man at the wedding of his sister Polly Jane, who was two years older than Henry. Polly married Frank Charles Cotton, a fisherman from Dawlish. The bride wore a cream dress and her younger sisters, Dolly

The Pond, Sampford Peverill

Mill House c 1905

and Minnie, were her bridesmaids. The presents were described as "very good and useful" and "the sun shone brilliantly during the ceremony". The marriage was to be short-lived; Frank Cotton started active service in France on 25th July 1915 and was killed in Flanders exactly two months later.

Of Henry's other sisters: we don't know what happened to Annie, who may have died young; Rosa married William Cork, also from the village, in 1921, and they had three children; and Edith married her cousin Frank Hayward in 1933.

Henry Heyward first entered service in WW1 as a private in the 8th Battalion Devonshire Regiment, and was in France by 1st Oct 1915. The local newspaper reported that he was home on leave in February 1917 after being wounded, but he returned to the war. We know that in 1917 he was still in the 8th Devonshires in 'C' company. This battalion was part of the 20th Brigade of the 7th Division, whose men took part in the third battle of Ypres, also known as Passchendaele, infamous for the terrible mud and for the scale of casualties.

According to the BBC history Passchendaele website[47]

> The infantry attack began on 31 July. Constant shelling had churned the clay soil and smashed the drainage systems. The left wing of the attack achieved its objectives but the right wing failed completely. Within a few days, the heaviest rain for 30 years had turned the soil into a quagmire, producing thick mud that clogged up rifles and immobilised tanks. It eventually became so deep that men and horses drowned in it.
>
> On 16 August the attack was resumed, to little effect. There was stalemate for another month until an improvement in the weather prompted another attack on 20 September. The Battle of Menin Road Ridge, along with the Battle of Polygon Wood on 26 September and the Battle of Broodseinde on 4 October, established British possession of the ridge east of Ypres.

In total about five miles were gained but it had taken over three months, 325,000 Allied and 260,000 German casualties.

According to a newspaper report Henry's parents were initially informed that he was in hospital suffering from shell shock, but they were later told that he died of wounds in hospital in the Boulogne area, the site of many of the military hospitals, on 7th October 1917. The log of the village school for that day recorded that: "News has come from France that Henry Heyward has lost his life in the advance now being made by Sir Douglas Haig. He, together with Walter Gale and Robert Hine, attended this school in the early years of this century."

An article in the Devon and Somerset News on 8th November 1917 reported:

> Concerning the death of Private H. Heyward, of Sampford Peverell, his sister has received several letters from France. The chaplain at a hospital sends his sympathy, and says the grave will be cared for. The sister in charge says the deceased was quite unconscious when admitted. Everything was done, but all was of no avail. She also sends her heartfelt sympathy.

Henry Heyward's medals, photo courtesy of a collector. The Military Medal is on the left.

---

[47] http://www.bbc.co.uk/history/wprldwars/wwone/battle_passchendaele.shtml

Henry Heyward was later awarded the MM (Military Medal) for bravery, as recorded in the London Gazette on 28th January 1918. We do not know exactly why it was awarded to him (most of the WW1 citations were lost) but the Military Medal was awarded to 'other ranks' of the British Army and Commonwealth Forces, the equivalent for officers being the Military Cross. The MM was an award for gallantry and devotion to duty when under fire in battle on land. On the reverse of the medal is inscribed "For Bravery in the Field".

Henry Heyward is buried in the Godewaersvelde British Cemetery in France, near the Belgian border. The inscription chosen by his mother, engraved at the foot of his headstone, is "Peace perfect peace".

Image © Local World Limited. Image reproduced with kind permission of The British Newspaper Archive (www.britis hnewspaperarchive.co.uk) '. Image © THE BRITISH LIBRARY BOARD. ALL RIGHTS RESERVED.

Henry Heyward is part of this family tree which we have created on ancestry.co.uk and which subscribers to the site can see here: https://www.ancestry.co.uk/family-tree/tree/52965763/family

Robert Hine

Robert Thomas Hine was born in October 1896 in Culmstock, about six miles west of Sampford Peverell, the oldest of 5 children of William James Hine 1869-1940, born in Holcombe Rogus, a Railway Plate Layer (like his father, another Robert) and Alice Stone 1872-1950 from Culmstock. Late in 1900 the family moved to Moor Cottages on the eastern outskirts of Sampford Peverell. By this time there were 3 children: Robert, Frederick William (born 1899), and Louisa Elizabeth (born 1900). A further two sisters (Rhoda May and Beatrice Mary) were born in 1902 and 1906 and baptized at St John's Church in the village.

We know from the log of the village school that Robert Hine was an attendee. When the Reverend Philip Rossiter, the village rector, died in 1910, he left many charitable bequests including £5 each to a number of local schoolchildren. Amongst these were Robert and Louisa Hine, for whom £5 would have been a very large sum of money.

By the time of the 1911 census the family had moved to Jersey Cottages, then a pair of cottages but now one cottage, in Sampford Peverell, on the road that goes down to the station, then a railway siding. The father still worked on the railway and Robert, then aged 14, was in "Domestic Service by the Day". In his 'next of kin' information on the Commonwealth War Graves site, his parents' address given in 1917 is 'Underdown, Sampford Peverell'.

Jersey Cottage, March 2015. It was originally a pair of cottages.

A newspaper article published on 11th September 1914 describes a recruitment meeting held in the courtyard of St Boniface Home in the village, which included stirring speeches, calls to patriotism, and much cheering. It reports that the recruiting sergeant returned the next day and took nearly twenty recruits to Tiverton including B (perhaps for 'Bob') Hine.

Robert Hine joined the 8th Battalion Devonshire Regiment as a private and first saw active service in France on 25 July 1915. He was in a machine gun corps, and at some point before 31st August 1917 he was promoted to Lance Corporal. A newspaper article published on that day reported that he was "home on furlough from the trenches".

After his leave Robert returned to France where the 8th Devonshires were part of the 20th Brigade of the 7th Division, who took part in the third battle of Ypres, also known as Passchendaele, infamous for the terrible mud and for the scale of casualties. This battle is described in the section on Henry Heyward who died the same day as Robert Hine.

Robert Hine was killed in action in charge of a machine gun on 7th October 1917, aged 20. A service was held in the village church in memory of Robert Hine and James Trevellyan, another casualty who died two days earlier. "Muffled peals were rung on the bells, and the Dead March was played by the organist".

Battle of Broodseinde 4 October: Men huddled in funk holes with corpses in front of them in a railway cutting at Broodseinde.   *Photo courtesy of the Imperial War Museum.*

153

Lnc.-Corpl. HINES.

September, 1914, at a recruiting meeting at Sampford Peverell. His parents live at Jersey Cottage, Sampford Peverell. His officer, writing to the parents says "He was a brave lad; when others were in their funk holes in the height of the most intense German bombardment, he was singing at his work."

LNC.-CORPL. HINES, Devons (Lewis Gun Corps), who was killed by a shell fragment in France during one of the recent advances. He joined up in

According to another newspaper report the Hines had another son serving in Egypt. This must have been Robert's brother Frederick William, who was only 18 when Robert died.

This newspaper article from the Western Times of 26th October 1917 records that Robert's officer wrote this to his parents: "He was a brave lad; when others were in their funk holes in the height of the most intense German bombardment, he was singing at his work".

According to the list of soldiers' effects on ancestry.co.uk Robert's outstanding pay of £13 1s 7d was paid to his father, William Hine, in March 1918, as was a war gratuity of £14 in 1919.

Like fellow Sampford Peverell men Percy Bradfield, Walter Brown, Wilfred Taudevin, and Charles Wallington, Robert Hine is commemorated at the Tyne Cot Memorial in Zonnebeke, Belgium. There is a picture of the memorial in the section on Percy Bradfield. Robert Hine's name is on stone 38A. Robert Hine is part of this family tree which we have created on ancestry.co.uk and which subscribers can see here:

https://www.ancestry.co.uk/family-tree/tree/68296702/family

Arthur Pillar

Arthur John Pillar was born on 5th January 1900, the younger of two sons of William Henry Pillar 1862-1940 of Sampford Peverell, a railway packer and Mary Grace Young 1866-1932, daughter of a Burlescombe wheelwright and carpenter. Arthur's father, William, is specifically mentioned in the baptism book of St Johns Church, Sampford Peverell, as being the first baby to be baptized in the newly restored old font on 29th June 1862! Arthur's father, William, was the oldest of 4 children of John Pillar 1841-1904, an agricultural labourer from Crediton and Jane Carnell 1834-1889 from Broadhembury. William had a brother James who also lost a son, Frederick (Arthur's cousin), during the war.

Arthur's parents were married in October 1890 and initially lived in Burlescombe. By the time of the 1901 census they were living at Jersey Cottages in Sampford Peverell, on the road that now goes down to the station, with their two sons: Arthur, and his older brother William Henry, born in 1892. There is a photo of Jersey Cottage in the section on Robert Hine, as his family lived there later. In the 1911 census they were living in 'Marchells' at Waterloo Cross, along with their maiden aunt, Charlotte Pillar. By late 1918, according to the military information, Arthur's parents had moved to Boobery *(2018: the site of 7, Boobery)* in Sampford Peverell, and we know from Gregory's Directory that they were still in Boobery in 1923.

Arthur's brother William signed up on 5th September 1914 to the 5th Somerset Light Infantry Regiment , and his cousin Frederick James Pillar, served in the Coldstream Guards during the war and was killed in action on 13 Apr 1918. He also had two second cousins, Ernest and Frederick Tucker, who died in the war.

Arthur Pillar would have been called up in the early months of 1918, and after training was sent to France to join the 1st/5th Battalion of the Devonshire Regiment. This battalion had previously served in India, but after the Germans broke through the allied lines after the collapse of Russia, this battle-hardened battalion was sent to France, via Egypt, arriving in Marseilles in June. The 1/5th Devonshires joined the 185th (2/ 1st West Riding) Brigade on 6th June 1918, and Arthur Pillar would have joined them soon afterwards. They were in action almost immediately, taking part in the second battle of Arras and the battles of the Hindenburg Line, also known as the Siegfried Line. According to cwgc.org these battles were a complex series of operations intended to advance allied formations towards the forward areas of a formidable system of German field defences called the Siegfried (or Hindenburg) Line, which the Germans had just re-garrisoned in a last-ditch attempt to prolong the fighting.

Arthur was wounded and was sent to a hospital but died of his wounds on 13th Sep 1918, aged just 18. There were a large number of military hospitals around Rouen during the war and most of those who died in one of these hospitals were buried in the St Sever cemetery. There were so many casualties that an extension to it had to be created in 1916, and it is in this extension that Arthur Pillar is buried. The inscription on his tombstone, "Rest in peace", was chosen by his brother "W.H.Pillar of Boobery, Sampford Peverell".

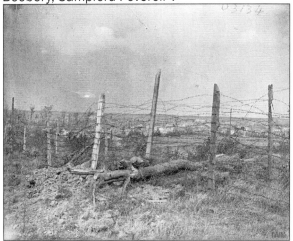

Battle of the Drocourt-Queant Line. Queant, to the NW, of which was the junction of the Hindenburg and Wotan Lines. 7 September 1918. Photo courtesy of the Imperial War Museum

A memorial service was held for Arthur Pillar in Burlescombe on 22nd September 1917. The newspaper report of it tells us that "Muffled peals were rung, and the church was filled with relatives and friends." His name is inscribed on the memorial tablet which was erected in the church in Burlescombe in August 1919.

According to the list of soldiers' effects on ancestry.co.uk Arthur's outstanding pay of £4 17s 11d and a war gratuity of £3 were sent to his father, William, in December 1918.

Arthur Pillar is part of this family tree which we have created on ancestry.co.uk and which subscribers can see here:

https://www.ancestry.co.uk/family-tree/tree/68538081/family

Frederick Pillar

Frederick James Pillar was the oldest of 5 children of James Pillar and Eliza Bell (1863-1940), who were married in Burlescombe in 1892. James Pillar had been brought up in Ayshford where his father was an agricultural labourer, whereas Eliza Bell came from Chevithorne, one mile northeast of Tiverton, - also from a family of agricultural labourers. Frederick Pillar was born on 15th September 1893 in Halberton and was baptized there exactly one month later. His father's occupation was recorded as a railway plate layer (i.e. someone whose job it was to maintain or replace railway track).

In the 1901 census Frederick was living with his parents; his brothers Albert and Walter; his sister Elda, and his maternal grandfather, Richard Bell. They lived in Lower Town, Sampford Peverell, in a group of eight cottages (*2018: the site of 16 Court Way*).

By the time of the 1911 Census the family had moved out to Waterloo, one mile east of Sampford Peverell, towards Uffculme. The father, James, was still a platelayer on the railway and Frederick, now 18, was described as a farmer. Frederick's younger brother, Albert, born in

Lower Town, showing the cottages on the right

1895, was working as a horse carriage driver at the Railway Junction Hotel in Willand in the 1911 census, aged 16. Frederick now also had a six-year-old sister, Beatrice. There is a possible WW1 service record for an Albert Henry Pillar of the Devonshire regiment, but it has not yet been possible to confirm whether this is Frederick's brother. Albert survived the war. Their younger brother Walter was just 18 when the war ended and it does not appear that he took part in it.

Frederick enlisted in 1915 and joined the 3rd Battalion Coldstream Guards, who in 1915 became part of the 1st Guards Brigade, Guards Division, who then transferred to 31st Division. This division was involved in a large number of battles in France and Flanders, including some at Ypres, Passchendaele and the Somme.

Frederick survived the fighting for nearly three years, but was killed in action on 13th April 1918, aged 24. He is remembered on panel 1 at

Battle of Hazebrouck. Collected stragglers of the 31st Division lining the railway line near Merris, 12 April 1918.   *Photo courtesy of the Imperial War Museum.*

the Ploegsteert Memorial in Hainaut, Belgium - a memorial for men with no known grave. According to the CWGC "most of those commemorated by the memorial were killed in the course of the day-to-day trench warfare which characterised this part of the line, or in small scale set engagements, usually carried out in support of the major attacks taking place elsewhere".

According to the list of soldiers' effects on ancestry.co.uk his outstanding pay of £9 12s 9d, which included a war gratuity of £7, was sent to his sister and sole legatee Beatrice in October 1919.

Frederick's cousin, Arthur Pillar, joined the army early in 1918 and died of wounds in September that year. He also had two second cousins, Ernest and Frederick Tucker, who died in the war. Arthur Pillar and the Tuckers are remembered on the war memorial plaque in Burlescombe church.

The Ploegsteert Memorial, Hainaut, Belgium

Frederick Pillar is part of this family tree which we have created on www.ancestry.co.uk and which subscribers to the site can see here: https://www.ancestry.co.uk/family-tree/tree/68538081/family

Arthur Scorse

Arthur Henry Scorse was the third child of Alice Scorse, who was born in Sampford Peverell in 1877 - the daughter of Charles Scorse, a railway worker, and Elizabeth, née Trevellyan. In the 1881 and 1891 censuses they lived in Tiddly Wink cottage in Whitnage Road.

In 1891 Alice, then 14, was a domestic servant at Landside Farm. When she was 16, and single, she had a daughter, Louisa Scorse, born on 28th March 1894 and christened in Sampford Peverell parish church in May that year. Two years later, and still single, she gave birth to Bertie Scorse on 1st July 1896. He was born in Tiverton Workhouse, where Alice was living at the time, but he was also christened in Sampford Peverell parish church in August 1896. After another two years, on 29th March 1898, Alice gave birth to Arthur Henry Scorse, again in Tiverton Workhouse, where she was still (or again) living. Arthur was christened on 22nd December 1899 at St Peter's church, Tiverton, and his abode was given as the "Workhouse". Several other workhouse children were christened on the same day.

By 1901 Alice was working as a domestic servant again, this time at Bishops Farm, Stawley in Somerset. Arthur Scorse, 3, and his sister Louisa, 7, were now living with their grandparents, Charles and Elizabeth Scorse, at Easton Cottage, Sampford Peverell. This cottage was demolished long ago, but it used to be down the lane or farm track which runs south-east opposite the house called 'Little Orchard' in Lower Town. Meanwhile Arthur's brother Bertie, aged 4, was still living at Tiverton Workhouse and he seems to have stayed there until he was a teenager.

Towards the end of 1903 Alice married Charles Tucker and she had three children with him: Elsie, Ernest and Francis. Charles Tucker died in 1908, and the following year Alice married Francis Brice. In the 1911 census Alice and Francis Brice were living at Lands Mill, Halberton, with her children Arthur Scorse, then 13, the three Tucker children, and an 8-month-old baby, Gladys Brice. Arthur's older sister Louisa Scorse was a general servant at Houndsmoor, Uplowman, and his brother Bertie was still in Tiverton workhouse.

In September 1914 a recruiting rally was held in Sampford Peverell, resulting in about twenty men joining the army, including Arthur Scorse who was just 16. Arthur enlisted at Exeter and served first with the Devonshire Regiment (No. 18232) and later with the 2nd Battalion, Dorset Regiment (No. 14256), which led to his being sent to Mesopotamia, like another Sampford Peverell casualty, Sidney Dunn.

A British 18-pounder Field Gun firing from an open position in the flat desert landscape of lower Mesopotamia.   *Photo courtesy of the Imperial War Museum*

From January 1917 to April 1918 the 2nd Dorsets came under the 9th Indian Brigade, 3rd Indian Division. This division, largely comprised of troops from India, arrived in Mesopotamia in April 1916 to fight the Turks, who were allies of Germany, and the action there continued until the end of the war. The following comes from the Long Long Trail website:

> Like Gallipoli, conditions in Mesopotamia defy description. Extremes of temperature (120 degrees F was common); arid desert and regular flooding; flies, mosquitoes and other vermin: all led to appalling levels of sickness and death through disease. Under these incredible conditions, units fell short of officers and men, and all too often the reinforcements were half-trained and ill-equipped. Medical arrangements were quite shocking, with wounded men spending up to two weeks on boats before reaching any kind of hospital. These factors, plus of course the unexpectedly determined Turkish resistance, contributed to high casualty rates. 11012 killed, 3985 died of wounds, 12678 died of sickness, 13492 missing and prisoners (9000 at Kut), 51836 wounded - Data from "Statistics of the Military Effort of the British Empire" (London: HMSO, 1920).

On 11th March 1917 the British and allied troops captured Baghdad and the Berlin-Baghdad railway, which was a significant achievement, but the conflict continued. Arthur Scorse was killed in action in Mesopotamia on 25th March 1917, a few weeks before his 19th birthday. His brother Bertie was also in the Army and he too was killed in action in the Middle East later that year. According to the Army Register of Soldiers' Effects, 1901-1929 (on ancestry.co.uk), in April 1918 Arthur's remaining pay, £9 13s 3d, was paid to his mother, Alice Brice, and a further £8 war gratuity was paid to her in 1920.

Arthur Scorse is remembered on the Basra Memorial. The Commonwealth War Graves Commission describes this memorial as commemorating more than 40,500 members of the Commonwealth forces who died in the operations in Mesopotamia from the autumn of 1914 to the end of August 1921 and whose graves are not known. It used to be on the main quay of the naval dockyard at Maqil, about 8 kilometres north of Basra, but in 1997 it was moved to a site 32 kilometres along the road to Nasiriyah, in the middle of what was a battleground in the first Gulf War. As it is not possible for the Commonwealth War Graves Commission to maintain this memorial, they have created a two-volume Roll of Honour listing all casualties buried and commemorated in Iraq. These volumes are on display at the Commission's Head Office in Maidenhead.

Arthur Scorse is part of this family tree which we have created on ancestry.co.uk and which ancestry subscribers can see here: https://www.ancestry.co.uk/family-tree/tree/75095332/family

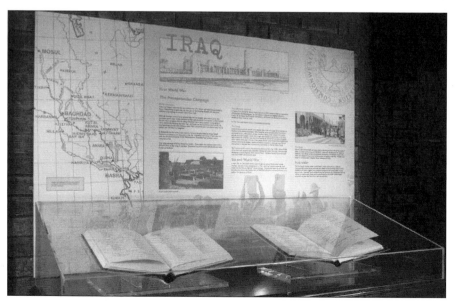

The Mesopotamia Roll of Honour in the CWGC headquarters. Photo courtesy of www.cwgc.org

Bertie Scorse

Bertie Scorse was the second child of Alice Scorse, who was born in Sampford Peverell in 1877 - the daughter of Charles Scorse, a railway worker, and Elizabeth, née Trevellyan. In the 1881 and 1891 censuses they lived in Tiddly Wink cottage in Whitnage Road.

In 1891 Alice, then 14, was a domestic servant at Landside Farm. When Alice was 16, and single, she had a daughter, Louisa Scorse, born on 28th March 1894 and christened in Sampford Peverell parish church in May that year. Two years later, and still single, she gave birth to Bertie Scorse on 1st July 1896. He was born in Tiverton Workhouse, where Alice was living at the time, but he was also christened in Sampford Peverell parish church on 5th August 1896. He was registered and christened as Bertie, not Albert. After another two years, on 29th March 1898, Alice gave birth to Arthur Henry Scorse, again in Tiverton Workhouse.

Tiverton Workhouse, main block in 2001. Photo courtesy of Peter Higginbotham and there is more info on Tiverton Workhouse on his web site: http://www.workhouses.org.uk/Tiverton/

A school admissions list shows that on 10th January 1901 Bertie Scorse was enrolled at Elmore School, Tiverton, the school normally attended by the children from Tiverton Workhouse. A few months later, when the 1901 census was taken, Alice was working as a domestic servant again, this time at Bishops Farm, Stawley in Somerset. Bertie's sister Louisa, aged 7, and his brother Arthur, aged 3, were now living with their grandparents, Charles and Elizabeth Scorse, at Easton Cottage, Sampford Peverell, but Bertie, the middle child, aged 4, was left at Tiverton Workhouse and he seems to have stayed there until he was a teenager. One has to wonder why his grandparents were unable to take him in.

Towards the end of 1903 Alice married Charles Tucker and had three children with him: Elsie, Ernest and Francis. Charles Tucker died in 1908, and the following year she married Francis Brice. In the 1911 census Alice and Francis Brice were living at Lands Mill, Halberton, with her children Arthur Scorse, then 13, the three Tucker children, and an 8-month-old baby, Gladys Brice. Her oldest daughter, Louisa Scorse, was a general servant at Houndsmoor, Uplowman.

Bertie, however, was still in Tiverton workhouse. He left it that same year, as we know from a newspaper article which appeared in the Exeter and Plymouth Gazette on 16th November 1912. It reports that:

> Yesterday, before the Tiverton County Magistrates, Bertie Scorse, aged 16, in the employ of Mr. Tarr of Boobier Hill Farm, Bampton, was brought up in custody charged with stealing 17s ½d, moneys belonging to Mrs. Hoare, saddler, of Brook Street, Bampton, on the previous morning. Defendant, a dull-looking youth, pleaded guilty. According to the evidence adduced by Mrs. Hoare and P.C. Evans, defendant went to Mrs. Hoare's shop with milk, and while she was absent he took the money from the till. Interviewed later, defendant told P.C.Evans that he intended going to Bampton carnival that evening. Defendant was bound over to be of good behaviour for six months. It was stated that Mr. Tarr took the defendant from the Tiverton Workhouse in April 1911, and that he was willing to try him again for another six months.

It seems surprising that he got off so lightly; perhaps the magistrate felt sorry for him.

Bertie's younger brother Arthur enlisted in the Army in late 1914, and Bertie must have signed up soon afterwards. Arthur was killed in action in Mesopotamia in March 1917.

Bertie Scorse enlisted at Barnstaple and joined the Royal North Devon Yeomanry (service number: 2326). Initially, according to www.longlongtrail.co.uk, the North Devon Yeomanry was a 'mounted' brigade, but in October 1915 they 'dismounted' and moved to Gallipoli, so Bertie would have gone there with them. This is confirmed by his medal card, which says he first entered the "2B" theatre of war on 23rd September 1915. 2B was the code for Balkans – Gallipoli (see http:// www.greatwar.co.uk/places/ww1-theatres-of-war.htm). Gallipoli was the scene of fighting between Allied and Turkish troops between April 1915 and January 1916, and is where the ANZAC (Australian and New Zealand) troops first took part in the Great War. British politicians thought it would be a 'back door' into Germany, but it turned into a disaster, resulting in massive losses on both sides, and a diversion of troops and supplies from the Western Front. The Long Long Trail website (www.longlongtrail.co.uk) describes the end of 1915, when Bertie was there, as follows:

Conditions on Gallipoli defy description. The terrain and close fighting did not allow for the dead to be buried. Flies and other vermin flourished in the heat, which caused epidemic sickness. In October 1915, winter storms caused much damage and human hardship, and in December, a great blizzard – followed by cataclysmic thaw – caused casualties of 10% (15.000 men) throughout the British contingent, and no doubt something similar on the Turkish side. Of the 213,000 British casualties on Gallipoli, 145,000 were due to sickness; chief causes being dysentery, diarrhoea, and enteric fever.

The British and Allied troops all left the area by 9th January 1916.

Bertie survived Gallipoli, and his section withdrew back to Egypt on 30th December 1915. In early 1916 they were absorbed into the 2nd Dismounted Brigade and were then merged with another group to form the 16th Battalion of the Devonshire Regiment (at which point Bertie was given service number 345727), under the command of the 229th Brigade, which became part of the Egyptian Expeditionary Force. In 1917 they took part in the 2nd and 3rd battles of Gaza, and then the capture of Jerusalem, in what was then Palestine.

Palestine was part of the Turkish Ottoman empire. Allied forces entered Palestine in December 1916 and over the course of the next twelve months they advanced towards Jerusalem. By 21st November 1917 they

A view of the landscape south-west of Gaza, 1917.   *Photo courtesy of the Imperial War Museum*

were about 5 kilometres west of the city, and very severe fighting followed, lasting until all the city's defences were captured on 8th December. Bertie Scorse was killed in action just a few days before this on 3rd December 1917, aged 21. Another Sampford Peverell casualty, Frederick Thomas, died at the same place on the same day. Bertie is buried in grave A31 in the Jerusalem war cemetery, where 2515 Commonwealth casualties are buried. The register of his gravestone suggests that they did not know his age or next of kin (perhaps he didn't either), so no personal inscription was used.

The list of soldiers' effects on ancestry.co.uk shows that in June 1918 Bertie's outstanding pay of £10 7s 4d was sent to Mrs. Lydia Leaworthy, his sole legatee, as was his war gratuity of £13 10s. In the 1911 census Mrs. Leaworthy was a 49-year-old "sick maternity nurse" at the Tiverton workhouse, so perhaps she was a mother figure for Bertie. Let's hope he experienced some affection in his short and eventful life.

Bertie Scorse is part of this family tree which we have created on ancestry.co.uk and which ancestry subscribers can see here: https://www.ancestry.co.uk/family-tree/tree/75095332/family

The Jerusalem War Cemetery.   *Photo courtesy of the Commonwealth War Graves Commission*

Wilfred Taudevin

Wilfred Taudevin was born and brought up in Sampford Peverell. He was the sixth of the nine children of Frederic William and Caroline Taudevin (née Lanyon, from St Goran, Cornwall) of Sampford Peverell. Wilfred's father Frederic Taudevin came from St Peter Port in Guernsey and moved to Sampford Peverell some time between 1871 (when he was still in Guernsey), and 1873 when his oldest son was born in Sampford Peverell. Around this time he took over the lease of the house and shop in Challis, Lower Town, which had previously been run by Joseph Jennings, and he bought the house and shop when they came up for sale in 1884. "Taudevin's" shop was the main shop in the village and sold groceries and haberdashery. Frederic Taudevin was a well-respected member of the community. As well as being a shopkeeper he was a member of the Parish Council for many years, a supporter of Liberal ideas, an active Nonconformist, and a Wesleyan preacher.

Wilfred was born in March 1881 (he was one month old at the time of the 1881 census). There are no christening records for the Taudevins because they attended the Methodist chapel, not the parish church. The rest of the family in 1881, as well as Wilfred and his parents, were: Frederic (7), Caroline (6), Sidney (4), Ethel (3) and Jessy (1). Other lodgers in the house were William H Shapland, a grocer's apprentice, and Sarah Whiton, a nurse.

By 1891 Wilfred had three more siblings: Ernest, Percy and Julia. An aunt, Grace Williams, 73, born in St Goran Cornwall, was also staying with them.

Taudevin's shop on the right, in Challis, Lower Town. A photo earlier in the book shows ladies outside it who are probably his mother and sister.

At some point in the late 1890s Wilfred and two of his brothers moved to Wales. In the 1901 census Wilfred, now a 20-year-old grocery assistant, was living in Caerleon Road, Newport, Monmouthshire, along with his younger brothers Ernest and Percy who were outfitters. They lodged with Charles Ambrose, a railway signal inspector born in Basingstoke, his wife Caroline and their daughter Rose Ethel, born in Reading, an 18-year-old dressmaker (who would later marry Wilfred).

Wilfred's brother Sidney died in the Sampford Peverell area in April 1903, aged 27. Two years later, in 1905, Wilfred's oldest sister, Caroline, died here too, aged 31, and Wilfred's father, Frederic, died suddenly in 1909. For some years his widow Caroline ran the shop; later it was managed by Wilfred's oldest remaining brother and sister, Frederic and Ethel, though their mother continued to live in the village until her death in 1925.

In 1911 Wilfred, now 30 and a grocery manager, was boarding at 8, Eastfield Road, Andover, Hants. Later that year, on 18th September 1911, he married Rose Ethel Ambrose in Newport Monmouthshire. They were married in the parish church of St Matthew, Newport, and the witnesses included Wilfred's younger brother Ernest and younger sister Julia.

The run of bad luck, or ill health, in the family continued and Wilfred's brother Percy died in March 1913 in Farnham, Surrey, aged 28. As a married man Wilfred would initially have been exempt from conscription when it was introduced in January 1916, but in May 1916 the act was extended to include married men, and Wilfred was probably called up soon afterwards.

He joined the Hampshire Regiment (service number 243118) but was then transferred to the 6th Battalion of the Duke of Cornwall's Light Infantry (service number 260187). They came under 43rd Brigade in the 14th Light Division, and Wilfred served with them in France and Flanders. The 14th Light Division were involved in the battles of Ypres, including the battle of the Menin Road from 20-25 Sep 1917, and the first battle of Passchendaele, on 12th October 1917.

Wilfred Taudevin was killed in action on 18th October 1917, aged 36, leaving his widow, Rose. They did not have any children. According to the Soldiers' Effects list on ancestry.co.uk his outstanding pay of £1 was sent to his widow. Probate of his will shows he left £221 8s 4d to Rose and her father Charles Ambrose.

A Sampford Peverell news item reported that his widowed mother had "another son serving in India". His oldest brother, Frederic, was running the shop, so if correct this must have been Ernest, who survived the war, but it may have been a mistake.

According to another newspaper report of Wilfred's death:

> Private Wilfred Lawson Taudevin, of Sampford Peverell, killed in action, was formerly employed at Andover as grocery manager, was 26 (sic) years of age, and leaves a widow but no children. A bursting shell killed him instantly, and his officer writes: "He died as he had lived out here, working hard and doing his duty conscientiously, like the true soldier I had always found him to be."

Like fellow Sampford Peverell men Percy Bradfield, Walter Brown, Robert Hine, and Charles Wallington, Wilfred Taudevin is commemorated (as W.L. Tau-de-vin) at the Tyne Cot Memorial in Zonnebeke, Belgium. His name is on stone 82A. There is a picture of the memorial in the section on Percy Bradfield. Wilfred Taudevin is part of this family tree which we have created on ancestry.co.uk and which ancestry subscribers can see here:

https://www.ancestry.co.uk/family-tree/tree/76123536/family

Assault on Passchendaele 12 October - 6 November: A line of infantry seen from the rear marching to a forward area along a muddy corduroy track strewn with debris at Westhoek.
Photo courtesy of the Imperial War Museum

William Taylor

William Henry Taylor was the only child of George Henry Taylor 1858-1917 of Sampford Peverell, and his first wife Lucy J Winsborrow 1859-1906 of Exeter. William Taylor was born on 12th March 1883 and was baptized in Sampford Peverell parish church six weeks later on 29th April 1883. His parents lived in Higher Town in the 1891 census, but by 1901 they had moved to Mount Pleasant on Whitnage Road where his father was a baker and farmer.

Mount Pleasant, mid 20th century

As a boy William was a pupil of the East Devon County School in Lower Town, Sampford Peverell. The premises later became the St Boniface home for boys. A newspaper article published on 14th February 1902 in the Exeter and Plymouth Gazette reported that "At the recent Veterinary College examination Mr. William Taylor, of Sampford Peverell, passed the first trial direct from the East Devon County School, and has taken tenth place among 80 students. He had no coaching beyond the usual school curriculum." He continued his veterinary studies and graduated from the Royal Veterinary College on 14th July 1905 (information thanks to the college librarian), after which he joined the Army Veterinary Corps (AVC) which later became the Royal Army Veterinary Corps (RAVC).

According to the London Gazette of 4th September 1906 he was made Lieutenant, effective from 5th

EAST DEVON COUNTY SCHOOL,
SAMPFORD PEVERELL.   *French & Son, Wellington.*

East Devon County School

September 1906. At the time of the 1911 census he still held the rank of Lieutenant and was on active service as an army veterinary surgeon in South Africa. The AVC had two sections in South Africa, one in Pretoria and one in Potchefstroom, but we don't know which one he was in. The London Gazette of 12th September 1911 announced his promotion to the rank of Captain.

William Taylor was transferred to France with the British Expeditionary Force at the very start of the war. Early in the war the Veterinary Corps was reorganized to provide a mobile veterinary section as part of each Division that went overseas. According to his medal card he was Officer Commanding No 3 Mobile Vet Section, 2nd Division. The Long Long Trail website explains that:

> A unit of the Army Veterinary Corps, the Mobile Veterinary Section came under command of the Headquarters of the formation known as a Division. It was in effect a first aid unit, providing medical care for sick, wounded or injured horses used by the units of the Division. If a horse required greater care that could not be provided by the MVS, the animal would be sent to a Base Veterinary Hospital and its place taken by a horse delivered from ASC Remounts.

Wounded horses arriving at No. 5 Veterinary Hospital at Abbeville, 22 April 1918.
Photo courtesy of the Imperial War Museum

Horses were essential to the army at the time, both for riding and for pulling carts and guns. The British army deployed and cared for over two million horses and mules during the war.

The 2nd Division was one of the first British formations to move to France and remained on the Western Front throughout the war. It took part in most of the major actions including, amongst many other battles, the first battle of Ypres in 1914, in which Major Taylor would probably have taken part.

The London Gazette of 19th Oct 1915 announced that from 31st July 1915 William Taylor was one of two "Captains to be temporary Majors whilst holding the appointment of Assistant Directors of Veterinary Services". According to his medal card he was on the Royal Army Veterinary Corps Staff at HQ No 2 Corps, so he would have been based at General HQ which was at St Omer at the time, and which moved to Montreuil-sur-Mer in March 1916. GHQ was an enormous administrative centre, staffed by both military and civilians, which decided strategies as well as coordinating the deployment of troops, munitions, supplies, and transport.

The Veterinary Section was responsible for the vast number of horses imported to, and used on, the Western Front, the Mobile Veterinary Sections, and the veterinary hospitals. They did an amazing job in the circumstances: 2.5 million animals were admitted to their care on the Western Front, and 80% of injured animals were treated and returned to duty.

The outside of the Ecole Militaire, the Central Office of the British GHQ between 31 March 1916 and April 1919, Montreuil.
Photo courtesy of the Imperial War Museum

The Army Veterinary Corps was given the prefix 'Royal' on 27th November 1918. The Quartermaster General stated: "The Corps by its initiative and scientific methods has placed military veterinary organization on a higher plane. The high standard which it has maintained at home and throughout all theatres has resulted in a reduction of animal wastage, an increased mobility of mounted units and a mitigation of animal suffering unapproached in any previous military operation." Horses were not the only animals for which the RAVC had responsibility; Britain deployed over 20,000 dogs on the Western Front. They were used as sentry dogs; for scouting (alerting soldiers to the presence of strangers); for finding the wounded and taking them medical supplies, and for carrying messages, for which they were much better equipped than humans, being faster and harder to detect.

On 17th December 1918 the London Gazette published a list of people 'Mentioned in Despatches'. The introduction to the list records that Field-Marshal Haig sent the following from General HQ on 8th November 1918, to the Secretary of State for War: "My Lord, I have the honour to submit a list of names of those officers, ladies, non-commissioned officers and men serving, or who have served, under my command during the period 25th February, 1918, to midnight 16th/17th September, 1918, whose distinguished and gallant services and devotion to duty I consider deserving of special mention". In the 'Commands and Staff' section the names include that of "Taylor, Capt. (T./Maj.) W.H., R.A.V.C."

Conditions at GHQ were good, and relations with the French were fairly cordial until prices and rationing put a strain on the local economy. In 1918 there was a huge influx of refugees to the area, hospitals became overloaded, and there were severe outbreaks of measles, dysentery and flu. William Taylor died in France on 11th Feb 1919, at the age of 35, after a short illness, most likely the epidemic of Spanish flu that swept the world shortly after the end of WW1 causing tens of millions of deaths. He is buried in Longuenesse, St Omer, a hospital centre. When he died (outliving both his parents) he was reasonably wealthy, and his probate was £5,280 12s 2d which he left to Walter John Winsborrow, his uncle.

Three dogs at the Central Kennel of the Messenger Dog Service, GHQ. Note the cylinder (attached to collar) in which the message was carried. Photo courtesy of the Imperial War Museum.

The London Gazette of 4th September 1919 issued a list of those who had been awarded the Croix de Guerre by the King of the Belgians, and this included, posthumously, Major Taylor. We don't know specifically what it was awarded for, but foreign nationals could only earn this medal for acts of heroism conducted while on Belgian soil.

This was not his only posthumous award. The London Gazette of 3rd October 1919 also listed him as recipient of the French 'Ordre du Mérite Agricole' as 'Chevalier', or Knight. This order is second only to the Légion d'Honneur, and is awarded to people who have rendered exceptional service in public duties or in the practice of agriculture, so his work may have included assisting French farmers during the war, and helping with the restoration of agriculture in Northern France in the immediate aftermath of the war.

Major Taylor's name is commemorated on the war memorial plaque in Sampford Peverell parish church, and also in the Royal College of Veterinary Surgeons in London on a memorial to those members who died on active service during WW1. The memorial lists nine members of the RCVS who were killed in action, twenty four who died of wounds, and thirty four who died of disease, including William Taylor.

William Taylor is part of this family tree which we have created on ancestry.co.uk and which ancestry subscribers can see here:

https://www.ancestry.co.uk/family-tree/tree/69315156/family

W H Taylor's name on the WW1 memorial in the Royal College of Veterinary Surgeons. This photo, courtesy of their librarian, was published in 1921 when the memorial was unveiled.

His gravestone at Longuenesse (St Omer) Souvenir Cemetery

173

Frederick Thomas

Frederick Thomas was born on 3rd December 1886 and baptized in Sampford Peverell Church on the 19th December, along with his brother Walter, born 18 months previously. They were the sons of William Thomas, an agricultural labourer, and his wife Louisa, of "Ridge" (described as "High Ridge" on the 1891 Census), a farm at the northern edge of the parish.

By 1901, Frederick, now 15, was a farm servant working for – and living with – Alfred Shattock and his family at Stallenge-thorne Farm, between Huntsham and Hockworthy. Perhaps farm work was not to his liking – or he sought a more adventurous life – for at some point before 1911 he joined the Army, enlisting with the 2nd Battalion, the Devonshire Regiment. The 1911 Census recorded him at a large military establishment in Malta.

On 3rd November 1913 Frederick married Ellen Hicks (known as "Nellie") in Uplowman. Nellie was the daughter of Henry Hicks, an agricultural labourer, and his wife Sarah. She was born on 11th September 1895 and was baptized in Sampford Peverell on 8th December. By 1901 the family had moved to Whittenhayes, Bampton, but in 1911 Sarah was living with

Palestine Campaign. Heavy Howitzers in action before Gaza. July-November, 1917.
Photo courtesy of the Imperial War Museum

her brother Albert, a farm labourer, at Charles Cottages, Kittisford (near Wellington). Frederick was already in the army and his service card records that he entered WW1 service on 22nd August 1914, in the 1st Battalion of the Devonshire Regiment. This battalion landed at Le Havre on 21st August. We cannot be sure where or when Frederick served for the next few years, or whether he was able to return home on leave to see his family. Fred and Nellie had one child – a daughter, Lizzie Ellen – who was born on 15th February 1915 and was baptized in Sampford Peverell on 3rd April 1915. Nellie's brother Benjamin, from Uplowman, was killed in action in Flanders on 21st April 1915.

In 1916 the 16th Battalion of the Devonshire Regiment came under the command of the 229th Brigade, which became part of the Egyptian Expeditionary Force. The EEF was a section of the British Army that fought battles in Sinai, Palestine and Syria during 1916 to 1918. Its successes played a major role in the destruction of the Ottoman Empire in the Middle East. In 1917 they took part in the 2nd and 3rd battles of Gaza, and then the capture of Jerusalem, in what was then Palestine, which was part of the Turkish empire.

At the time of Frederick's death, the EEF, under General Edmund Allenby, and supplemented by a large Indian army contingent and ANZAC mounted troops, had broken through the Ottoman defences and advanced towards Jerusalem. By 21st November 1917 they were about 5 kilometres west of the city, and very severe fighting followed, lasting until all the city's defences were captured on 8th December.

Frederick Thomas was killed in action just a few days before this on 3rd December 1917, as was Bertie Scorse, another Sampford Peverell casualty. Frederick died on his 31st birthday and is buried in grave A14 in the Jerusalem war cemetery, alongside another 2515 Commonwealth casualties. There is a picture of the cemetery in the section on Bertie Scorse. The inscription on Frederick's gravestone, chosen by his widow, is "Them asleep in Jesus will God bring so shall we ever be with the Lord".

At some point after Lizzie's birth in 1915, Nellie had moved to Tiverton, where her address (shown on the Commonwealth War Graves Commission Debt of Honour record) was 9, Curwood Court, Westexe. She received a (significant at the time) war gratuity of £19 in addition to his outstanding pay. Nellie died in 1933, aged 38.

Frederick Thomas is part of this family tree which we have created on ancestry.co.uk and which ancestry subscribers can see here: https://www.ancestry.co.uk/family-tree/tree/116744290/family

James Trevellyan

James Trevellyan was born in January 1877 in Uplowman. He was baptized in the church there on 21st January 1877 as his parents lived in Whitnage, a hamlet near Uplowman, but his family had strong Sampford Peverell roots. His surname was spelled in a variety of ways and in the Uplowman parish register it is "Trevillian", but we will use Trevellyan here.

James Trevellyan's grandparents were William Trevellyan, a labourer, and his wife Martha. They lived in a small cottage in Boobery, Sampford Peverell, next door to William's brother and his family. In 1851 their children were Henry, Martha, Ann, Jessey and William. This youngest son, William, James Trevellyan's father, was baptized in Sampford Peverell church on 25th March 1849. He grew up in the village and on 30th November 1870 he was married in Sampford Peverell church to Eliza Warren from Tiverton, before moving to Whitnage.

In the 1881 census William and Eliza Trevellyan were living in Chapel Cottages, Whitnage, with 4-year-old James and his sisters Martha, Mary Jane and Alice. By 1891 14-year-old James Trevellyan was an agricultural labourer working for Edward Pearce, farmer, at Boehill Barton, Sampford Peverell. His parents, William and Eliza Trevellyan, were still in Whitnage with their other children including William and Charles (actually their grandson but brought up as their son) who were also later to take part in WW1.

As was the case with many men in those days, James left agriculture to work on the railways. In the 1901 census he was living in Whitnage with his parents and younger siblings. James was now a "platelayer on GWR", i.e. an employee of the Great Western Railway whose job it was to maintain or replace railway track. On 31st March 1902, in Uplowman, James married Edith Ann Ford, who was born on 3rd April 1881 in Poltimore, the daughter of Edwin Ford, a wagoner, and his wife Mary Ann. James was still a platelayer on the GWR. According to the parish register they both lived in Uplowman, but the marriage announcement in the Western Times of 11th April reported that he was "of Witnage [sic]" and she was "of Poltimore". They probably moved to Sampford Peverell soon after their wedding because their daughter, Ivy Nester Trevellyan, born on 6th January 1903, was baptized in Sampford Peverell church on 1st February 1903.

In the 1911 census James Trevellyan was still a platelayer for the GWR, and he and his wife and daughter lived in Buckland Cottage, Sampford Peverell. This is the cottage next to Buckland Bridge over the canal in Whitnage Road

(*2018: Fair View Cottage*), which was also referred to as Wharf Cottage in some documents. James Trevellyan rented the cottage from Mrs Spear, who also owned the adjacent playing field.

In 1915 James' daughter Ivy Trevellyan was one of many Sampford Peverell children to take the Exeter Diocesan Church of England Temperance Society examinations. They included intermediates and juniors, and in the juniors Ivy obtained a mark of 55 (other marks went from 24 to 87). The "Big Brother's Prize" for the youngest child with the highest marks went to Denis Cluett, Sampford Peverell, aged 7. These exams are explained by Denis Cluett himself in his memoirs.

As a married man, James Trevellyan would have been exempt from military service when conscription was first introduced in January 1916, but not enough men were being recruited so on 25th May 1916 conscription was extended to include married men, and at the age of 39 James became a sapper with the Royal Engineers 268th Railway Company (service number 201978). On 28th April 1917 his daughter wrote a postcard to him which included "Hope you are alright. It is six months ago yesterday that you went away", so he must have left home on 27th October 1916. The railway companies were mainly made up of railway workers assembled and trained in groups, and that particular company embarked for France on 19th December 1916.

Around that time James wrote a short note to his wife on a Friday saying that all leave had been cancelled and there were rumours flying around that they would be going to France the next Thursday. He said he would send her some money and a longer letter, and ended: "I remain your ever loving husband Jim". James sent his daughter, Ivy, a postcard from Southampton, postmarked 20th December 1916 (a Wednesday), saying (spelling and punctuation exactly as written) "Dear Ivy just a line to let you now that we stoped Southampton last night had a nice strool around the town I quite remembered the places were we had been before we are off this morning Wensday good by from your ever loving Father. love to all".

Back home we know from a newspaper article on 2nd Feb 1917 about a child's death in Merriemeade House Sampford Peverell, that James' wife, Edith Trevellyan, worked there for the Norrish family and was a witness at the inquest. The house is now The Merriemeade pub. Later Edith went to work at the St Boniface Home for Waifs and Strays. Edith and Ivy continued to live in Wharf Cottage, with their dog, Spot, who is mentioned fondly in the correspondence between James and his family.

The longest letter we have from James Trevellyan was written on 25th February 1917. He wrote it in pencil on YMCA paper. This is a transcript of it, with the original spelling but with some punctuation added for the sake of readability:

"My Own Dearest Wife and Daughter
just a few lines hoping it will find you quite well as it leaves me at present.
We are having this afternoon off so I am been busy washing. I have washed
two shirts and twol and pants and have had my hair cut so you can see that
I have been quite bussy. What a change we have had the last few days. It
has been mild and very fogy but the frost isn't all gone out of the ground
yet and it his up over our boots with mud and water and my feet are wet
every day but I change my boots every night when I leave off and put on
dry socks. Their his a lot of our men with bad fingers and feet caused by
the frost but, thank goodness, mine are keeping alright. Dear Edith how
are you getting on with the money I alow you do you get it alright? Can
you make both ends meet? I don't supposed you will get any more for Ivy
- I see on the paper it his for they under 14 years of age. You asked me

about my living on the last letter, well we could make I do if we had a little more bread. We haves 1 little loaf between three every day. I could eat all mine for my breakfast if I had some more. We goes in the village every other night and gets a loaf of bread. We have to scramble for it and then have to pay a frank and 3d for it – that his 13/- English money. I supposed it his a lot dearer in England, than it was when I leave home. All they wants his your money. Dear Edith you said you wish that I could have a few days leaf. I only wish I could come home alltogether with you.   I am afraid I shall never get my work up after again if I stop away to long,

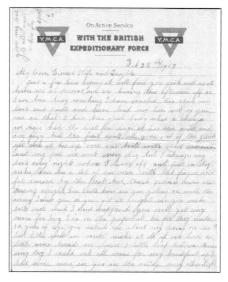

the gardening will get in such state. But cheer up o dear I will make up for it some day. I should like to take you and dear Ivy for a walk this afternoon and pick some primroses. I think about you all the day long and wonder how you are getting on, and am thinking of you half of the night long. Dear Ivy I am sending you and Mam a little card each wish I hope you will like. I wish I could send you something better but I will try to get you a better present when this wicked war his over. I had a letter from Brother Bill this last week. He wishes to be remembered to you all. He his expecting to be shifted from were he his shortly, but I hope we shall stay were we are and then I think we shall be safe. Tell mam not to worry about me. So now I must sine off. Wishing you health and happyness from your ever loving Father and Husband xxxxxxxxxxxx Give my love to all and a kiss for Spot xx"

There is a lot of information about the railway companies on the longlongtrail website. One section in particular helps paint a picture of the situation:

As the various campaigns and battles unfolded, RE Railway Companies were engaged all over the British sector, joined by Dominion RE Railway Companies. Close examination of the period maps bear testimony to miles of what was to be temporary track that criss-crossed the area. Howitzer Spurs, Ambulance Train Sidings, Tank Enablements and bridges were all constructed, in addition to the constant maintenance and line doubling.

Work in progress was always a potential target for enemy artillery and also there were the attentions of the German Air Force to contend with. Zeneghem Yard, for instance, was a natural target and sappers from RE Railway Companies are recorded as having to help extinguish serious fires resulting from air raids. A primary objective was always to take standard gauge railways as close to the front as possible, to lessen the demands on light railway systems, horsed transport and manpower. For the sappers, work could mean toiling around the clock, especially where lines had been cut by shellfire.

James Trevellyan died in France on 2nd October 1917. A newspaper reported that: "Trevelyan was attached to the Royal Engineers, and while actively employed in France was wounded so severely by a bomb from an aeroplane that death followed shortly afterwards."

He is buried in the Dozinghem military cemetery in Belgium and the registration of his grave refers to his parents who were in Whitnage, Uplowman, and his wife Edith who was in Wharf House, Sampford Peverell. The inscription ,"Until the day break", was chosen by Edith.

James Trevellyan's name appears on the GWR memorial to employees who died in WW1, under the engineering department based at Burlescombe. This memorial can be seen at major GWR stations including Exeter St. David's.

The probate summary of his will records that he died at 61st Casualty Clearing Station France, leaving £125 9s 5d to his widow, Edith. According

British troops laying a light railway line near Boesinghe, 28 July 1917.
Photo courtesy of the Imperial War Museum

to the list of soldiers' effects on ancestry.com his outstanding pay of £5 2s was sent to Edith, in December 1917, another 2 shillings in March 1918, and his war gratuity of £3 was sent to her in November 1919.

Edith never remarried and continued to live with Ivy in Buckland/Wharf cottage for many years. Ivy kept in touch with a boy from St Boniface Home, Ernest Johnson, who served during and just after WW1 in Palestine and India. They were married in Sampford Peverell church on 22nd April 1924.

James Trevellyan is remembered on the memorial plaque in Sampford Peverell church. We are not sure exactly when the plaque was erected but we hope it was there by 1924 so that at some point during her wedding service Ivy could look up at her father's name on the memorial plaque and share that moment with him. Ivy became a teacher, and she and her mother bought Woodbine Farm in Culmstock in 1935, which they lived in and ran with Ivy's husband, Ernest. During the Second World War they got help on the farm from some Italian prisoners of war, one of whom returned to the farm after the war with his young family. Ernest and Ivy did not have any children so they loved having the family with them and built them a house on the farm. Edith died there in 1965, aged 84. Ernest died in 1986 and Ivy in 1988. They left the farm to the youngest son of their 'adopted' Italian family, who was kind enough to lend us the photos and letters, kept all together by Ivy, which have helped tell us so much about James Trevellyan and his family. They also said that Ivy could never bear to see anything about Remembrance Day and if it came up on the TV she would go to her room and shed tears for her beloved father.

There are photos of James and his family, and also photos of letters, cards, his medals and other items, on this web page: http://spsocresearch.weebly.com/trevellyan-photos.html

James Trevellyan is part of this family tree which we have created on ancestry.co.uk and which subscribers can see here: https://www.ancestry.co.uk/family-tree/tree/75014822/family

Stanley Trevelyan

Stanley William Trevelyan (sometimes spelt Trevellyan) was baptized in Sampford Peverell parish church on 26th July 1896. The parish records show that he was born on July 5th 1896 and was the son of William Edward Trevelyan and Mary Ann Trevelyan (née Radford), living in Sampford Peverell. Stanley's father, William, was born in Sampford Peverell (William's father, George Trevelyan, was a carpenter who lived in Always cottage), and Stanley's mother, Mary, was born in Culmstock. They married in the second half of 1895 in the Wellington area.

In the 1901 census the family was living in Lower Town, Sampford Peverell, in one of a group of eight cottages (*2018: the site of 16 Court Way*). Stanley's aunt, Caroline Trevellyan, would later marry Sidney Dunn, another WW1 casualty, who grew up in the Hare and Hounds. Another WW1 casualty, James Trevellyan, was a second cousin of Caroline and Stanley's father, William. William worked as a carter on a farm, and the other family members in 1901 were Stanley's mother, Mary Ann, Edith Radford (aged 14, servant, a relation of his mother), and Stanley's younger brother George Charles, known as Charley, aged 2. Like Stanley, Charley was born and christened in Sampford Peverell.

At the time of the 1911 census Stanley's parents were living in "Whitnage, Sampford Peverell" with children Charley (12), Percy (10), and William (2). Percy and William were both born in Sampford Peverell and christened at St John the Baptist Church there. Stanley, now 14, was working as a "cow boy" for George Lock, a dairyman, in Brithembottom, Cullompton. He must have moved from there to work in a quarry, as he was described as a quarryman when he enlisted in 1914.

Stanley's service number was PLY/16549 and he served as a Private in the Royal Marine Light Infantry. His service record on findmypast.co.uk contains the following pieces of information:

- Enlisted: Exeter on 14th Jan 1914, aged 18 yrs, 6 months, 3 days [but see below].
- Date of birth: 11 July 1895 [note this is a year earlier than that recorded in the parish register and birth registry, so he was actually 17 when he enlisted].
- Where born: Sampford Peverell, Tiverton.
- Trade: quarryman.
- Religion: C of E.
- Next of kin: mother Mary, Witnage [sic], Uplowman, Tiverton.

- Stature: 5' 6½"
- Complexion: fresh
- Eyes: blue
- Hair: brown
- Marks, wounds and scars: Nil
- School Certificate: 3rd class, on 3rd March 1914
- Able to swim: Yes, tested on 23rd March 1914 in Deal

The record tells us that he did the following drills (training): Infantry (9.9.14, Very Good), Signalling (Army), Gunnery (Sea Service) (20.10.14, Very Good), Musketry (War Office class) (twice in 1914 and again on 30.10.17), Field Training (29.1.18, Very Good), and RMA Gunnery (bombing) (29.1.18, Good)

Initially he was in the recruit depot in Deal from 14 Jan 1914 until 12 Sep 1914, when he was transferred to Plymouth. Stanley was in the Plymouth division from 15 Sep 14 to 11 Nov 14, his embarkation date. He then served on HMS Louvain from 17 Nov 1914 to 10 July 1917. Throughout this time his character was described as very good and his ability as satisfactory. HMS Louvain was formerly a passenger ship called the SS Dresden. Like many civilian ships the SS Dresden was taken over by the Admiralty in 1915 as an Armed Boarding Steamer, a type of warship designed for boarding an enemy vessel, and she was renamed HMS Louvain. We don't know exactly where the ship was operating but six months after Stanley left her, on 21 Jan 1918, she was torpedoed in the Eastern Mediterranean, with the loss

HMS Louvain

of nearly all on board amongst whom were many Maltese nationals, so it is likely that the ship was involved in the conflicts around Greece and Turkey when Stanley served on her.

Stanley was transferred back to the Plymouth division in July 1917, probably for extra training judging by the drills on his service record, and was there from 11 Jul 1917 until 20 March 1918 when he re-embarked. This time Stanley is described as being on "President III DAMS" (Defensively Armed Merchant Ships) from 21 March 18 to 10 August 18. "President III" was not a ship; it was an administrative centre for the Navy, and is all that appears on the records of servicemen assigned to defend merchant ships, probably because they regularly changed ship. They received increased pay for being with DAMS; technically they were lent to the Board of Trade and received Mercantile Marine rates of pay, which were considerably higher than Naval rates. They also wore civilian clothes in harbour, and apparently there has been some debate as to the legality of this and of the arming of merchantmen. They had authority to move from ship to ship as and when needed.

At the time of his death Stanley was on board the SS Tatarrax, a British steam tanker built in Greenock. In 1916 she was purchased by the Standard Transportation Company, Hong Kong. "On August 10th, 1918, Tatarrax, on a voyage from Port Said via Alexandria to France with a cargo of spirit, was sunk by the German submarine UC-34 (Hans Schüler), off Rosetta. 61 persons were lost."

The Western Times reported his death on 27th September 1918 as follows:

> News has been received from the Admiralty by Mr. and Mrs. Wm. Trevelyan, 2, Whitnage, Uplowman, formerly of Sampford Peverell, that their eldest son, Stanley William Trevelyan, has met his fate whilst serving on the s.s.---. The ship caught fire, blew up and sank. There were no survivors.

It also reports that a memorial service was held at Uplowman Church.

Stanley is remembered on panel 29 of the Plymouth Naval Memorial. The Commonwealth War Graves Commission website records that he was "killed by internal explosion of vessel off Alexandria 10 Aug 1918". Rank – Private. Age 22". The Plymouth Naval Memorial is one of three memorials (the other two are in Chatham and Portsmouth) to those members of the Royal Navy who died during the war and had no known grave. His name is also amongst those on the memorial plaque in the church at Uplowman.

The Royal Marine medal roll 1914-20 on findmypast.co.uk shows that he was awarded the 1914-15 Star, Victory, and British War medals, which were sent to his father.

Stanley's brothers Percy and Charley also fought in WW1: Percy was in the Royal Navy, and Charley was in the Royal Field Artillery. Both emigrated to Australia after the war: Percy in January 1921 and Charley in December 1921. Charley had come back from the war with problems, and apparently went into the bush and lost touch with the family. Percy's daughter has

The Plymouth Naval Memorial

stayed in touch and has been back to visit the area. Stanley's other brother, William, was too young to be involved in WW1 but he joined the RAF in WW2. William's son, another Stanley, who still lives in Sampford Peverell, often visited his Trevelyan grandparents when they lived at 4, Boobery, and he remembers them with great affection. He can recall his grandmother, the mother of Stanley, Percy, and Charley, telling him that the boys joined up during WW1 for the excitement, but that, sadly, it turned out badly for all of them.

Stanley Trevelyan is part of this family tree which we have created on ancestry.co.uk and which subscribers to the site can see here: https://www.ancestry.co.uk/family-tree/tree/75014822/family

Ernest Tucker

Ernest Tucker was the son of Richard Tucker, who married Jane Cottey in St John the Baptist Church, Sampford Peverell in 1894, both declaring themselves to be resident in Sampford Peverell at the time. Their first child, Herbert, born in June 1895, was baptized in the same Church, although by that time they were living in Hayne, Cullompton. Frederick Tucker was born in Cullompton in 1897 but they moved back to Sampford Peverell and their third son, Ernest James, was born on 11 November 1898 in Sampford Peverell and was christened in the parish church a month later.

In the 1901 census the family was living in 'Smoke Alley', one of a pair of adjoining cottages in Boobery (*2018: 22-24 Boobery*). These cottages were owned by the Trustees of the Poorlands Charity and were let out at a 'market' rent in order to provide an annual income to distribute among the poor of the Parish. The Tuckers' cottage was actually let to John Bowden, a prominent local farmer, for whom Richard Tucker undoubtedly worked. Judging by the censuses and Land Tax Returns, the Tucker family continued to live in Smoke Alley until around 1917 so it was the home of the Tucker boys throughout their childhood, probably in the right hand (easterly) cottage. There is a photo of Smoke Alley in the first part of the book.

In 1907 when Ernest was 8, his mother, Jane, died soon after childbirth and was buried on 15th October with her two-day-old baby boy, who was placed in his mother's coffin. The funeral was reported in the Sampford Peverell section of the Exeter and Plymouth Gazette as follows:

> There was a large assembly at the funeral of Mrs Richard Tucker who with her two days' old baby, was interred in the parish churchyard on Wednesday. All Mrs Tucker's sisters and brothers-in-law followed the coffin, as well as the bereaved husband and six children, the latter all under the age of 13 years. The deceased was the daughter of Mr and Mrs Cotty, who are old and respected inhabitants.

It must have been a very difficult time for the family, but a few years later, on Feb 11th 1911, Richard remarried. His new wife was a widow, Annie Wotton. In the 1911 census they were still living in Boobery with Frederick (now a yard-boy) aged 14, Ernest, 12, Gussie (Augusta), 11, Arthur, 7, and Florrie (Florence), 6, all born and christened in Sampford Peverell. Ernest's oldest brother, Herbert, was now working as a farm boy for the Dennis family at Jurishayes near Tiverton.

We can see from Ernest's military record on ancestry.co.uk that when he enlisted in Tiverton on 1st May 1915 he said he was a carter, aged 19 years and 5 months. In fact he was only 16. He was 5' 4½" tall, weighed 130 pounds, his chest girth was 36", and his physical development was 'good'. His complexion was fresh, his eyes hazel, and his hair brown. Ernest's references were provided by his employer, Mr. G Dennis, a farmer of Jurishayes, who was also his brother Herbert's employer in 1911. Mr. Dennis said he employed him as a horseman and car driver "anytime when required" and that Ernest left his employ "to join the army". Asked if he believed Ernest to be sober and honest he answered "yes", and asked for information as to his character he wrote "Very good man on the whole". You wonder what was implied by that 'on the whole'...

According to Ernest's military record he joined up at Aldershot on 3rd May 1915 and was in the Army Service Corps 208 regiment as a driver, serving overseas. He left Devonport on the 'Caledonian' on 24th July 1916 and disembarked at Salonika on 8th August 1916. At some point his brother Frederick was also sent to Salonika and the two brothers must have been there at the same time for a while between late 1916 and late 1917. Frederick died there of malaria on 5th September 1917.

On 10th July 1918 Ernest voluntarily transferred to the Devonshire Regiment. This might have related to a couple of minor offences on his service record: of being 'drunk in charge of a pair of mules' in May 1918, and on two occasions (26th May and 5th June 1918) 'parading with a dirty harness', for which he was fined 7 days' pay. Bearing in mind that he was young, in a war, a long way from home, and that his brother had recently died, some minor misdemeanours are understandable.

Ernest was still in Salonika in July 1918, and on 1st September 1918 he was compulsorily transferred to the Cheshire Regiment, 12th Battalion, for special duties. He was killed in action in Salonika on 18th September, aged just 19. In the memorandum about where his effects should be sent (to his father, Richard Tucker, Ashford Road, Sampford Peverell) someone has written 'no effects'. The records include an acknowledgement from his father of receipt of his British War Medal and Victory Medal.

The Royal British Legion has provided the information that Ernest Tucker was killed on the first day of the third battle of Doiran, which took place in Macedonia between the Greeks and British on one side, and Bulgarians on the other. The first two battles had ended with the allied side being driven off, and in the intervening period the Bulgarians had strengthened their already strong positions. So in spite of a heavy bombardment from the British, the allies were again driven off after two days of bitter fighting.

During the fighting the brigade to which Private Tucker's battalion belonged lost 65% of its soldiers. Nevertheless, several days after the end of the battle, it was noticed that the Bulgarian positions had gone quiet. When the British sent patrols to investigate, it was discovered that the Bulgarians had withdrawn. The reason was that their rear was threatened because a Serbian and French army had defeated the Bulgarians at the battle of Dobra Pole, and were advancing on Doiran.

British 18-pounder field gun firing from a camouflaged position on the Doiran Front.
Photo courtesy of the Imperial War Museum

The following is from an account of the fighting in Doiran from The Long Long Trail website: www.longlongtrail.co.uk

> The offensive began in July 1918 but the British contingent did not play a significant part until early September. Then the British attacked a series of fortified hills. The final assault began along the whole front on 15 September 1918; the British being engaged in the Lake Doiran area. This battle was really on the 18 and 19 September 1918 and was a disaster for the British Divisions. They had to frontally assault 'Pip Ridge' which was a 2000 foot high heavily defended mountain ridge with fortresses built on some of the higher mountains, notably Grand Couronne. (This was what the Bulgarians had been working on in the first months of 1916 and early 1917.) They sustained very heavy casualties.

The article includes an eye-witness account specifically mentioning Ernest Tucker's battalion, the 12th Cheshires. This is just a small part of that account:

The Battle of Doiran is now a forgotten episode of the Great War, overshadowed by the doings of Haig in France and Allenby in Palestine. There was no full contemporary account of the Battle in any British Newspaper. Sir George Milne's dispatch was not published and did not appear in the Times until January 23rd 1919, and then only in truncated form. The very name of the battle is unknown to most. Yet, in singularity of horror and in tragedy of defeated heroism, it is unique among the records of British arms.

Our attack on ' Pip Ridge' was led by 12th Cheshires. The battle opened with a crash of machine-gun fire, and a cloud of dusty smoke began to blur the outline of the hills, Almost immediately the advancing battalion was overwhelmed in a deadly stream of bullets which came whipping and whistling down the open slopes. Those who survived were followed by a battalion of Lancashire men, and a remnant of this undaunted infantry fought its way over the first and second lines of trenches - if indeed the term " line " can be applied to a highly complicated and irregular system of defences, taking full advantage of every fold or contortion of the ground. In its turn, a Shropshire battalion ascended the fatal ridge. By this time the battle of the " Pips" was a mere confusion of massacre, noise and futile bravery. Nearly all the men of the first two battalions were lying dead or wounded on the hillside. Colonel Clegg and Colonel Bishop were killed; the few surviving troops were toiling and fighting in what appeared to be inevitable and immediate death. The attack was ending in a bloody disaster. No orders could reach the isolated cluster of men who were still trying to advance on the ridge. Contact aeroplanes came roaring down through the yellow haze of dust and smoke, hardly able to see what was going on, and even flying below the levels of the Ridge and Grand Couronne. There was only one possible ending to the assault. Our troops in the military phrase of their commander, 'fell back to their original positions'. Of this falling back I will say nothing. There are times when even desperate heroism has to acknowledge defeat.

Ernest does not have an individual grave but his name is engraved on the Doiran Memorial to the Missing in Salonika, Greece. The panel list gives his name as being in column 3 of the west face of pylon 1. The grave registration records that he was 18, and that his parents were "Mr R and Jane Tucker of Goldsmoor Cottage, Westleigh, Wellington, Somerset".

According to the list of soldiers' effects on ancestry.co.uk his outstanding pay of £13 13s 2d and a war gratuity of £15 10s were sent to his father, Richard, in 1919.

Sad Coincidence

ERNEST.   FRED.

MR. RICHARD TUCKER, of Ashford Court Cottages, Sampford Peverell, has lost two sons in the war. Pte. Ernest J. Tucker, Cheshire Regt., was killed in action at Salonika on Sept. 18th last, and Pte. Frederick William Tucker, A.S.C. (Transport), died from fever at Salonika twelve months previously.

Western Times, 25 Oct 1918. Image reproduced with kind permission of The British Newspaper Archive (www.britis hnewspaperarchive.co.uk) '. Image © THE BRITISH LIBRARY BOARD. ALL RIGHTS RESERVED.

Both he and his brother, Frederick, and his second cousin Arthur Pillar who also died in the war, are remembered on the war memorial plaque in Burlescombe church. Another second cousin who died in the war, Frederick Pillar, is remembered on the Sampford Peverell church plaque.

This is the article from the Western Times of 25th October 1918 about the two Tucker brothers. Headlined 'Sad Coincidence' it reads: "Mr. Richard Tucker, of Ashford Court Cottages, Sampford Peverell, has lost two sons in the war. Pte. Ernest J. Tucker, Cheshire Regt., was killed in action at Salonika on Sept. 18th last, and Pte. Frederick William Tucker, A.S.C (Transport), died from fever at Salonika twelve months previously."

Ernest Tucker is part of this family tree which we have created on ancestry.co.uk and which subscribers can see here: https://www.ancestry.co.uk/family-tree/tree/74511558/family

The Doiran Memorial to the Missing, Salonika, Greece

Frederick Tucker

Frederick Tucker's father, Richard Tucker, married Jane Cottey in St John the Baptist Church, Sampford Peverell in 1894, both declaring themselves to be resident in Sampford Peverell at the time. Their first child, Herbert, born in June 1895, was baptized in the same Church, although by that time they were living in Hayne, Cullompton. Frederick William Tucker was born in Cullompton in the first quarter of 1897 but it seems they moved back to Sampford Peverell and their third son, Ernest James, was born on 11 November 1898 in Sampford Peverell and was christened in the local church a month later.

For more information about the family during Frederick's early years, see the previous section on his brother Ernest.

We don't have a detailed service record for Frederick, but we know he enlisted and, like his brother Ernest, became a driver in the Royal Army Service Corps. At some point Frederick was sent to Salonika in Greece, as was Ernest, and the two brothers must have been there at the same time for a while between late 1916 and late 1917.

The Long Long Trail website gives this summary of events there in 1917:

> During 1917 there was comparatively little activity on the British part of the front in Macedonia, due in part to complex political changes in Greece throughout the year. The main fighting took place around Lake Doiran, where the line was adjusted several times by each side early in the year. In April 1917, the British attacked, gained a considerable amount of ground and resisted strong counter-attacks. In May, the Bulgarians attacked the British positions, but were firmly repulsed. The British action in May triggered a series of attacks elsewhere on the front by the other Allies, known as the Battle of Vardar.

In September 1917 a newspaper reported that Mr Richard Tucker heard that his second son Frederick had died of fever in Mesopotamia, possibly a mistake for Macedonia as the Commonwealth War Graves registration document records that Frederick died of malaria on 5th September 1917 in Salonika, in Greece, officially aged 23 but we know he was actually aged 20. It also tells us that his headstone information is: "God has called him to his eternal rest. Mr R Tucker, Ashford Court, Sampford Peverell, near Tiverton".

Frederick is buried in the Salonika (Lembet Road) Military Cemetery in Greece. Both he and his brother, Ernest, and his second cousin, Arthur Pillar who also died in the war, are remembered on the war memorial plaque in the church in Burlescombe.

A convoy of lorries from 689 Motor Transport Company (ASC) halted on the Seres Road whilst the drivers have a tea break, ca.1917.   *Photo courtesy of the Imperial War Museum*

An article concerning his death, including a photo of the two brothers, is reproduced in the previous section on Ernest Tucker. Frederick Tucker is part of this family tree which we have created on ancestry.co.uk and which ancestry subscribers can see here: https://www.ancestry.co.uk/family-tree/tree/74511558/family

The Salonika (Lembet Road) military cemetery

Charles Wallington

Charles Harold Wallington was born in Horfield, NW Bristol, in January 1882. He was the fourth of the six children of Charles Wallington and Bright Jordan. His father's family came from Wotton-under-Edge in Gloucestershire, where they ran the local wine and spirits shop for several generations, and his mother was the daughter of a single mother and was born in Worcestershire. She grew up in her grandmother's boarding house in Great Malvern and was married in 1874, aged 20, to Charles Wallington (senior), who was a draper's assistant. Charles then became a commercial traveller for the drapery firm before a dramatic career change in the 1880s when he joined the clergy and became Reverend Charles Wallington. Tragically he died aged 37, leaving his widow with six young children.

The widowed Bright Wallington moved with her children from the outskirts of Bristol to Dawlish in Devon, where she ran a boarding house for about 20 years – as her grandmother had done in Great Malvern, Worcestershire. Bright would have been very familiar with the workings of a boarding house having been brought up in one.

Some time before 1911 Bright Wallington left the boarding house in Dawlish and moved to "Morrels House" on Lower Town, Sampford Peverell – just opposite the Globe Inn. There is a photo of it earlier in this book. The house became a girl's boarding school, with her daughter, Dorothy, being the schoolmistress.

Charles Harold Wallington, however, did not move to Sampford Peverell. Instead he moved to London where he was working as a butcher's assistant in the 1901 census, near Carnaby Street, and by 1911 he was a Butcher's manager, working in the Strand but living at Charing Cross.

In July 1912, in Barnet, Middlesex, Charles married Gladys Putnam. Gladys was born in 1888 so was 6 years younger than her husband. While he was in the army his wife lived at 166 Hoppers Road, Winchmore Hill, London, N21. They did not have any children and she never re-married. Gladys died in 1971 aged 83, staying in Middlesex all her life.

Charles had an older brother, William, who enlisted in 1915. At the time, William was a bank cashier working in Cardiff and was 39 years and 3 months old when he joined up in Dec 1915, having "given away" his sister Florence in June that year when she was married to Mr Trevor Matthews at St John's Church, Sampford Peverell. Two of Florence's sisters were bridesmaids, along with the sister of the bridegroom, and the reception was held in Morrells, the home of the bride's mother. Charles and his wife Gladys were probably at the wedding.

Charles appears to have enlisted early in 1917, aged 35, joining the Devonshire Regiment. By June he had been promoted from Cadet to acting second Lieutenant. He went to the front in Belgium in August 1917 where he was attached to the 1st/6th battalion of the King's Liverpool Regiment. They in turn were attached to the 165th (Liverpool) Brigade of the 55th (West Lancashire) Division. Between 20th and 23rd September 1917 this brigade took part in the battle of Menin Road Ridge, part of the third battle of Ypres (also known as Passchendaele). In the battle of Menin Road Ridge alone, between 20th and 26th September over 20,000 Allied and over 25,000 German troops were killed or injured. The report of the action on 20th September from the Commonwealth War Graves Commission reads:

> Wet through by overnight rain the infantry were on their start positions by early morning of 20 September. At 5.40am 65,000 troops advanced on an eight mile front, screened by heavy mist and a stupefying bombardment. Keeping close to the barrage, the initial rush, across slippery ground, quickly overran enemy outposts; retaliatory fire strengthened and skilful fighting was needed to negotiate surviving strongpoints. By midday the four attacking Divisions on the Gheluvelt Plateau were on their final objectives. The simultaneous attack by Fifth Army kept up alongside on the left. The newly won positions were co nsolidated in anticipation of expected German counter-attacks. Clear afternoon weather offered reconnaissance flights near perfect visibility; German threats were quickly spotted and between noon and 7.30pm numerous counter-attacks were dispersed by viciously accurate British barrages. By evening the battle-ravaged forward slopes of the Gheluvelt Plateau were in British hands.

The casualties that day included Charles Wallington who was killed in action, aged 35, after just one month at the front. His death was reported in the local newspapers on 5 Oct and a memorial service was held for him at St John's church, Sampford Peverell on 7th Oct 1917. A local newspaper reported that "muffled peals were rung on the bells at the close of the service, and the Dead March was played by the organist".

Charles Wallington is remembered on this individual plaque in Sampford Peverell parish church, which was probably paid for by his family.

Like fellow Sampford Peverell men Percy Bradfield, Walter Brown, Robert Hine, and Wilfred Taudevin, Charles Wallington is commemorated at the Tyne Cot Memorial in Zonnebeke, Belgium, where his name is on stone 38. There is a picture of the memorial in the section on Percy Bradfield.

A view of the newly captured ground taken from the main road to Zonnebeke during the Battle of the Menin Road Ridge, 20 September 1917. Shells can be seen bursting in the distance.
Photo courtesy of the Imperial War Museum

Charles Wallington is part of this family tree which we have created on ancestry.co.uk and which ancestry subscribers can see here:

https://www.ancestry.co.uk/family-tree/tree/74092134/family

Charles Wallington's plaque in Sampford Peverell parish church.
Photo supplied by the Sampford Peverell Society, 2014

Postcard sent from Edith to James Trevellyan

The village after the War

The First World War came to an end with the German surrender on 11th November 1918 at 11am. News of the cessation of hostilities reached the village that same day, within one hour of the German surrender. The Sampford Peverell school log records that the children were assembled, sang the National Anthem and were then given the afternoon and the following day off by way of celebration.

The return of those who served

Within three days of the start of the war the Devon patriotic fund had been established to pledge allegiance to the Crown and to provide support for serving men and their families at home. At the urging of the Lord Lieutenant of Devon, each village and town had been encouraged to establish their own local fund or committee. On 27th August 1914 in Sampford Peverell, in a meeting attended by 40 people and chaired by Mr J G Pedler, a fund was duly formed. The necessity to support our serving men was clearly recognised at the outset of the war. During the course of the war 122 men and 3 women helped directly in the war effort. 24 of these lost their lives and there is an article about each of these brave men elsewhere in this publication.

98 men and 3 women returned from the war. 51 of these, about half, definitely returned to Sampford Peverell, but there are a number of men whose exact residence after demobilisation we have not been able to establish.

Demob Year	Number
1914	0
1915	1
1916	2
1917	1
1918	11
1919	67
1920	9
1921	3
1922	1
1923	1
1924	1
1925	0
1926	0
1927	2
1928	1
1929	1
Total	**101**

The above table shows when 98 serving men and three women were discharged from the forces. There were seven men who were discharged before hostilities were over on 11 Nov 1918; all were discharged due to medical issues and being unfit to continue serving. A further eight men were discharged in the last six weeks of 1918. The vast majority of men returned during 1919, largely between March and July. Men holding rank were usually retained until 1920 and those with specialist skills such as nursing were retained until 1921. The seven men who stayed with the military after 1921 were all "professional" soldiers and sailors and had signed up for at least 12 years' service when they initially enlisted.

Some men were categorized as 'Z Class', a category introduced on 3rd December 1918. There were fears that Germany would not accept the peace treaty, so the government decided it should be able to recall trained men rapidly if war broke out again. Soldiers who were being demobilized, especially those who had signed up 'for the duration', were classed as "Z class reserves": they returned to civilian life, but with an obligation to return if called upon. The Z Reserve was abolished on 31st March 1920.

The serving men (and women nurses) did not all return to the village immediately after hostilities had ended as can be seen from the table above. A newspaper report in the Tiverton Gazette, dated 15 Apr 1919 stated that "There are about 20 demobilised soldiers returned to our village, some of whom have gone back to their old vocation in life....."

Before a soldier left his unit, he was medically examined and given a form, if needed, to claim for any disability caused by his service. He also received forms concerning his employment in the army. He would be transferred to a transit camp and then given a railway warrant or ticket to get him home, still wearing his uniform, helmet and greatcoat. He also received a policy insuring him against unavoidable unemployment for up to 26 weeks in the first 12 months after demobilization. He was given a fortnight's ration book (to be exchanged for a civilian one), a voucher for the return of his greatcoat (in return for £1) to a railway station during his final leave and could choose a clothing allowance of 52s 6d or a suit of plain clothes.

In addition, a land settlement plan was announced to provide small areas of land, or land and a cottage, for men to become self-sufficient. Financial incentives were offered for young commissioned officers and those who had interrupted their education to serve in the war. Given that one in three of the serving men from Sampford came from an agricultural background anyway, there appears to have been little need for such a scheme in our rural community.

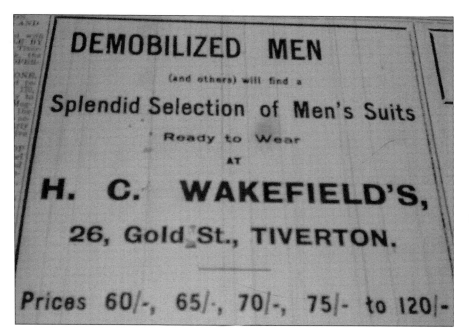

In the Tiverton Gazette, 1 Jul 1919, courtesy of Tiverton Museum

A number of the survivors had been injured during the war, contracted diseases as a result of the conflict, been poisoned by gas, or suffered from psychological problems: their traumatic experiences affected many of them for life, a problem which became known at the time as 'shell-shock'. Using an arbitrary age of 50 as a measure of "early death", ten men (10% of the survivors) died before their 50th birthday. Two were discharged early from the army with TB and were aged just 29 and 33 when they succumbed to the illness. Three had been invalided out with wounds and died aged 37,39 and 46 - with the presumption that their wounds precipitated an early death. Three have no record of war injuries but were all involved in particularly ferocious areas of combat – with the royal marines, machine gun regiment and royal field artillery. The disturbing psychological impact of their wartime experiences can only be speculated upon. Indeed, one of these men was discharged from the war in January 1918, so it is highly likely that he was incapacitated. Of the two remaining "early" deaths, one was almost certainly due to physiological issues giving a short life expectancy – he was just 3' 7¼" tall. The other individual had served as a stoker in the Royal Navy during the war, drifted in and out of work on the railways and was unemployed for a 15-month period. He died aged just 29.

Memorials and celebrations

The UK government strongly suggested that each individual local village and town might like to consider a suitable memorial to commemorate the end of the war and those who served in it. They suggested that playing fields and recreation grounds would be an appropriate lasting memorial. They also suggested that the local community would like to fund these initiatives as there was no money available centrally, taxpayers' money having been totally spent on the war effort. Memorials were particularly needed after this conflict, in which so many thousands of men died and were buried abroad or were reported as missing presumed dead. Their families needed somewhere local to remember them.

As Todd Gray points out in 'Lest Devon Forgets'[48], every Devon town and village wanted a memorial, but it took committees a long time to agree on such issues as what form the memorial would take, where it would go, what it should commemorate (some put more emphasis on peace than on war), or who should be named on it. It could be difficult to say clearly where someone came from, as families were often dispersed across an area, and names in a church might not include men from other religious backgrounds. Some communities wanted to include the names of all participants, but early in 1920 the Bishop of Exeter stated that only those who died could be remembered in churches in the diocese. Some got round this by listing all participants in the church porch or listing everyone on a memorial outside the church. Finding agreement amongst all concerned was difficult. There was controversy in Halberton where the vicar stated that the memorial should take the form of an extra aisle for the church. The residents of Halberton disagreed, wanting a village hall instead, and they eventually won the day.

In Sampford Peverell a public meeting, chaired by Mr J G Pedler, chairman of the Parish Council, was called at the school in January 1919 to consider a 'War and Peace Memorial'. Suggestions included Recreation grounds, reading rooms, playing fields, tablets in the chapel and church, a public memorial in the centre of the village for all who had served, endowment of a bed in Tiverton hospital, a village nurse, electric lighting for the village and the church, and a general holiday or day of feasting[49]. At a follow up public meeting, reported on 11th February it was unanimously decided to:

---

[48] Gray, T. (2010). Lest Devon forgets : service, sacrifice and the creation of Great War memorials. Exeter, The Mint Press.
[49] Tiverton Gazette, 21st Jan 1919

a) erect a commemorative tablet in the chapel and the church
b) install 2 extra bells in the church
c) form a public library

At a Sampford Peverell Parish Council meeting in April 1919 Mr C Radford asked the chairman if anything further was likely to result with regard to the War memorial propositions decided at the earlier meeting. There was much discussion and the Parish Council then resolved to call another public meeting to formulate a scheme.

In May 1919 a third public meeting was held to consider the question of a war memorial for the village. The proposals made earlier had fallen through for lack of support. There was a unanimous vote to rescind all former proposals and start afresh! The meeting decided to purchase a recreation ground and erect a granite monument. A group of councillors, led by Mr Pedler, were tasked to meet and talk with Mr & Mrs Spear of Boehill Barton, who owned the sports field, with a view to buying it as a war memorial for the village. This meeting took place but no decision was made at the time by the Spears' (the sports field was eventually gifted into trust for the village in 1952).

Saturday 19th July 1919 was declared a national public holiday for "Peace Day". At a Parish Council meeting in May 1919, the chairman, Mr Pedler, decided to celebrate the end of the war by giving a free tea to all children in the parish below 14 years of age and a dinner to all demobilised men, their wives and sweethearts. Independently Dr & Mrs W M Browne of Turberfield House, Lower Town were already arranging a sports day, to take place on the cricket field, for village children and demobilised men. The celebrations would be followed by tea, dinner and dancing and then finally nighttime illuminations on Connigar Hill, just north of the village.

Peace Day arrived, and so did torrential rain. The comprehensive sports programme had to be abandoned at the last moment, but the crowd transferred to the pre-prepared large room at St Boniface Home and had a wonderful tea, then dinner and dancing in the evening for the demobilised men and their "wives and sweethearts". At 11pm a bonfire was lit on Connigar Hill followed by a display of fireworks – both of which had been banned during the war under the draconian measures of DORA (Defence of the Realm Act). There was a collection made during the course of the day which raised £71. After paying for expenses incurred in organising the day, it was resolved to divide the balance between the soldiers from the village who had not yet been demobilised and therefore had been unable to take part in the celebrations.

The hastily re-arranged sports day took place on Monday 21st July 1919, and prizes were given out by Mrs Browne, who had organised the occasion with her husband, Dr William M Browne. A sumptuous tea was once again provided for the children. There was also a plan to take the children for a day out to the seaside as part of the Peace celebrations, but we have been unable to verify whether this event actually took place or not.

A War Memorial Fund collection was organised to pay for the cost of installing a memorial tablet to be placed in the church. There were 64 recorded donations to the fund, two of them anonymous. The amount raised was just under £225, with the 12 biggest donations totalling £175. The list of the subscribers was duly recorded, as was the dispersal of the funds. It can be seen on our website: https://spsocresearch.weebly.com/ww1.html Intriguingly only 20% of the funds were used to actually purchase and install the memorial plaque in St John the Baptist church. Nearly all of the rest was used to provide new electric lighting for the church – which had previously been illuminated by around 100 candles. There was no plaque erected in the Methodist Chapel and no purchase of a recreation ground, yet alone erection of a Granite Memorial Stone for those who served in the war. Nine men are listed on the memorial tablet in the church as being from this parish and having died in the war between 1914 and 1919, and another has a separate brass plaque, presumably privately funded by his family. There is no record of how these names were arrived at, and we now believe there should have been 24 names altogether.

The hoped-for purchase of a recreation ground as a commemorative memorial did not proceed with any due speed! In April 1929 Sunnyside Garage on Lower Town *(currently the hairdresser's in 2018)* and the adjoining land east of it, as far as the stream - amounting to 1.18 acres - were sold to Charles Radford, the proprietor of the garage. At some point, believed to be 1932, part of this land was purchased by local trustees of the British Legion. This was paid for with funds raised by public subscription to create a memorial to WW1 participants and included money to build the hall on the other side of Lower Town. The land was then sold by the Trustees in March 1946 and ended up being owned by William Henry Norrish, the owner of the large Dairy Company in the village. He died in 1947 and in June 1948 his executors sold the land for £137, together with 0.5 acre of land to the East of the stream (where the tennis courts now exist) for £90 to Sampford Peverell Parish Council. There was a covenant that the land was to be used *"for the purpose of Public Playing fields and Village Hall for the use of Societies or organisations having athletic, social or educational objects...".* In 1948 funds of £2,300 were raised (£1,100 from local taxpayers and the balance from UK taxpayers). It was used to construct two hard tennis courts and adjacent pavilion, a children's playground with a slide and four swings, and a cricket pitch which could be converted into a skittles alley! The park was opened in December 1949 by Derick Heathcoat-Amory, the Tiverton MP, as a memorial to those in the village who died in both the World Wars. In 2017 the play park was renovated, and a sign near the entrance now records its origins as a memorial.

An earlier transfer of land occurred around 1932. The land on the opposite (south) side of Lower Town was part of a plot of land used as a garage, owned and run by Mr Fred Vickery. The Uplowman and Sampford Peverell Branch of the British Legion erected the Memorial Hall between 1932 and 1935 to commemorate the men of both villages who lost their lives in the Great War. A plaque set into the face of the building records the completion date of 1933. The funds for this were raised by the British Legion themselves, but the hall was expensive to run and to maintain so it was later handed over to the Parish Council.

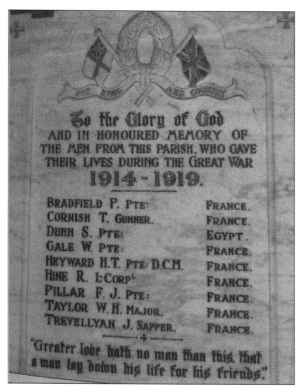

Memorial tablet in the church

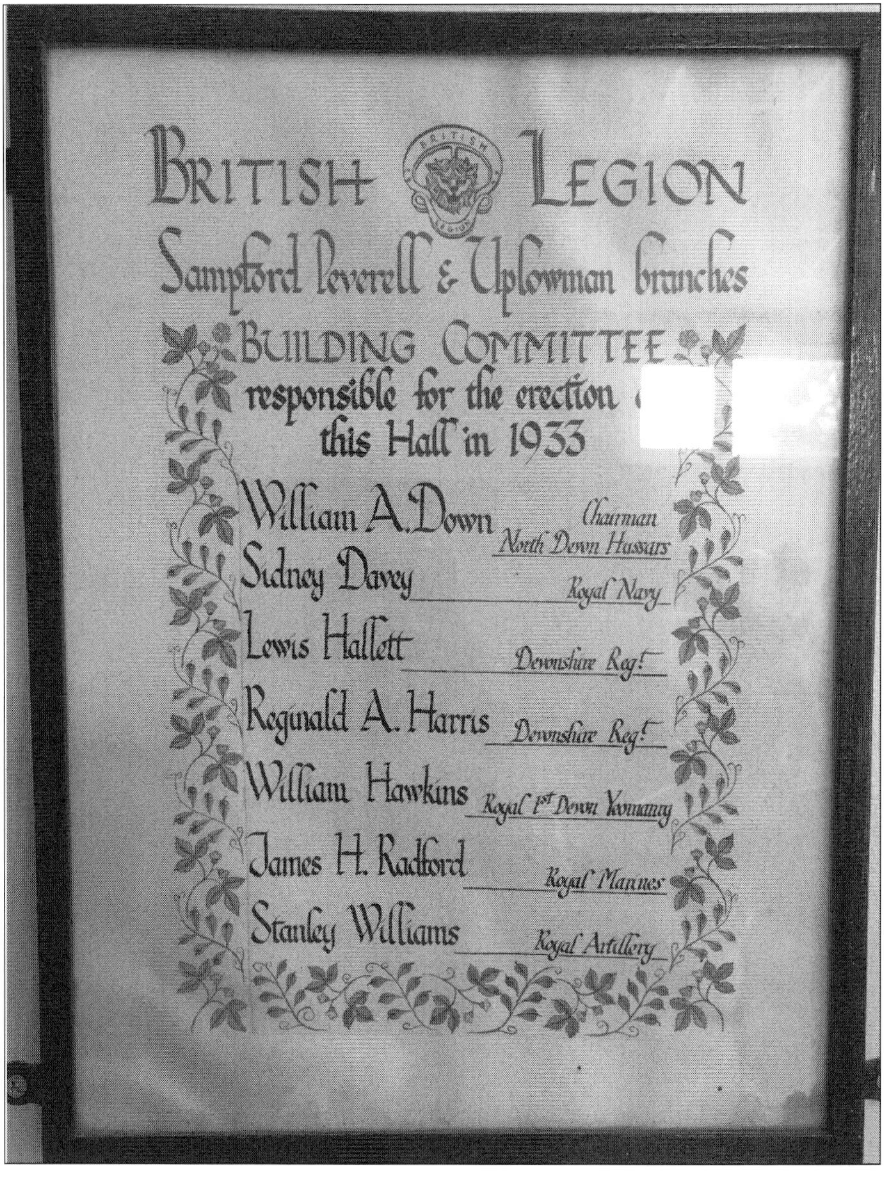

List of names of the men who founded the village hall

Sampford Peverell WW1 participants who survived

Introduction

Below is a list of ninety-eight men and three women with a Sampford Peverell connection who served in WW1. 80% of those who served were born in Devon. Indeed half (50) had been born in Sampford Peverell, had continued to live in the parish before the war, and then returned to the parish afterwards. In addition to these 101 survivors, there are twenty-four men who lost their lives during the war. An extensive write-up on each of these men can be found above.

Our findings are in an abbreviated form below, but fuller descriptions and more pictures for some of these WW1 participants may be found on our website: https://spsocresearch.weebly.com/ww1.html

For many of the participants we have created family trees on ancestry.co.uk which can be seen by those with subscriptions to the site.

The St Boniface boys are not included in this list unless they had another local connection, but where we have found more information we have put it on our website. A significant number of the St Boniface boys emigrated to Canada when they reached 14. When WW1 broke out, a large proportion of these young men who had by then reached, or said they had reached, the age of 18, joined the Canadian forces and came back to Europe to fight. A few lost their lives, but most returned to Canada after the end of the war. We have very little information about their birth places and dates to help identify them, and in some cases they confused matters themselves, for instance Frederick Henry James Chivers, born in 1899 in Paddington, London, was a St Boniface boy who moved to Canada in 1913. Men with that name signed up to the Canadian Expeditionary Force in July 1916, and again in October 1916, and again in September 1917! All with the same name, address and date of birth, but giving different heights, eye colour and hair colour. We presume these were three different boys using one shared ID.

Service records for all those who took part in WW1 were stored in the War Office, but it was bombed during WW2 and 60% of the records were lost. This is why in some cases we have not been able to find military records for likely participants. In other cases we have only brief details, and if a name is not unique it may be impossible to prove which of several people might be the one from Sampford Peverell. With common names there can be too many to choose from.

Electoral Rolls (lists of those entitled to vote) were issued up to 1915, and then again from 1918 onwards. Also a 1919 'absent voters' list was created to cover those people who were normally resident in the village but were still away on service. From 1918 onwards those still on war service were marked NM for Naval or Military, so in some cases below where we have not found the details of a person's military service, we can tell from the electoral roll that they were away from the parish on military duty.

If you know that we have missed out somebody who should be in this list, or if you have more details or photos about any of our participants, we would be very happy to hear from you, as we can still add information to the website. The Sampford Peverell Society website has a 'contact us' page: http://www.sampevsoc.co.uk/contact-us.html

Abbreviations used below:

b = Born, bp = Baptized, d = Died, m = Married

Ag Lab	– Agricultural Labourer
ASC	– Army Service Corps (it became RASC in 1918)
AWOL	– Absent Without Leave
BEF	– British Expeditionary Force
DOB	– Date of birth
dr	– daughter
ER	– Electoral Roll
GWR	– Great Western Railway company
LAC	– Leading AirCraftman
LI	– Light Infantry
NM	– on Naval or Military duty (see explanation above on Electoral Rolls)
Q1, Q2, Q3, Q4	– 1st, 2nd, 3rd or 4th Quarter of the year.
RASC	– Royal Army Service Corps
RAVC	– Royal Army Veterinary Corps
RE	– Royal Engineers
RFA	– Royal Field Artillery
RFC	– Royal Flying Corps
RFR	– Royal Fleet Reserve
RN	– Royal Navy
RND	– Royal Naval Division
RNAS	– Royal Naval Air Service
SP	– Sampford Peverell

Surnames A-E

ANDREWS William J was a most unlikely recruit to the army! He was b May 1859 in SP and bp on 12 Jun at St John the Baptist Church. He was 7th/10 children of William Andrews, b Jan 1818 Morchard Bishop, Nr Crediton, Devon (ag lab and sometimes Labourer for the Great Western Railway) and Jane Woodhouse b 1819. His parents married around 1840. Their first child, Mary Jane was b Sep 1840 and bp 21 Feb 1841 in Morchard Bishop. The family moved to Exeter St Davids, then Stoke Cannon and to Lee Ditch, SP, around 1853. There were six children b in SP (including William in 1859). Around 1870 the family moved to Hillfarrance in Somerset and were there for both 1871 and 1881 census. William's occupation in 1881 was "Groom", single and living with his parents.

In 1883 William married Bessie b 1863 Otterford, Devon. They had a daughter, Mabel J. b 1886 in Taunton, Somerset. In 1891 the family lived at Norton Fitzwarren, Somerset and William was in the census as a farmer. By 1901 they were at Wilton, Somerset - occupation once again a groom. His widowed mother Jane, aged 82 lived with them. By 1911 the family had moved into Taunton where he listed his occupation as Groom – out of work. His daughter Mabel had married and left home. Shortly after the War broke out he made the extraordinary decision to enlist – at the age of 55 (although he declared that he was only 53!). He was subject to extensive medical examination before being accepted, with the proviso that he must not march more than 10 miles a day.

He was accepted into the 4th Battalion of the Somerset Light Infantry, #3989. His military service started on 22 Feb 1915 and he declared that he was previously in the national reserve and had served in both the ASC and 3rd Somerset LI. He was at home in the UK for the duration of his military service of 1 year and 44 days. He was then discharged 5 Apr 1916 in Portishead as being medically unfit - having been diagnosed with Tuberculosis (Phthisis and Pleuritic Effusion). His medical record goes into gory detail of the illness. It was judged that his condition had been aggravated by Normal Military Service and on discharge (then private #21818) he was awarded an invalidity pension of 15 Shillings/ week. He died in Wandsworth, London in Nov 1921.

AUTHERS {ARTHURS} Archibald – b 17 Jul 1888 SP and bp 12 Sep 1888 SP. One of 9 children of Walter John Marshall Authers, b Dec 1857 SP and his wife Ellen Needs (1858-1898). The family moved around the area frequently and the father, Walter, had many different occupations before his death in 1929. In the 1901 census, 3 years after the death of his mother, Archibald was living with his aunt, Rosa Selina Sparkes née Authers b 1879 (younger sister of his father) and her husband Sylvanus at their farm in Holcombe Rogus. Archibald later became a baker before enlisting in the army. In the 1911 census he was based at Aldershot Barracks. He served in France with the ASC, occupation cook, from Aug 1914 to Jan 1915. On 27 May 1915 his elder brother Albert William lost his life at sea on HMS Princess Irene. There is a memorial plaque in Uffculme church. In Aug 1915 Archibald married Alice Maud Taylor in Cambridge and they had a son Ronald b Jul 1917. Archibald returned to France with the RASC Nov to Dec 1917, then transferred to the Royal Flying Corps on 24 Dec 1917. He transferred again to the newly formed RAF on 1st Apr 1918 – still with occupation cook. He stayed in France until he was demobbed 21 Mar 1919. He returned to Devon and died in the Tiverton area in Dec 1954. Family tree: https://www.ancestry.co.uk/family-tree/tree/55070480/family

BASS Arthur Stanley – b 29 Mar 1896 Burlescombe was the 2nd/5 children of John Bass (carpenter then farmer, b Cullompton) and Sarah Ann Arthurs (b Leonard Moor). The family lived on Leonard Moor in both the 1901 and 1911 census (next to the current M5 Junction). Arthur attended primary school in Higher Town, SP at the very beginning of the 20th century. He then assisted his father on the farm. He received call-up papers in March 1916, when he was 19 and appealed against his military conscription as he was the only son working on the farm run by his 57-year-old father, who was suffering from a ruptured hernia, but the appeal was refused and he was then enlisted in the 9th Devons – Private #26301. His sisters took over much of the farm work. He wrote home regularly and there is a fuller account of his war experience on our website, written by his son. These are just some of the interesting details.

Arthur left Devon by train, seen off from Exeter by an aunt who gave him plums and a cake. After training he moved to 3rd Devons in Devonport. He said they all had colds – Recent training had included being stood up to the waist in water for two hours. By November 1916 he was in France and was lucky enough to be billeted in a barn. In February 1917 he was a guard at a POW camp and complained that the French were over-charging them for milk. He was in good health other than being plagued by fleas:" I am boiling up my cardigan while I am writing this as the little beggars are everywhere and the blankets are full of them". He often mentioned the food parcels the family were sending him, but also mentions the potato rot at home, the shortage of men on the land, and the bad news from Mespotomia. In May he left the front line, as the officer to whom he was then a batman was sent on a course. Back near the front line he was continually trying to reassure his mother that he wasn't really in danger. In September 1917 we learn from the letters that Lou Gale (see Lewis Gale below) visited Arthur's parents when he was home on leave. The friends obviously kept in touch with each other's families.

Arthur Bass

In November 1917 the battalion was moved by train to Italy and Arthur wrote back about an incident of the soldiers finding vats of wine at a siding – bayonets were used to make holes and some of them got very drunk! Their time in Italy was seen as a wonderful break from the grim days in France. They were still getting food parcels from home - Arthur wrote that "The cream would have been alright if I had been in France, but it had just turned by the time it had got here. The dough cake was alright however and I can butter it if it gets dry." They were nearly sent back to France in early 1918 but plans were changed at the last minute. Food parcels continued to arrive including butter and sponge cakes. Arthur's former teacher from Uffculme wrote to him about how much he loved mountains, but Arthur wrote to his mother "give me the dear old country with hills you can jump over and hang the Alps"! Despite this he did retain a love of Italy in later life. They did not return to France until September 1918 and entered a particularly bloody phase of the war. No letters exist from this period. He survived uninjured and was eventually demobbed on 3rd February.

In later years he often talked to his son about the war. One close shave he had was when he had finished his day's work at a command post and his officer asked him whether he was going to stay there the night or return to the lines. He went back to the lines. Overnight the command post was hit by a shell, and the officer was brought out mortally wounded. Arthur's battalion often came into contact with Scottish regiments, and he came to love the sound of the bagpipes. He also met a lot of Australians, and said they stuck closely together and took no notice of any officers other than their own, but they were always very friendly.

After the war Arthur's sister, Minnie, married William Saunders, another WW1 participant. In Jun 1926, Arthur married Winifred Vickery from Westleigh, but she died a few years later. In Jun 1933 he married Dorothy May Snow and their son was born the following year. Arthur farmed, and his family still farm, Leonard Moor farm. Arthur Bass died Apr 1970. Family tree: https://www.ancestry.co.uk/family-tree/tree/64235835/family

BATER Stanley – b SP 7 Jul 1895; son of John Bater, a railway packer. The family lived in Boobery. On the 1911 census Stanley was a farm servant for Mr Lucas at Houndaller Farm, Waterloo Cross. He tried to join the army (Somerset Light Infantry) in May 1912 by giving false DOB, but was rejected. On 5 May 1914 he joined the RN and signed up for 12 years. He did land service on Vivid II et al to Nov 1917 then served on HMS Dublin as Leading Stoker #22477. Demobbed 15 Mar 1920. He got a job on the railway (like his father, John) and served as a labourer in the Mill shop – I believe this was in Manchester, until Apr 1922. He left voluntarily and was unemployed until 19 Jul 1923 before he re-joined the railway in the same job. He died in the first week of May 1924 in Exeter.

BROWNE William Mitchell (Dr) b 14 Jan 1877 Londonderry – 1914 Captain in Royal Army Medical Corps; he was also the village Doctor and lived at Turberfield House, Lower Town. He was the son of Dr David John Browne and Jane Osborne, both of Londonderry, Northern Ireland. William was the second of 6 children and qualified as a doctor in 1900. In Oct 1906 in Londonderry, aged 30, William married Hester Mary Beattie (1879-1965) and they had a son David Terence Alexander Mitchell Browne on 11 Sep 1907. Dr Browne was made lieutenant on probate in the Army Medical reserve in 1907. Two years later his appointment in the RAMC as lieutenant was confirmed. Dr Browne was in Dublin in 1911, but he and his family must have moved to the Falkland Islands, as the family travelled back to England in May 1913 on the 'Oransa'. They moved to Sampford Peverell soon afterwards and by September 1913 they were living at Turberfield House, Lower Town.

Dr Browne was still in Sampford in Spring 1915 but must have been called back into service as a medal card for him shows that he was promoted from Lieutenant to Captain in the RAMC, and entered the European theatre of war in December 1915. He was back in Sampford by September 1916 when he was appointed certifying surgeon for the Uffculme district of Devon. After the war they moved to the newly built "Namora" (later to become Green Headlands, then the Parkway hotel) on Lower Town/ Whitnage Road. Dr William Mitchell Browne died in May 1929, as a result of septicaemia from a rose thorn in his finger. His son David married Violet Norrish from the Creamery family. There is more about him, including a photo, in our chapter on Public Services. Family tree: https://www.ancestry.co.uk/family-tree/tree/120247555/family

BRYANT Charles Bow b 23 Dec 1889 Berry Pomeroy, Totnes, Devon youngest of 7 children of John Henry Bryant (1849-1934), a Blacksmith and Emma Bow 1848-1890. His mother died in Q1 1890, shortly after giving birth to Charles. In 1901 census he was living in Totnes with his widowed father (a farrier and Blacksmith) and one elder sister. By the 1911 census Charles had left home and was the assistant gamekeeper at Huntsham Court, just north of Tiverton. His connections with Totnes were far from over as on 23 Mar 1912, in an independent chapel, he married Elsie Smith (b 1890, Totnes). He joined up with the army in Bristol on 3 Jun

The smithy in Lower Town c 1920. Charles Bryant is probably in the photo

1916, (Reg #20520 then 33299) where he gave his next of kin as Elsie Bryant, his wife - address Boobery, Sandford Peveril (sic). He qualified as a skilled shoeing smith in the army in Sep 1916. Served in France with the BEF from 1916 to 1919. Initially with the Southern Cavalry Depot, then Oxford 7 Bucks Light Infantry, then the Army Veterinary Corps. Demobbed 22 March 1919. He is listed in the 1918 & 1919 autumn electoral roll for SP as a resident, with "NM" next to his name. He appeared in various trade directories (Gregory's, Kelly's) from 1920 to 1930 where his occupation was shown as a Blacksmith, living at Lower Town, SP. In 1926 he became part owner of the new 'Sampford Peverell Motor Company' with WH Norrish, but it folded after a few years. In 1928 they had a baby girl and his occupation on her baptism record was "Motor Engineer". In the 1939 Register the family were living at Fore St Torquay, where his occupation was shown as Foreman Blacksmith and Fitter (Quarrying trade). He died Jun 1972 in Torbay, Devon aged 82. Family tree: https://www.ancestry.co.uk/family-tree/tree/154322107/family

CASE William b 30 Jun 1891, Chevithorne was the youngest of 7 children of Richard Case (b1845) and Mary Hill (b1852). His parents were farmers and in the 1911 census he lived at Little Turberfield Farm, SP with William and an elder brother Sidney assisting on the farm. We do not have details of his service but in the 1918 ER he was listed as NM. In Q4 1919 Tiverton he married Sophia Bessie Authers/Arthurs. He returned to SP (1920 ER) where he worked as a dairyman with his father at Lower Turberfield dairy. He was still living there in the 1939 Register. He died Mar 1976 in Exeter, aged 84. Family tree: https://www.ancestry.co.uk/family-tree/tree/55070480/family

CAUDWELL Archibald Thomas – b 12 Nov 1899, Shepton Mallet, Somerset. Son of Thomas Caudwell and Bessie née Sowden. His father, a salesman for Suttons Seeds in Reading and a widower, married Bessie when she was his young housekeeper, but he committed suicide the day after the wedding. Bessie returned to her parents in Somerset, where she gave birth to Archie later that year. In 1906 Bessie married Walter Cluett and they had a son, Denis, in 1907. The family moved from Somerset to Sampford Peverell in or soon after 1911, where Walter Cluett took up the role of chief clerk at the creamery. Archie's half brother was Denis Cluett, whose memoirs of SP have been published by the SP Society as "A Village Childhood". In 1914 Archie was apprenticed to an engineering firm in Tiverton, travelling there from the family home, initially in Roberts Cottage (*2018: 16 Boobery*) and later at Kerslake House (*2018: 4 Chains Road*). On 25 Aug 1917, shortly before his 18th birthday he was called up and sent to Ireland for training. He initially joined the 47th Reserve Battalion Devon Regiment (#71791). He later joined the RASC in Exeter in 1918 (#418467). He was discharged from the army in Nov 1919 in Germany. In 1920 he lived in Turnpike, SP where his parents lived in 'Tyrella'. After the end of WW1 he joined the RN, having nominally signed up for 12 years – (#35300). He first saw active service on HMS Defiance on 12 Jan 1920. He was a fitter and turner. He then had a spell on HMS Hood and his last service date

Archie Caudwell on HMS Defiance in 1919

was 14 Nov 1929. He is shown as a freemason at the St Aubyn Lodge, Devonport on 14 Jun 1921. On 3 Jan 1927 he married Sybil Bessie Pauline Palk (b 31 Dec 1903) at St Johns, SP. In 1939 register Sybil was living with her parents May and Henry at Howards Road, Bournemouth. Archibald is not shown – assumed away. He died in Bournemouth Nov 1995, aged 96. Family tree: https://www.ancestry.co.uk/family-tree/tree/154324189/family

CAUNTER Henry Ernest b 1879 Newton Abbot, Devon – the son of William H Caunter (b 1857, painter) and his wife Elizabeth. In Q2 1900 Tiverton Henry m Elizabeth Chapman. They must have moved to SP as on 21 Feb 1906 his son Harold William was baptized in SP. In 1911 census he was an Ag Lab and lived at Holiwell Cottages, Tiverton. He joined the war as a private in the Queens Own (Royal Kent) 1/5th #241296 (Ancestry) or #241292 (FMP). After the war he returned to Tiverton and lived in Broad Lane, working as an agricultural labourer. He died in 1948.

CLARIDGE Reginald Algernon Aubrey b 7 Nov 1898, Staines, Middlesex son of Bryant Henry William Claridge (1869 Kilburn, London) - accountant and Company Secretary and Fanny Willis. His father moved to SP at the end of WW1 to run the Globe Inn in Lower Town. Reginald enlisted with the London Regiment in 1916 and was transferred to ASC (Transport) with Reg #393057. He was discharged in 1919 with heart problems and neurasthenia. He was listed on the 1919 electoral roll for SP, living at the Globe Inn with his father who was then the landlord. In Sep 1920 in Bristol he married Annie Dorothy Flemming (b 1898). Reginald died Sep 1980 in Bristol.

COLWILL (COLWELL) John – b SP 10 Aug 1888 to William Colwill (Shepherd) and Lucy (née Jones). Lived at Barton Cottage (*2018: 4 Boobery*), 1891 and 1901 but cannot be found in any UK 1911 census – possibly because he joined up in the RFA early in 1909 where he served as a gunner for three years until the death of his father, William, in Jun 1912. When war broke out he joined the reserves and served in France. There are three possible service records for a John Colwill – with Somerset LI, Cornwall LI or a sapper with the RE working on the railways. We cannot be sure which is "our" man. He was wounded in the head and invalided out. In the 1920 & 1926 Gregory's Directory for SP he was living in Higher Town with his widowed mother, Lucy Colwill and working on the railways as a packer. He was buried 6 Jun 1934 in SP, aged 45.

COOK Wilfred Thomas – b Burlescombe 15 Aug 1885, son of William Cook, Yeoman. In 1891 and 1901 census he lived with his parents and siblings at Heazille Barton, Rewe. On 14 Mar 1907 he signed up to RN (#347642) and was posted to HMS Defiance. He worked as an electrician and in 1921 was promoted to RN Electrician 1st class. His last service date (still on HMS Defiance) was 29 Nov 1928 – 21 years after signing up. On 16 Oct 1916 in SP he married Edith Hanna Pedler, b 20 Dec 1879, youngest sister of the other Pedler family members mentioned in this book, based at Sampford Barton farm, SP. He was 31, she was nearly 37. After leaving the navy he returned to SP and lived at "Tyrella", Turnpike, but no occupation shown in Directories. He died Sep 1968 in SP, aged 83. Family tree: https://www.ancestry.co.uk/family-tree/tree/107786313/family

CORNISH Albert James – b 1892, Hillfarrance, Somerset; eldest of 8 children of Eli Cornish (canal worker) and Elizabeth Maria Rossiter from Taunton. 1911 census he was living with his parents in Higher Town (*2018: 30 Higher Town*). He joined the 3rd London regiment (#3983) as a private, later promoted to Lance Corporal. He then transferred to the Guards (#2327) where he was part of the machine gun regiment. One of his younger brothers - Thomas (b 1897) died in Mar 1917 during the war. In

1920 he resided with his mother in Higher Town (his brother William Henry lived with him). Albert was working as a Newsagent and Shoemaker. By 1926 his sole occupation was shoemaker. He did not marry and was buried 1 Feb 1936 in SP, aged 44. Family tree: https://www.ancestry.co.uk/family-tree/tree/75458494/family

CORNISH William Henry – b 31 May 1896, Hillfarrance, Somerset to Eli Cornish and Elizabeth Rossiter. Younger brother to Albert James above. In 1911 census he lived with his parents at Higher Town (*2018: 30 Higher Town*) and was shown as a general labourer. In 1914 his occupation was shown as Dairyman. In 1915 at Devonport he enlisted in the RN (K28842). He was a stoker on HMS Revenge and last saw service 31 May 1919. In 1920 and 1926 he lived with his widowed mother and his brother Albert James at Higher Town. Occupation shown as factory hand – actually a cheese maker at Norrish creamery in Chains Road, SP. In Mar 1919 in Taunton he married Rose Mary Burgess (1895-1976). They had three children all b and bp in SP. In the 1939 Register William was living at Highland Terrace (far end of Higher Town) with his family and was a Maintenance Engineer. Family tree: https://www.ancestry.co.uk/family-tree/tree/75458494/family

COUPLAND-SMITH Frederick Geoffrey – b 1872 Peckham, London. A merchant of Private Means. 1911 census lived at High Cross House, Higher Town. His son Frederick Vivian C-S b 1896 was a pupil at Blundell's school Tiverton, who joined the army and lost his life in July 1917 in Belgium. The father, Frederick Geoffery, was an orderly with BRCS (British Red Cross Society) and served initially in France on 10 Aug 1915. Later he served in Salonika, even though he was 43 at the start of the war. He died in Mar 1924 in Hove, Sussex but his home address given as Catcott, Bridgwater, Somerset. Family tree: https://www.ancestry.co.uk/family-tree/tree/73887918/family

DAVEY Sidney – b 5 Feb 1869, Templeton, Tiverton son of Edwin Davey (1839-1914, Ag Lab) and Harriet Alford (Also 1839-1914). Sidney was the 2nd of 6 children and a "professional" sailor with the RN. He joined the Navy in Plymouth on 3 Feb 1885, 2 days short of his 16th birthday. He became an Able Seaman 1 Oct 1887, a Leading Seaman 1 Jul 1891, a PO (2nd class) 10 Jan 1894, 1st class 18 May 1894, acting CPO 6 Apr 1900, and full CPO (Chief Petty Officer) 6 Apr 1901. He was pensioned off on 1 Jan 1909 after nearly 24 years service, but within 2 months had re-enlisted and joined RFR Devonport in the capacity as onshore trainer- with service on Vivid I,

Jupiter, King Alfred, Vivid III and finally Vivid II. He retired for the second time on 30 Jan 1919. In Q4 1890 in Plymouth, Sidney married Mary Louisa (b 1871 Plymouth) and they lived in St Andrews, Plymouth in 1891 census. They had three children- all b in Plymouth William Edwin (1891-1976) -who also served in the RN in WW1, Elsie Elizabeth (1893-1975) and Olive Mary (1895-1944). Shortly after his "first retirement" in 1909, the family moved to Boobery, SP – except for William who was an apprentice wheelwright in Plymouth, before he signed up in 1915, giving his residence as Quay Head, SP. Perhaps the family moved to be closer to Sidney's parents – who had moved to SP then on to Lowman Cross, Uplowman. Sidney's parents and siblings left Templeton in 1873 and moved to Hockworthy for 3 years before moving to Uplowman around 1885. His parents then moved to SP and in the 1901 census were living at Rose Cottage but returned to Lowman Cross by the 1911 census. Both were buried in Uplowman in 1914 – within 6 months of each other.

Sidney's wife Mary Louisa died in SP in Nov 1931. He was part of the British Legion committee responsible for setting up the village hall in 1933. In the 1939 register he was shown as a widower, Navy Pensioner, living at Parker's Cottages, Higher Town with James and Olive Cotterell. Sidney died in 1955 at the age of 86 in Tavistock, Devon.

DIMENT John – b 30 Apr 1885 SP and bp at St John's church 24 May 1885. He was the third child of Mark Joseph Diment (a dairyman b 1856 Clyst St George) and his first wife Elizabeth (1857-1889 Jersey Farm, SP). His father remarried Jan 1891 to Mary Ann Thorne (b 1859 Cheriton Fitzpaine). The family lived at Jersey Farm (Waterloo Cross) when John was baptized. By 1891 census the family had moved to Poltimore Village. By 1901 John had left his parents house and was working as an agricultural labourer at Raddon Court, Thorverton.

In 1908 John married Lucy Chapman (b 8 Jun 1884 Exmouth). John and Lucy moved to Withycombe Raleigh (near Exmouth) and in Aug 1910 they had a son, Ernest. In the 1911 census they lived at 7 Princes Street, Exmouth – deemed to be part of Withycombe Raleigh! John was a van driver for Port House laundry company. His brother in law and his niece were living with them at the census date. In Q1 1913 John and Lucy had a son, Leslie F Diment, b in St Thomas, Exeter. On 6 Aug 1914, almost as soon as war was declared, John enlisted, giving 7 Princes Street, Exmouth as home address (as per 1911 census) and married to Lucy. He enlisted with the 1/7th (cyclists) battalion with the Devonshire Regiment – service no 1786. He only saw "service" at home and he was discharged 14 May 1915 in Totnes, having served just 282 days - having elected for course (C) under war office letter no.9 / cyclists / 475(T.F2) of 29 /1/15. John died Sep 1959 in Exeter, aged 74.

DINHAM Albert Ernest – b 7 Jun 1891 Tiverton, second son of Albert and Lucy. Lived at Moor cottage, Lower Town, in 1911 census with parents and siblings where his occupation was shown as Railway clerk. On 6 Oct 1914 he married Millford Holloway (b 24 May 1886) at the Wesleyan Chapel in Higher Town. Her step-brother was Samuel Cromwell Holloway who also served in WW1. Albert enlisted in the army as a private in the Machine Gun Corps (#65733). After demob in Mar 1919 he returned t o live at the Mount, Higher Town with occupation Factory Operative. He and his wife left the village before 1923. In the 1939 register they lived at Ilminster Road, Taunton with occupation retired foreman, dairy factory. He died in 1967 in Taunton, Somerset. Family tree:
https://www.ancestry.co.uk/family-tree/tree/76142649/family

DINHAM Frederick Guy - b 30 Jul 1889 Tiverton, eldest son of Albert (1858 Wellington-1920) and Lucy (1861, Exeter). His father was a signalman on the Railway. In 1911 Frederick lived at Moor End Cottage, Lower Town, with his parents and three younger brothers – Albert Ernest 1892, James Stanley 1896 and William Clifford 1897. Frederick was a clerk on GWR, having started working as a railway clerk in Dec 1906 where he was based in Leominster. By Feb 1909 he was in the telegraph office at Pontypool, Wales.

Frederick first saw service in the RN on 19 Jun 1916 with VIVID1 – a shore-based installation. He worked as a clerk and his last service was also at VIVID1 – on 4 Jun 1919. His enlistment record shows that his height was just 3 (Three) feet 7 ¼". On 1919 Electoral Roll (Absentees) occupation/rank was shown as 3rd writer M21241, RND, Port Said (Egypt). In Q4 1920 in Taunton he married Leila Emily Jewell. His brother James Stanley Dinham also married a Jewell – sister to Leila Emily! Frederick died 1 May 1925 and left £811 to his widow Leila and his brother James. Family tree:
https://www.ancestry.co.uk/family-tree/tree/76142649/family

DINHAM James Stanley – b 4 Oct 1895 Tiverton, the third son of Albert and Lucy. 1911 lived at Moor cottage, Lower Town, where he was an apprentice. He initially enlisted in the West Somerset Yeomanry (private 1591) then changed to the Labour Corps (809 Company, #621632). In 1921 he married Susannah Jewell – b 28 Jul 1895 (his oldest brother Frederick had married her elder sister Leila Jewell Q4 1920). James and Susannah had two children. In 1923 James was living at Moor Cottage – his parents having died a few years earlier. In the 1939 register the family lived at Prospect Road, Brixham, where James was a Goods Checker with GWR. James died aged 74 in Taunton in Dec 1969, his wife Susannah died 1978. Family tree: https://www.ancestry.co.uk/family-tree/tree/76142649/family

DREW Thomas - AKA Thomas HODDER. B 15 May 1888 as Thomas DREW – Son of Sarah Drew (B Oct 1862 Uplowman; daughter of Thomas and Sarah Drew) who married 18 months later in Oct 1890 to Frank Otter (B 5 Nov 1860 SP; son of William and Sarah Otter). In 1891 Census Thomas was living at Winks Cottage, Whitnage Road, with parents - father a labourer. In 1901 Census Thomas HODDER was living at Lower Town (*2018: site of 16 Lower Town*) with his "parents" (father a Railway Labourer) and 4 younger siblings: Charles 1892, Caroline 1893, Mary 1895, Frank 1897. Also living there was his widowed maternal Grandfather – Thomas Drew b 1834 Hatherleigh. In 1911 Census Thomas had left SP, but his parents and even more siblings lived at Lower Town. His father Frank HODDER was now the Canal Keeper and his mother a Laundress. Frank died in May 1916 at Exeter Lunatic Asylum. He was admitted sometime post 1915 Electoral Roll, but we do not know why he was admitted. Thomas seems to have reverted to his true surname of Drew (the maiden name of his mother, Sarah) at around this time.

Thomas Drew was Rifleman #553536 in the 16th London Regiment. On 16 Sep 1917, at St John's Church, SP, Rifleman Thomas Drew married Annie Dunn, b 10 Aug 1891, d of Frederick Dunn (deceased) a coal merchant. Annie was the sister of Sidney Dunn – who lost his life in WW1. Intriguingly the marriage record shows the name of Thomas' deceased father as Frank DREW – rather than Frank OTTER or HODDER. Thomas was on leave from hospital, having been wounded in the face / shoulder in France in May 1917. He was on the absent voters list on the 1919 Electoral register, with address Lower Town. He continued to live in Lower Town, occupation labourer, with his wife Annie and was still there in 1934 electoral register. They do not appear to have had any children. In the 1939 register he lived at Downs Cottages, SP, occupation Quarry Worker, with his wife Annie. He died in Mar 1965 in Taunton, Somerset, aged 74. Family tree: https://www.ancestry.co.uk/family-tree/tree/118211823/family

Surnames F-K

FEWINGS Percy Victor b 12 Jan 1897 North Tawton ; 2nd of 5 children of William Thomas Fewings (1867-1950) and Catherine Jane Stoneman (1867-1947) . His father was the SP village policeman from 1898 to 1909, but had come from an agricultural background – he was one of 5 children bought up on a 108 acre farm at Rose Ash (North Tawton). In the 1901 census the family were living in the Lower Town police house (*2018: 21 Lower Town*) with four children under the age of five. In 1909 Percy, his siblings and parents moved to Stoke Canon, just N of Exeter and in the 1911 census his father was the village police constable there. Shortly after the census Percy left Stoke Cannon school, aged 14 and moved to Exeter National School. He stayed there for 14 months then on 21 Jun 1912 his school record reads "Left; gone to work". Percy started work with GWR but on coming of age (18) he enlisted (probably Q1 1915) with the Army Service Corps (ASC) as Private #M2/200251 and served with them for the duration of the war.

On 27 May 1918 his younger brother, Herbert Reginald Fewings lost his life in France and Flanders - near Reims. See the earlier section on those who died for more details. After the war Percy followed in the family tradition and became a farmer - at East Worlington, Witheridge, just south of where his grandfather used to farm. In Sep 1928 at St Thomas, Exeter he married Florence Rhoda Hore (b Dec 1901, Exeter), daughter of Frederick George Hore, a Brass finisher and Alice Vicary. In the 1939 Register Percy lived at Prospect Park, Exeter where he was a "hire car proprietor". Percy died in 1986 in Exeter, his wife Florence predeceased him in 1982. Family tree https://www.ancestry.co.uk/family-tree/tree/116827186/family

FOXFORD Albert Edward b 24 Apr 1887 SP; youngest of 4 sons of James Foxford (ag lab/lime burner/gardener) (b 1850 Molland) and Jane Kerslake (1841-1901). Lived in Higher Town (*2018: 15 Higher Town*) in 1901 census with parents and 2 surviving brothers. Widowed father still in SP in 1911, and Albert gave SP as his home address when he signed up 19 Feb 1917 to Royal Engineers (#240325) for road building. Gave his occupation as steersman on tractor. Served in France. In hospital Sep 1917 and Jan 1918. Demobilized 26 Mar 1920. In Q2 1920 he married Ethel F Sleeman in Redruth, Cornwall. She died 8 years later in Redruth. He continued to live in Cornwall, whilst his parents still lived in SP. Albert died Jun 1958 in Penzance, Cornwall. Family tree:
https://www.ancestry.co.uk/family-tree/tree/74614375/family

GALE Lewis b 7 Feb 1892 Bampton, Devon was the eldest of 8 children (3 died as infants) of George Robert Gale (an Ag Lab from Bampton) and Blanche Banbury of Templeton. Lewis's brother Walter (1894-1916) was the first SP man to lose his life in WW1. The family moved to SP around 1900 and lived in a cottage in Lower Town (*2018: site of 16 Court Way*). In the 1911 census Lewis was working as a blacksmith. A recruitment meeting was held early Sep 1914, 2 months into the Great war, in the courtyard of St Boniface Home in Lower Town. Twenty men from the village signed up, including both Lewis and Walter Gale. They both joined the 8th Devon Regiment (Lewis Private #10803) and both first saw active service in France 25 Jul 1915. Exactly two months later, in the battle of Loos, both brothers were involved in a poisonous gas incident – from their own side. It was the first time the British had used poisonous gas and it did not go to plan. Fortunately both survived, but nearly a year later Walter was to lose his life whilst helping wounded colleagues from the battlefield. Lou (as he was known) Gale visited the parents of Arthur Bass when he was home on leave in September 1917. The young men of Sampford obviously kept in touch with each other and their friends' families.

Lewis survived the rest of the war and was discharged from the army 25 Mar 1919. He returned to the village, lived in Boobery in Spring 1920, then moved back with his parents at Jersey Cottage by Spring 1921. The whole family then left the village before Spring 1922 and moved towards Wellington, Somerset. In Dec 1929 in Tiverton, aged 37, Lewis married Annie Maunder (1894-1944). At exactly the same time & place his younger brother, William Harold Gale, married Violet Mabel Maunder – younger sister of Annie. Lewis and Annie did not have any children.

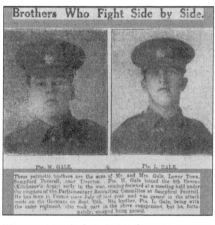

Water and Lewis Gale Article from the Western Times 29 Sep 1916: Image reproduced with kind permission of The British Newspaper Archive (www.britishnews paperarchive.co.uk) '. Image © THE BRITISH LIBRARY BOARD. ALL RIGHTS RESERVED.

In the 1939 register he lived at Leonard Moor, SP with Annie, occupation Council Roadman. Lewis died Mar 1976 in Exeter, aged 84. Family tree: https://www.ancestry.co.uk/family-tree/tree/76011902/family

GLANVILLE Ira b 1 Jun 1888 Plymtree, Honiton – one of 13 children of William Glanville (b 1845, Ag Lab) and Elizabeth (b 1852). He was a bricklayer / mason and lived in Plymtree with his parents until just after 1911 census. On 13 Mar 1913 in SP he married Florence Elizabeth Morrell (b 1886), dr of John Morrell, ag lab. They lived in SP and had a son Ira Morris / Maurice on 3 Feb 1914 but the baby died aged just 2 months old and they had no more children. In 1915 Electoral Roll they lived at Higher Town *(2018: 30 Higher Town)*. He enlisted in Exeter on 9 Dec 1915 aged 27 years and 192 days – reg no 177232 then 3072787. He joined the Royal Engineers and was then transferred to the 16th Battalion of the Tank Corps on 19 Jan 1918. He served for 2 years 5 months in England and 2 months in France – leaving Southampton for Le Havre 9 Sep 1918 and then suffered from infected nerves in left leg caused by exposure – medical report dated 18 Oct 1918. He was returned to England Nov 1918 and treated in a military hospital in Devonport with burns to thumb and fingers on left hand – possibly the same incident which damaged his left leg. His medical report said he was healed 20 Dec 1918. He was transferred to the army reserve, "Class Z", 18 Feb 1919. The Glanvilles continued to live in Higher Town until 1926. Ira died Jul 1927 in Tiverton hospital aged just 39 and his wife Florence left the village shortly afterwards.

GOFFIN Wilfred John - b 9 Jan 1892, SP. Youngest of 7 children of Frederick Goffin (1851-1932) plumber and Elizabeth Ponsford Farr (1851-1923). Wilfred worked for GWR for a week and then became an engineer's fitter, living with his parents at Turnpike *(2018: number 8)* in the 1911 census. Wilfred signed up to the RN 11 Aug 1913 at Devonport for a period of 12 years as a fitter and turner. He was initially based on VIVID II, a shore-based training facility, before moving around many different vessels. Leander Nov13-Oct14, Indefatigable Oct 14-Jul15 (this ship was sunk in Battle of Jutland 1 year after he had left with all but 2 of the 1,079 crew killed), Diligence (Marmaduke) Jan16-Oct16, Dalhousie (Royal Indian Ship based in Basrah) Dec 16-Mar18, Dolphin Aug 18-Oct18. He then had several more years' service - repairing / maintaining RN ships in the dockyards. He appeared on the SP 1919 absent electoral voters list with ref ERA III M6488 HMS Revenge. Last service date was 15 Nov 1927. In 1920, aged 28, he married Alice Jane Dodd (1893-1977) in Plymouth. They had one daughter, Audrey Hilda (1922-2005). In the 1939 Register Wilfred lived in Plymouth, occupation "Armament Fitter" (retired RN Pensioner). He died Sep 1967 in Plymouth, aged 75. Family tree: https://www.ancestry.co.uk/family-tree/tree/54003725/family

GOFFIN William – b 10 Feb 1870 in SP to George Goffin (ag Lab at Whitnage farm) and Elizabeth Trevelyan. He was 7th of 8 children, but three older siblings all died as infants in 1864 in a scarlet fever epidemic which decimated the younger population of the village and surrounding areas. William enlisted in the RN 29 Apr 1885 as a 15-year-old. His mother had died 18 months previously. He first saw service on HMS Impregnable as a cabin boy. He gradually rose through the ranks – ordinary seaman, able seaman, leading seaman and was made Petty Officer Apr 1894, aged 24. His "last" service on his first tour of duty was on HMS Ganges on 31 Oct 1898, three weeks after the birth of his first son (who also later served in the RN).

William re-enlisted less than a month after his previous term with the RN. His second tour of duty started on HMS Thunderer and ended 12 years later in Nov 1910 on HMS Blake where his rank was shown as Boatswain. At the age of 40 he then re-enlisted in the Royal Fleet Reserve and had the rank of Chief Boatswain. During WW1 he was the Chief Warrant Officer at the HM Naval Base at Stornoway. On 4 Jul 1921, aged 51, he retired "for good" from the RN with rank Lieutenant. He married in Aug 1897 at SP to Lily Trevelyan who was his first cousin. They lived at Chains Cottage (*2018: 8 Chains Road*) and had three children, the eldest of whom also served in the RN in WW1 (see below). William died Nov 1949 in SP, aged 79, nine years after his wife Lily died. Family tree: https://www.ancestry.co.uk/family-tree/tree/54003725/family

GOFFIN William Charles – b 11 Oct 1898, SP. Oldest son of William Goffin (1870-1949, RN career) and Lily Trevellyan (1875-1940) and lived at Chains Cottage (*2018: 8 Chains Road*). Before the war he was a fitter and turner. He signed up, aged 18 ½, in Mar 1917 to the RN (F26765) serving on the land-based President II which provided accounting services etc to the RN. He was based at Crystal Palace (an RND training centre), then Cranwell (an RNAS training centre) and finally Wormwood Scrubs (an airship station). Last accounting service date 31 Mar 1918. On 1 Apr 1918 he transferred to the newly-formed RAF, Air Mech I #227675 then from 1919-1920 was a turner. In Nov 1919 he was in Baghdad, then HQ India. 1921 promoted to LAC (still a turner); March 1922 went from Iraq to Port Said, Egypt in 208 Squadron until finally discharged 14 Jun 1923. In Mar 1925 in Biscot, Bedfordshire he married Winifred Maud Tew. They had 3 children in Luton, then the family moved back to Devon in the late 1940's. William died Dec 1978 in Tiverton, aged 80. Family tree: https://www.ancestry.co.uk/family-tree/tree/54003725/family

GUNN Ernest George b 20 Feb 1899 Rackenford, eldest of 5 children of Allen George Gunn (b 1862 S Molton) and Emma Pincombe (b 1879 Rackenford). His father was originally a thatcher, but by the 1911 census he was manager of the Hare and Hounds Inn, Lower Town, SP (*2018: 11-17 Lower Town*). On 31 Jan 1916, aged nearly 17, he started work with GWR as a cleaner. He enlisted 7 Sep 1916 in the Bedfordshire Regiment, aged 17, and served in France. He was discharged 3 Jun 1919 and awarded the silver medal badge. After the war he returned to SP. On 19 Oct 1921 at St Johns he married (declaring occupation as chauffeur) Beatrice May Gale, b 9 Jul 1898 Bampton, but who lived with parents in SP from just after birth. Beatrice had an elder brother, Walter Gale, who lost his life in 1916 in France during WW1 and a brother Lewis Gale who also served with the 8th Devons. In the 1939 Register Ernest lived with his wife Beatrice at Westcott Cottage, Westleigh – his occupation lorry driver. Ernest G Gunn died there on 16 Dec 1984 with probate £48,957 to his widow Beatrice who died in 1988. Family tree: https://www.ancestry.co.uk/family-tree/tree/76011902/family

HELLYER / HELLIER (Richard) Sidney – b SP 20 Jul 1879, bp 11 Sep, to Nicholas Hellyer (ag Lab b 1824 SP) and his second wife Jane Wright (b 1835, Holcombe Rogus). His parents married Oct 1856 Burlescombe and Sidney was the youngest of 10 children. The family lived in Boobery (*2018: 3 Boobery*). He initially joined the army in Feb 1896, where he gave his age as 18 yrs 1 month – 18 months older than his true age. He joined the 4th Devonshire Regiment on a short service attestation - no 4697. In 1899 he extended his army service and enlisted for a further 21 years. In Sep 1899 he transferred to the ASC #T15188. In Feb 1900 he was transferred to South Africa where he spent the next 10 years. In 1909 in Johannesburg he married Christina Allan McLaren,b 1883 Hunslet, Leeds to Scottish parents – David McLaren (engine driver) and Jessie Fairey. The family returned to England – Bulford Barracks, Wiltshire, where their first Daughter Jessie was b Sep 1910. In the 1911 census he was at Bulford Barracks, Wiltshire, married, now declaring his year of birth as 1881 and serving as a company quarter master sergeant for the 28th Army Service Company (ASC). His wife and daughter were also living at the barracks in married quarters. They had a second daughter in May 1912 (Ethel). When WW1 commenced he was posted to France, mentioned in despatches in Dec 1915 and was given the Meritorious Service medal Jan 1917. By 1918 he became Staff sergeant major, but now with dob as 27 Jan 1878! He was demobbed Sep 1920 and then moved to Southampton where he became a transport clerk. His wife Christina died Apr 1939 in Lambeth. In the 1939 register he was shown with another dob – 2 Jul 1878, as a widower, a Clerk for a timber broker and lived in Lewisham. 6 months later in London, aged 60, he remarried - to Ivy Victoria Davis 18 years his junior. She predeceased him in Oct 1962, age 65, whilst Richard Sidney died Mar 1967 in Braintree, Essex, aged 87. Family tree: https://www.ancestry.co.uk/family-tree/tree/116240277/family

HESLOP Cyril George - b in Rotherfield, Sussex 7 Feb 1882. In 1901 he and his brother Eric (see below) were living with his widowed mother Leera or Lerra Heslop (née Martin) - b in Calcutta, India and of private means, in Lewisham, London. How they came to be living at "Ivydene" (*2018: Worths, 3-5 Turnpike*), in 1911 is not known. His occupation was shown as ex- stock-jobbers clerk. However, in 1916 Cyril married Dorothy Wallington b 7 Jun 1886, who in 1911 was running the small private school set up by her retired mother at "Morrells" in Lower Town, SP. Dorothy was also not Devon-born, being from Accrington in Lancashire.

Cyril enlisted in the Northern Cyclists' Battalion in January 1917, but was discharged in September 1918 as "no longer physically fit for War Service" [he suffered from varicose veins]. Interestingly, his 'trade' was given as 'Director' and the address of next-of-kin [wife, Dorothy Heslop] was 40, Mercers Road, Holloway, London. In the 1939 register Cyril and his wife Dorothy were at Hendon, Middlesex. Occupation : Managing Director window cleaning company. Cyril and Dorothy clearly returned to Devon at some point after the War because they both died in Honiton – Cyril in 1960 (aged 78) and Dorothy in 1968 (aged 82). Family tree: https://www.ancestry.co.uk/family-tree/tree/74092134/family

HESLOP Eric Charles - B in Hornsey 20 Jan 1881 to Charles Henry Heslop and Leera or Lerra Heslop (née Martin), parents were mechanical engineers and lived in 1881 at Rotherfield Sussex, with Leera's widowed mother, Louisa L Martin (annuitant of private means). In 1901 census in Lee, Lewisham, London Eric lived with widowed mother and once again widowed grandmother. In 1911 census he lived in "Ivydene", (*2018: Worths, 3-5 Turnpike*) with his widowed mother (b in Calcutta) and his younger brother Cyril; occupation shown as ex-stockjobbers clerk. A possible military record is for a Lieutenant Eric Charles Heslop in the Manchester Regiment, but another man with this same name was born in Manchester in the same year. There is also a Private E.C. Heslop in the Durham LI, wounded in

1916. He returned to SP and is shown in Gregory's Directories. He married, aged 49 in 1930 to the 16-year-old Pauline Faye Price (b 12 Apr 1914) at St Thomas (Exeter); she was the daughter of Reginald J.S. Price and his wife Ellen Frances (née Bodenham). In the 1939 register he lived with his wife Pauline at Priscillas Tea Rooms, Alton, Hants where he was the proprietor. Eric died in Alton, Hampshire in Jun 1955 (aged 74) leaving effects valued at £434 to his wife Pauline, who died in Surrey in 1974 (aged 60). Family tree: https://www.ancestry.co.uk/family-tree/tree/74092134/family

HEYWOOD Henry Edward – b 30 Dec 1895 SP (bp St John's 19 Feb 1896) to John Heywood (carpenter/wheelwright/farmer) and Susan Elizabeth. Henry was the youngest of 5 children and lived in Kerslake House (*2018: Chains Road*) in 1901 and in Boobiers (Turnpike) in 1911 – when his father had changed his career from master wheelwright to farmer. Henry was helping on the farm. He signed up but we have not found a definite military record. He may be 210787/204046 in the Devons and then the S Staffs – no birth info to say for sure. A newspaper report in Feb 1917 reported him home on leave with a poisoned hand. In the 1918 electoral roll he has the suffix "NM" but gave his home address as Boobiers, SP. His parents continued to live there until 1924 when his mother died. His father moved away 18 months later. Henry moved to Somerset (Brent Knoll) where he was a railway signalman, living with the "Fox" family. Surprisingly though in 1946, aged 50 and a bachelor, he went to Gothenburg in Sweden and married the 45-year-old spinster Margareta Wahlstedt. They returned to Somerset and there is a burial record in Sep 1977, Weston-super-Mare for Margareta and in Dec 1957 for Henry.

HEYWOOD Walter Arnold - b 1894 Taunton was next eldest brother to Henry (above). Walter and indeed his elder brother John Baker Heywood b 1891, lived in SP up to 1911, in Kerslake House, Chains Road, and Boobiers, Turnpike (*2018: 14 Turnpike*), but emigrated

It is worth while going out to the trenches when you get treated like this on your return.

Postcard sent from Ivy to James Trevellyan

to New Zealand around 1912 where he became a shepherd. Four years later, in 1916, Walter later joined the New Zealand Infantry 4th Battalion #14813 and sailed to Europe and fought in France. He was wounded in the Messines battle and had his foot smashed. A newspaper report dated 4 Jan 1918 stated that his parents lived in SP but he was recovering in a hospital in Bethnal Green, London. He recovered and returned to New Zealand. He died in 1947 in Horowhenau, New Zealand.

HINE Frederick William – b 24 Apr 1898, Sampford Arundell, Somerset to William James Hine (platelayer GWR) and Alice Stone. He was the 2nd of 5 children. The family lived in one of the two Jersey Cottages in SP. His elder brother, Robert Thomas Hine lost his life on 8 Oct 1917 in Flanders. We have not been able to find a definite military record, but he may be Frederick Hines, Private in the Devons, 203875, or Private Frederick Wm Hine SE/1946 in the RAVC who served in France from December 1914 onwards. We know he signed up as he shows on 1918 electoral Roll as serving with the military, address shown as Lower Town. After the war he worked as fireman for GWR, based in Taunton 1920-1939. In Jun 1927 Taunton he married Nora Lavinia Baker (22 May 1905-1995). They had 4 children. In the 1939 register Frederick, his wife Nora and one son lived at Roman Road, Taunton. He is probably the Frederick W Hine who died in1966 in Taunton. Family tree: https://www.ancestry.co.uk/family-tree/tree/68296702/family

HODDER Charles – b 22 Jan 1892 SP to Frank Hodder (aka Otter) and Sarah Drew. He was older brother to Frank and cousin to Charles Henry (see below). He also had an older brother Thomas who served – but Thomas used his mother's maiden name and was therefore known as Thomas Drew - see earlier in this list.

In the 1901 and 1911 Census Charles lived in a Lower Town cottage (*2018: site of 16 Court Way*) with his parents and siblings. In 1911 he was a packer with GWR. Shortly after the census he moved to Worle, Axbridge, Weston-Super-Mare, Somerset. On 18 Nov 1915 he enlisted with the Somerset LI (Machine Gun Corps) with reg # 26699. He was posted to France and served with the BEF from May 1916. On 1 Sep 1916 he was promoted (unpaid) to Lance Corporal. On 28 Mar 1917 he was transferred to 38th Battalion and reverted to Private. He was discharged in Nottingham on 11 Mar 1919 to Z reserves.

He gave his home address on discharge as Cockymoor Farm, South Brewham, Somerset. In Dec 1919 in Axbridge, Weston-S-M he married

Ada Maud Williams (née Davis, b 1882) whose husband had died in 1914 leaving her with 4 young children to bring up. Charles and Ada did not have any more children. In the 1939 register they lived at Church Road, Weston-S-M with two children from Ada's first marriage. Charles' occupation shown as general labourer (heavy work). Charles died in Dec 1948 in Weston-S-M, aged 56. His wife Ada lived for a further 20 years and died Sep 1968. Family tree:
https://www.ancestry.co.uk/family-tree/tree/118211823/family

HODDER Charles Henry- b 6 Oct 1889 SP as Charles Henry **OTTER**. He was the second illegitimate son of Lucy Otter (b Feb 1868). He was first cousin to the brothers Charles Otter (later Hodder) and Frank Hodder, who were both born in SP and served in WW1 – see records above and below. NB Many researchers have got Charles Henry Hodder and Charles Hodder muddled up!! In the 1891 census Charles Henry and his older brother William Frank were being looked after by their widowed grandmother Sarah Otter in Higher Town (*2018: 8 – 10*). Charles' mother, Lucy, had moved to Bridgwater in Somerset and was working as a domestic servant and lodged there in 1891 census. 4 months later, in Axbridge, she married Henry Palmer who was 20 years older than her. They had three children in close succession and in the 1901 census Charles was living in Hutton, Somerset with his mother, stepfather and step siblings.

Charles Henry Hodder enlisted in September 1908 initially in the 10th (Princess of Wales Own) Hussars. In the 1911 census he is with the military unit, stationed in India. On his return he married Lillian Ann Parsons in Weston-super-Mare in October 1914, before serving two tours of duty with the B.E.F., returning in January 1919. He was discharged in September 1920 and awarded the usual 3 medals: 1914 Star, British War Medal and Victory Medal.

Charles and Lillian had two children (Lucy 1916, Charles 1919) prior to his discharge from War service and four more afterwards - born between 1921 and 1931. In the 1939 register he lived with his wife Lilian and 4 of his 6 children in Weston-Super-Mare. His occupation was foreman at a coal and timber yard. Charles died in Weston-super-Mare in May 1963, aged 71, having outlived his wife by 8 years. Family tree: https://www.ancestry.co.uk/family-tree/tree/118211823/family

HODDER Frank b 1 Jul 1897 SP to Frank Hodder (previously Frank Otter) and Sarah Drew. In the 1911 census he had left his parents' Lower Town cottage (*2018: site of 16 Court Way*) and was working as a farm servant

(Cow Boy!) to the Gater family at Jersey farm. He had two elder brothers who served in the war – Thomas Drew and Charles Hodder above, but we have been unable to find his military record. He may be 4469/18824, Machine Gun Corps then Devon Reg (medal card found on thegenealogist website but no birth or date details so can't be sure). He was home on leave in Feb 1917 according to a newspaper report with "frozen feet". A Western Times report on 17 Aug 1917 stated that he had been wounded a second time. On discharge he returned to the village and lived with his widowed mother Sarah in Lower Town from 1920 until her death in 1928. He continued to live in Lower Town and in Jun 1929 in Tiverton he married Florence Annie Pook, b 11 Sep 1900 Blackborough, d of Philip and Sarah Ann Pook.

The newly weds lived in Lower Town up to 1934. In the 1939 Register they lived at Laurel Cottage, Higher Town, SP. Frank gave his occupation as "Permanent Way Labourer". At some later stage they moved to Weston-super-Mare, close to where his brother Charles lived. Frank and Florence do not appear to have had any children. Frank died Sep 1972 in Weston-S-M, whilst Florence died 10 years later in 1982, also in Weston-S-M. Family tree: https://www.ancestry.co.uk/family-tree/tree/118211823/family

HOLLOWAY Samuel Cromwell b 28 Mar 1896 SP to Samuel Holloway (butcher and grocer) and Susanna Kerslake Bowden. In 1911 the family lived at Higher Town (*2018: 14 Higher Town*) where they ran Holloways shop. Cromwell signed up 27 Aug 1915 in Exeter, Reg No 89195 -WX CC Hation (RAMC) – unit 32MAC. Within 1 month of signing up he was treated for gonorrhoea. His home address was given as 36 Parr Street, Exeter, where there was also a Stanley Holloway living. After 16 months in the UK he was posted to Salonika, Greece and worked there as a cook for the duration of the war. Whilst serving he contracted Malaria, after 9 months in Salonika in Sep 1917. His medical record indicates that in 1917 he also was treated for syphilis. He had 7 further documented attacks of malaria, the last in a B.M.H. in the UK in 13 Jan 1919. He was "disembodied" 12 Apr 1919 under paragraph 392 section xvi(a) –medically unfit for further service and was assessed as being 20% disabled, receiving a weekly pension of 5s 6d. In Autumn 1919 he was on the absent voters electoral roll, home address given as Mount View, Higher Town, SP.

In 1915, before enlisting, he got engaged to a Taunton girl, Gladys Minnie Evans. He sent her love letters and poetry while on service in Macedonia. She moved to London but in 1920 he jilted her and informed her by letter that he had married someone else! There was a court case in May 1920 (where he neither appeared nor was represented) for breach of promise, and the scandal was reported in newspapers across the country. He was found guilty and ordered to pay £100 damages. He moved to St Pancras, London - on ER 1921.

In Dec 1938, age 42, he married Annie Hayes in St Pancras, London – 18 years after the birth of their daughter. Both Annie and her daughter however used the surname "Holloway" from 1920. In the 1939 Register Samuel lived at Mornington Crescent, St Pancras, occupation butcher, with his wife Annie and daughter, who was then a hospital ward orderly. In 1950 he was on the Stepney ER. No death record found. Family tree: https://www.ancestry.co.uk/family-tree/tree/74614375/family

HURFORD Lionel George – b 5 May 1898 in SP, third child of John Charles Hurford (a GWR Packer/Platelayer) and Loveday (née Sandercock). He lived in Higher Town (*2018: in or near number 40*) with his parents and siblings in the 1901 and 1911 censuses. On the "Royal Navy Register of Seamen's Services 1900-1928", Reg # K28848, his date of birth is recorded as 5 May 189**7** -so he declared himself to be exactly one year older than he actually was. His occupation was first given as "Horse Driver" later changed to "Engine Driver (stationary)". He served on three separate vessels: HMS Vivid II 8.11.1915 -2.2.1916 (shore based), HMS Centurion 3.2.1916 -18.2.1916 (shore-based), HMS Vivid II 19.2.1916 -25.4.1916 (shore based), HMS Bellerephon 26.4.1916 -16.7.1919 (Battle of Jutland et al). He did not return to the village. He married Ivy Parkhouse (b 30 Nov 1897 in SP, daughter of shoemaker Tom Parkhouse) in London in 1922. In the 1939 register he was a civilian carpenter living at the Barracks, London Road, Hertford. He died in Hertford aged 51 on 23 Dec 1949. Lionel and Ivy had five children (3 boys and 2 girls) between 1923 and 1934.

HUTCHINSON Jack – b Apr 1896 Tiverton was the 4th of 6 surviving children of John Hutchinson (Farm Carter, b 1861 Hastings, Sussex) and Augusta Ann Bird (b 1865, Shaldon). In the 1901 census the family lived in the Lowman Ward of Tiverton – at Putson Cross. Before 1911 Jack (aka John) had left home, but his parents and 3 siblings still lived there. By 1913 his parents had moved to Kings Cottages, Lower Town, (*2018: site of 5-7 Lower Town*) where they stayed until the end of 1924. Jack enlisted in the Devon Regiment as private #11909 and first saw active service in France on 22 Sep 1915. Later he was promoted to Lance Corporal – recorded as HuNtchinGson. He was included on the 1919 absent voters list as Corporal J. Hutchinson #11909, 10th Devon Regiment and gave his address as Lower Town, SP – where his parents lived. He does not appear on any subsequent Electoral Roll for SP. He appears to have married a Lily Gardner (b 5 May 1885) in Mar 1920 in Tiverton. In the 1939 register they lived at Rembarton Cottage - Cullompton where his occupation was "farm Carter". Lily must have died shortly after this register. In Mar 1941, Tiverton Jack remarried to an Edith Charlotte Smith. Jack died in Jun 1959 in Halberton, Tiverton, aged 62, leaving probate to his widow Edith Charlotte.

HUTCHINSON Sidney, b 16 May 1892, Uffculme, was the elder brother of Jack (above) and 1ˢᵗ child of John and Augusta. He was still living with his parents in 1911 census, aged 18 at Putson Cross, Lowman Ward, Tiverton where his occupation was Carter on Farm – just like his father John. By 1913 his parents had moved to Kings Cottages, Lower Town, (*2018: site of 5-7 Lower Town*) where they stayed until the end of 1924. In Jan 1912, aged 19 years 8 months, Sidney signed up for 12 years military service with the 15th Hussars #8077– Hussars of the Line. He was invalided out on 27 Jul 1912 as being medically unfit for further service. There is a record later in 1912 for him as a Chelsea Pensioner. He must have re-enlisted - as on 1 Dec 1917, Shoesmith Sydney (sic) Hutchingson (sic sic) was home on 10 days leave from France after 15 months service - to attend the wedding of his sister Augusta (same name as his mother) to Francis George Evans (a sailor). A Sidney Huchinson, Reg #J71673 received the standard victory war medal at the end of the war – but this is a Navy Record – so as he was previously recorded as serving in France – an Army, not Navy theatre of war, he may have changed regiments once again. In Oct 1914 Tiverton, an ordinary Seaman J71673 called Sidney Hutchinson married a Beatrice Maud Bradford (b Jan 1895 Exmouth). They had two children. In the 1939 register they lived at Shillands, Tiverton where Sidney was employed as a Crepe Worker, Textile. Sidney died 5 Mar 1969 in Tiverton.

Shoeing horses.
Photo courtesy of the Imerial War Museum

JOHNSON Alfred b Q4 1895 Kingstone, Uttoxeter, Staffs. In 1901 census he lived at Heath Union Workhouse, Uttoxeter with elder brother John b 1892 and younger brother Ernest (see below). No parents were shown, but our research shows them to have been Henry Johnson, plate layer and Elizabeth (née Plant) from Manchester. In 1911 census, Alfred and his younger brother Ernest (see below) were at St Boniface Home for Waifs and Strays. His age was recorded as 14, but was in fact 15. He signed up before May 1915, initially in the ASC as M2/077750, serving in France , then transferred as a private to Ox & Bucks Light Infantry #33817. In 1919 Electoral Roll he was at West Pitt farm, in 1921 ER at Wharf Cottage and in 1922-1927 ER at Higher Town. He left the village in 1928. He may be the Alfred Johnson who was doing munitions work in Uttoxeter, Staffs in 1939. Family tree: http://trees.ancestry.co.uk/tree/75014822/family

JOHNSON Ernest (aka Jack) b 5 May 1898 Kingstone, Uttoxeter, Staffs – younger brother to Alfred above. 1901 census he was at a workhouse in Uttoxeter (no parents) and by 1911 he was at St Boniface home for Waifs and Strays in Lower Town. He enlisted with the Somerset Light Infantry (date unknown, but during WW1 as he received WW1 medals) # 26677/0338. He served with the 8th platoon and was in Acre, Egypt on 2 Nov 1919, where he sent a postcard to Ivy Nester Trevellyan, of Wharf House, SP (*2018: Fairview Cottage*) who was 16 at the time. Her father, James Trevellyan, had died in the war (see earlier for more details). In 1921 and early in 1922 he was still serving with the Somerset Light Infantry – in India. In the 1922 electoral roll Ernest was recorded as NM with home address Wharf Cottage, Turnpike - occupiers Edith Ann Trevelyan and Edwin and Sarah Vickery. On 22 Apr 1924 SP, Ernest (a gardener) married Ivy (see above) who later became a teacher. By 1935 Edith Trevellyan and her daughter Ivy

Ernest (Jack) Johnson

(Ernest's wife) had completed the purchase of Woodbine Farm, Culmstock. The family lived there until their deaths. Ernest died Feb 1986 and his wife Ivy died two years later. They did not have any children. Family tree: https://www.ancestry.co.uk/family-tree/tree/75014822/family

KEELEY William Daniel b 24 Sep 1874 Preston 5/6 children to William (a Gunner in the Royal Artillery for 21 years then a blast furnace man, b Wicklow, Ireland) and Catherine (née Galvin) from Ashton-under-Lyne, Manchester. His family moved around the country, but William enlisted in the army in Chester 28 Jun 1898, no 5770 in the 3rd battalion of the Cheshire regiment. He was promoted to Lance Corporal, then Corporal, however he was found guilty of being AWOL and reduced to the ranks. He then served in South Africa Jan 1900 - Jul 1902, before being discharged as medically unfit in Aug 1902. He married in Jul 1903 to Lucy Bellis in West Kirby, Liverpool. He was working as a clerk at that time. In the 1911 census they were in Lincoln where he was head of the St Hugh's Boys home for waifs and strays (one of his prior clerical jobs was in a waifs and strays home in Chester). In 1913 William and Lucy moved to SP where he became master and Lucy later became Matron of the St Boniface Home for waifs and strays on Lower Town. Almost immediately after war was declared in Aug 1914, William enlisted in the 8th Devons Labour Corps, aged 40, and within two months had the rank of Sergeant. His initial role was training of military recruits at Aldershot camp. He first saw active service in France 26 Jul 1915. Due to a shortage of officers he led his platoon in the battle of Loos and on 25 Sep 1915 his platoon was badly affected by gas - from shells fired from his own side for the first time in battle. Two other SP soldiers (brothers Walter and Lewis Gale – see entries above), were also caught up in the botched gas attack. William was shot in the shoulder and due to the weight of his kit and the mud was unable to move. He was released from his kit by a "kiltie" from the 2nd Gordon Highlanders. He then crawled 4 miles to a dressing station before being taken a few days later to the hospital ship SS Egypt and back to England. He recovered and by Jun 1916 he returned to the front with rank of acting Quarter Master Sergeant. In Oct 1917 he was promoted again to acting 2nd Lieutenant and on taking charge of the company on 17 Sep 1918 he was promoted again to acting Captain. When he relinquished the command of the company on 30 Jun 1919 he reverted to the rank of Lieutenant and shortly afterwards was discharged from active service. He did not return to SP, but in the 1939 register he was superintendent at the Talbot Boys home, Bournemouth where his wife Lucy was Matron. Shortly afterwards he retired and Willam and his wife

Lucy moved to Broughton, Lancashire. William died in Horwich, Lancs on 9 Jun 1940 and his wife Lucy died 1 Sep 1945 and was buried in Hindley, Lancs.

KEMP Frank Wallis - b Oct 1884, Bampton, the son of Frank Kemp, b 1852 Hockworthy a farmer and his wife Catherine (née How). The family lived at Cudmoor Farm, Bampton in 1891. Frank, snr. died Jul 1893, aged 41 and Catherine re-married to George Palfrey, a farmer 11 years her junior, in 1897. Catherine had probably inherited Cudmoor Farm, where she and George were living in 1901 with Frank, his sister Catherine Mary and their baby step-brothers Harold and Herbert. By 1911, Frank was farming at Churchwalls Farm, SP, with his sister (identified on the Census form by just the initial 'M'). He married Edith M Heard in 1914 (Q2 Tiverton, 5b 973). Frank signed up as a gunner with RFA (#69318). He returned to the village after demobilisation and was on 1918-1920 ER at Churchwalls with his wife, Edith Mary. They left the village and don't appear to have had any children. Frank died in 1927, aged 42.

KERSLAKE Ernest John b 13 Nov 1891 SP to Lydia Mary Kerslake, a single mother, b 30 Sep 1873 and bp 23 Feb 1892. In 1901 census he lived with his mother Lydia, who had by then married an Eli Crook and they lived with Ernest's widowed grandmother, Charlotte Kerslake, at Winks Cottage, Whitnage Road SP. By 1911 census he was gardener to the vicar and lived at the (newer) Rectory on Higher Town. In Nov 1911, aged 19, he married Ellen Harriet Heyward (b Oct 1892) who was pregnant at the time. Their baby Louisa Lydia Ellen Kerslake was b 1 Mar 1912. He started active service in France 16 Mar 1915 as private 7647 in the 2nd Devons – 5 days before the baptism of their second child, Ernest. He later moved to 1st Gunnery Battalion, Devons, and was home on leave in August 1917. Discharged exactly 3 years after enlisting on 16 Mar 1918. However on the 1919 Electoral roll he was shown as absent from the village on military service - #176436 Gunner with RFA, home address Higher Town. He and his wife continued to live in Higher Town, having a third child, Laura, in 1924. Last record available for residency being 1934 Electoral Roll. In the 1939 register they lived at Mounts Cottages, Higher town where his occupation was lorry driver, creamery. Their married daughter Louisa Lydia Ellen Smith also lived there, as did their son Ernest F Kerslake. Ernest John Kerslake died in Q1 1961 at Waterloo Cross, shortly after the death of his wife Ellen Harriet. His occupation shown as shop assistant. Family tree: https://www.ancestry.co.uk/family-tree/tree/74614375/family

KERSLAKE Frederick James b 1892 SP was the eldest of 13 children of Frederick James Kerslake (1872-1934, Manager Lime Kilns) and Annie Salter (1872-1950). His brothers Henry and Herbert also participated in the war. He lived with his parents at Hill Kilns, SP, in 1901, worked as a quarryman after he left school, then enlisted in the army for 12 years in Taunton in Dec 1910 as gunner #34097 in the Royal Garrison Artillery. He first entered the theatre of war 22 Jun 1915 in the Balkans (SE Europe) and would have provided long range artillery fire from behind the front lines with target guidance from Morse code messages from the RFC (Royal Flying Corps). Whilst on leave, on 4 Oct 1918 in Halberton he married Emily Mary Osmond (1890-1981). He was disembarked in Dover 17 Mar 1919 and transferred to the reserves. He returned to Kings Cottages, Lower Town (*2018: site of 5-7 Lower Town*). Their first child, Frederick Harold, was b 7 Sep 1919 in SP and at his christening a month later, the father gave his occupation as "Coal Yard Manager". Their second son was b 31 Jan 1922 in SP. Frederick's 12-year period with the army officially ended on 28 Dec 1922.They had two further children in 1927 and 1929. An Osmond relation remembers him delivering coal by horse and cart. It must have been thirsty work as he was known to stop at the odd pub or two on his round. She also remembers a tattoo of a woman on his arm, which he could make dance by twisting his arm! In the 1939 register he was still living at 1 Kings Cottages, Lower town with his wife and the two younger children – the two elder boys had left home. His occupation had reverted to Quarry labourer. He died in Dec 1969 in SP, and his wife died 1981. Family tree: https://www.ancestry.co.uk/family-tree/tree/74614375/family

Fred Kerslake

KERSLAKE Frederick John b 6 Mar 1896 SP was the eldest of 6 children of John Kerslake (1867 SP, Carter on Farm) and his second wife Elizabeth Upham (1870 Halberton). His father was actually born John Kerslake Pillar to the single woman

Sarah Ann Pillar (b 1848 SP). The father of John Kerslake Pillar could well be John Kerslake, a lime burner, living nearby at Hill Kiln, who was two years older than the unmarried Sarah Ann Pillar. Sarah had another son, William Thomas Kerslake Pillar, b 16 Nov 1870 and baptized 28 Apr 1871. The assumed father John Kerslake married a Charlotte Walker on 5 Apr 1871. In the 1901 census Frederick lived at Barton Cottages (*2018: 4 and 6 Boobery)* with his parents and 2 siblings. In 1911 census the family (now 6 children) had moved to Park Cottage (which no longer exists, but was near the former pond at Sampford Barton). Frederick (age 15) was employed by a Market Gardener. He joined the Devon Regiment in 1916, initially as 2663 then Private 201630 with 1 / 4 Devons. The regiment moved to Iraq Feb 28 1916 and over 400 men were hospitalised due to heat related illnesses – including Frederick who suffered a sandfly attack. He was on the SP absent voters' electoral roll in Autumn 1919, home address Pond Cottage – which was where his parents lived. He was demobilised Oct 1919. His father died in Apr 1920, but Frederick continued to live at Pond Cottage with his widowed mother, Elizabeth until Spring 1924. In the 1939 Register his mother Elizabeth was at Kings Cottages, Lower Town, SP, but Frederick was living in Exmouth with his wife, Florence (née Wakeham), and was working as a brickworks labourer. He died in 1983. Family tree: https://www.ancestry.co.uk/family-tree/tree/68538081/family

KERSLAKE Henry John b 13 Sep 1896 SP - 3rd of 13 children of Frederick James Kerslake (1872-1934, Manager Lime Kilns) and Annie Salter (1872-1950). He lived with his parents at Hill Kilns in 1901 and 1911, then later moved to The Square, Uffculme where he became a baker. He served with the 87th RASC (Royal Army Service Corps) Private 314095 – enlisted Nov 1916 aged 19 and 60 days. He married Emily Mary Webber (1891-1948) on 8 Apr 1917 in Uffculme and gave his occupation as baker. After the end of the war Henry and Emily returned to SP and lived at his parents' former house – Hill Kiln Cottage, until Autumn 1922. In Spring 1923 they moved to the newly constructed Council Houses (number 2), later to become Beaufort Close, where he died Jan 1960, aged 63. His occupation was factory dairy hand, Creamery. His wife Emily died 12 years earlier in 1948. They had no children. Family tree: https://www.ancestry.co.uk/family-tree/tree/74614375/family

KERSLAKE Herbert b 19 Jul 1895 SP – 2nd of 13 children of Frederick James Kerslake and Annie Salter. His brothers Frederick and Henry also took part in the war. Herbert lived at Hill Kiln cottage with his parents and siblings in 1901 and 1911 census. He enlisted #2350078 as a private with 449 Ag Co Labour Corps – details in 1919 SP absent voters electoral roll where he gave home address as West Pitt (farm). In Jun 1920 Cullompton he married Alice Doble (b 1895) and they had two girls. Alice died in 1930, aged just 36. Herbert remarried the following year in 1931 to Florence Harris and they had four children. In the 1939 register he lived at Widhayes Cottage, Uplowman with his son Dennis and 3 others. Herbert lived to the age of 86, whilst his second wife, Florence, died in 2002 aged 96. Family tree: https://www.ancestry.co.uk/family-tree/tree/74614375/family

Surnames L-R

LEGG(E) Albert George b 4 Feb 1900, Halberton to Charles Legg (b 1863 Milverton, Somerset) - ag lab and Mary (née Cook) b Oct 1860 SP. Albert was the youngest of 5 children – the first 4 were born in Willand. In 1898/9 the family moved from Willand to Halberton and were living there for the 1901 census. His mother Mary d Nov 1904, aged 44 and was buried in SP 18 Nov. The family moved to Boobery (*2018: number 3*) SP and the widowed father, Charles, appeared on Electoral Rolls of 1908, 1910 and 1912. Charles – ag lab and widower and three children, including Albert, were recorded in 1911 Census in Boobery, SP.

It appears that Albert's father, Charles, remarried in Exeter in Apr 1911, just after the census date, to Elizabeth Skinner. The whole family, with the exception of Albert, emigrated shortly afterwards to Canada. No information has emerged to explain why Albert stayed in the UK and indeed who looked after him after his father and siblings emigrated. However Albert travelled to Devonport in Sep 1915 where he signed up to the RN as a cabin boy, aged just 15 ½.

He enlisted 6 Sep 1915 and spent a year on Impregnable, a month on Pembroke and then 2 ½ years on Penelope to Mar 1919. On his 18th birthday (4 Feb 1918) he enlisted for 12 years and was made up to AB (Able Seaman). He was paid a war Gratuity. HMS Penelope was renamed Indomitable and he served there until Jun 1919 before returning to Vivid 1, a shore-based installation at Plymouth. He continued to move round ships and although he passed the educational sufficiency test to become a Petty Officer, he remained an AB. It appears that after his 12-year service expired in Feb 1930 that he re-enlisted – although there are no records available to confirm this.

In 1926 in Taunton he married Florence Elsie Daley (1902-1994), daughter of Frederick Daniel Daley, Ag Lab, and Alice Gill. Florence was residing at Bishops Hull, near Taunton at the time of Albert's death. They had one son b Mar 1928 Taunton. However Albert George Legge died at sea in WW2 on 17 Jan 1942. He was on board the Destroyer HMS Matabele on convoy duty between Iceland and Mirmansk in Russia. The ship was sunk by a U-boat torpedo and 236 men perished of 238 crew. It was reported that many died of hypothermia in the icy cold sea before they could be rescued. His name is recorded on a memorial in Plymouth – panel 65. Family tree: https://www.ancestry.co.uk/family-tree/tree/117570145/family

LOCK George James - b 4th April 1890 Uplowman, the youngest of 7 children to William Lock (1849-1903) an "Agricultural Labourer/Herdsman" (1891 Census – living at Green End, Uplowman) and Mary Ann Bradford. They were married in Uplowman in 1875. On the 1901 Census, the family were living in Whitnage, which George gave as his place of birth on the 1911 Census when he was an "Assistant Butcher" boarding with George Hodges (Butcher, aged 43) and his family at 7 New Buildings, Frome.

He served as a bombardier in the RFA. The Western Times of 24 Dec 1914 carried an interesting letter which he wrote to his mother in Higher Town (*2018: site of 29, 31 or 33*). This letter is quoted in full in the earlier section on recruiting for the war. George later worked on the railways: UK Railway Employment Records 1833-1956 (Ancestry) reveal that he was a "Porter" at Blaina (Ebbw Vale, S.Wales) (6 May 1919) and a "Brakesman" at Aberbeeg (a few miles down the valley) (9 Feb 1920), and that he was "Recalled to Army" (11 Apr 1921).   His record sheet shows him back at Aberbeeg as a "Goods Guard" only seven weeks later (9 Jun 1921) and still employed up to 9 Jun1924, but with no indications as to where or in what capacity. By this latest date he had married May Williams (reg. Pontypool Q4 1923) and they had two children, both registered in Pontypool. The 1939 Register shows the family in Wells, with George a "Great Western Railway Guard" and his wife May on "Unpaid Domestic Duties". George died Q3 1946 (reg. Wells, Somerset).

LOVELL Henry James b 16 Dec 1883, Burlescombe to James Lovell (GWR plate Layer) and Lavinia Holley. In Feb 1900, aged 16, he joined GWR as a "Uniformed Lad Porter". In Q3 1906 Tiverton he married Mabel Lavinia Norman (b Sep 1895) from Watchet, Somerset. In 1911 Census he lived in Lower Town (*2018: 23 Lower Town*), with his wife and 2 children -Phyllis and Ronald and worked for RS Norrish and Sons as a "Butter Packer". They had a third child, Evelyn May in Oct 1913. His application for exemption from Military Service was turned down in May 1916. He enlisted 16 Jun 1916, and gave his occupation as factory engineer. He joined the Military Transport Division of the RASC (#M2/193950) and saw service in India, South Africa and Salonika. He contracted dysentery and was transferred out of the army Feb 1919. He returned to SP after discharge and in 1919 he was a cycle maker / dealer on Lower Town. In 1920-1926 trade directories he still lived in Lower Town, but occupation now shown as "Chauffeur". In 1930-39 directories (Kelly's) he once again returned to cycles – as a dealer / distributor. In the 1939 register he was a commercial traveller, cattle feedstuffs, lived at Rockfield, SP with his wife Mabel and married daughter Evelyn May Palfrey. He died in Mar 1969, aged 87.

MARLEY William b 16 Jan 1900 SP, first child to Samuel Marley (Labourer) and Martha Rosina Scorse. He was first cousin to WW1 casualties Bertie and Arthur Scorse. In 1911 census the family lived at Higher Town, (*2018: 29, 31 or 33*) father's occupation shown as "farm carter". On 14 Feb 1916 William joined GWR at Tiverton. On 28 Jan 1918 William was "called to the colours". On sign up he was #39522 in 12th Gloucester Reg, then #29511 in E Surrey Reg. He was awarded the Victory and British medals. He is shown on 1919 SP absent voters lists as Private 29511, 1ˢᵗ East Surrey's, home address - his parents' house in Higher Town. He rejoined GWR after demobilisation in Apr 1920, but was initially based in Cardiff, then transferred to Newport in 1923. His parents Samuel and Martha continued to live in Higher Town, but William moved out of the village permanently. He died 1982, aged 82 in Newport, South Wales. Family tree: https://www.ancestry.co.uk/family-tree/tree/75159961/family

MILTON Edward James b Jul 1891 Wellington was the second of 6 children of Albert Edward Milton {Milton-Twose} (labourer 1867-1911) and Sarah Amelia Boucher Vickery (b 1860, South Molton). The family moved to Royal Oak Cottages, Higher Town, (*2018: space between 14 and school*) around 1895. The family were there in both 1901 and 1911 censuses. Edward joined the army in Taunton on 29 Dec 1910 – height 5'6" and weighing less than 9 stone - and stated his occupation as baker. He was enrolled into the corps of Dragoons of the Line (2nd Dragoon Guards – known as the "Queens Bays") #3435. He started at Aldershot and obtained a third-class certificate Mar 1911. He served at home until 8 Sep 1914 and was then posted to France with the BEF. The 2ⁿᵈ Dragoon Guards were renamed the 1ˢᵗ Cavalry Division shortly after arriving in France. They served on the Western front in France and Flanders. In Apr 1917 he was appointed Lance Corporal (unpaid). In Nov 1917 he became ill and was sent back home to Birmingham War hospital with suspected pleurisy. He was formally discharged from the army 5 Feb 1918 when it became apparent that the illness was actually Phthisis – now known as Tuberculosis. His condition deteriorated and he died 6 May 1920, aged 28.

MILTON Francis Percy b 15 Feb 1895 Burlescombe, 4ᵗʰ child of Albert Edward and Sarah Amelia; brother of Edward James (above). Lived with parents in Higher Town (*2018: space between 14 and school*) in 1901 and 1911 census- occupation general labourer. Enlisted 17 Nov 1911 in Plymouth (gives 15 Feb 1894 as DOB) with Royal Marines Light Infantry (Plymouth Division) Reg No 15499. He was transferred initially to Deal before returning to Plymouth Aug 1912. In Feb 1913 he was posted to

"Roxborough" until Nov 1917. He was then based at Plymouth until Jan 1919. On the night of 22 &23 April 1918 he took part in a raid on Zeebrugge and Ostend and later participated in a ballot for the award of the Victoria Cross – but only two Marines actually received the award. From Jan 1919 he served on "Cornwall" where he was awarded his war gratuity of £29 in Aug 1919. He returned to Plymouth until 26 Jan 1920 when his service ended. He immediately re-enlisted into the Royal Fleet reserve and served for a further 5 years until he left 26 Jan 1925. In the 1939 register he lived at Fir Close, Tiverton, occupation butcher / slaughter house man. His wife, Florence b 21 Oct 1894 was also there. It appears that his widowed mother Amelia left SP and moved to Coldharbour, Uffculme whilst he was serving. He died in Heavitree, Exeter in 1941. Florence d Q2 1963 also in Exeter.

MILTON William Thomas b 5 Mar 1897 SP – 5th child of Albert Edward Milton {Milton-Twose} and Sarah Amelia – brother to Edward James and Francis above. Lived with parents in Higher Town (*2018: space between 14 and school*), in 1901 census. In the 1911 census William (aged 14) was an apprentice Baker, living on the premises, but still in Higher Town, SP. He served with the 1/4th Devons, private #1698 then #200240. He was Demobbed 26 Oct 1919 and was awarded the standard Victory and British War medals. In Q4 1920, Tiverton he married Winifred L Elworthy and they had a son, b Feb 1921. In the 1939 register the family lived at Stone Cottage, Uffculme. William was a wool comber and Winifred a wool spinner/winder- presumably at Coldharbour Mill. William died in Sep 1967 in Exeter.

MOON (Enos) Enoch b Oct 1883 Uplowman To William and Elizabeth, elder brother to Mark (below). He enlisted into the army around 1900, adding two years to his age. In 1901 he was a private with the Devon Militia in Jersey. By 1911 he had returned to his parent's house in Lower Town (*2018: number 19*) where he worked as a limestone quarryman. He served in the army as private 10752 in the 8th Devon Regiment. He was in France in 1915 and was home on leave from the trenches in Oct 1917. In Sep 1921 Burlescombe he married Blanche Davey – 6th of 8 children of John and Elizabeth. Enos and Blanche had 5 sons - all baptized in SP, between 1921 and 1929. Enos worked as a quarryman and by 1926 the family moved to Hill Kiln Cottage, where Enos was foreman at the adjacent Quarry. He continued to work as a quarryman. By the 1939 register he had moved to Highland Terrace (Western end of Higher Town) and lived there with his wife Blanche and 4 children. He died in 1967, aged 84.

MOON Mark b 4 Sep 1888 SP to William Moon (Labourer, b Hockworthy) and Elizabeth (née Candy) – who later became a nurse and a midwife. In 1901 the family lived in Boobery and by 1911 they had moved to Lower Town (*2018: number 19*) where Mark was an Ag Lab. In May 1914 he joined GWR as a packer, but on 27 Sep 1915 he enlisted into the army and was assigned to the Royal Engineers, 116th Railway Troops Company as a sapper. After training he was sent to Egypt where he spent the rest of the war. He had two short spells of illness and was finally demobbed in Feb 1919. He returned and lived briefly in Halberton, then married 29 Oct 1919 to Florence Ponsford (b Nov 1886) in SP. The family moved to Boobery in 1920 and had a son.

WW1 Royal Engineers badge

Mark returned to work on the railways until retirement aged 65. In the 1939 register he and Florence lived at the War Memorial Institute in Tiverton. He died in 1961 aged 73.

MORRELL Herbert Thomas b 8 May 1892 SP to John and Ellen, younger brother to John Henry Morrell (above). In 1901 he lived with his widowed father and 4 siblings at Barton Cottage (*2018: 6 Boobery*). In 1911 census he was a live-in servant working in Uffculme. We have not found a military record but he was away from SP during the war. Herbert returned to SP Spring 1923 ER and lived in Boobery. By Autumn 1923 he had moved to Always Cottage on Chains Road and lived there until Spring 1926. In Spring 1927 he moved to Rose Cottage, Higher Town where he was shown as a newsagent. Remarkably he was blind, but still managed to deliver the newspapers by bicycle! He was not recorded as being blind in the 1911 census, so his blindness may have been caused by the war. There is much more detail about this remarkable man in a Sampford Peverell Society book on SP businesses. In Apr 1927 in SP, aged 34, he married Eileen Daisy Hawkins, known as Ida, (1893-1942) of SP. In 1939 they still lived at Rose Cottage, Higher Town. They do not appear to have had any children. He continued to live there, working as a newsagent, until his death on 25 Apr 1959.

MORRELL John Henry b 14 Mar 1890 Burlescombe was son of John Morrell (1865, Uplowman, Ag Lab) and Ellen Cottey (1864-1896), who died Aug 1896 in childbirth - the baby survived. In 1901 the widowed father and his 5 children lived at Barton Cottage (*2018: 6 Boobery*). By 1911 John Henry was a Groom / gardener for Henry Wood (Saddler) and lived at his house – Rose Cottage, Turnpike. He applied for exemption from war service, but this was refused in Feb 1916. He enlisted as private 202013 Devons 2/4 and he then went on to join the Wiltshire Regiment, also as a Private, service number 0150. He was on the 1919 absent voters list with his father's address in Boobery.

By 1920 Henry John (rather than John Henry!) had returned to Rose Cottage Turnpike with Henry Wood (Saddler). In SP Mar 1921 he married Maude Frampton Wheeler (b 22 Jun 1900 SP) and he gave his occupation as chauffeur. He lived at '2 Rose Cottage, Boobery' and continued to live there, occupation chauffeur, until at least 1934. A daughter was born in 1930. In 1939 he and Maud lived at 10 Council Cottages (later named Beaufort Close). His occupation was lorry driver Milk Factory/ provender Millers. Later in life he became a gardener as evidenced by the 1959 probate of his brother Herbert Thomas Morrell. Henry died Sep 1963 in SP, aged 73.

NEEDS William b 18 Oct 1894 Chevithorne, 4th of 6 children of Thomas Needs (b 1861, Washfield, Ag Lab) and Jane Davey (b 1862 Withycombe, Somerset). In 1901 he lived with his parents and siblings including brother Thomas, at Chevithorne. In 1911 he was at Uplowman as a waggoner at Hill farm. His parents moved to Ashford Court dairy. He joined the army and was stationed in Jersey at the outbreak of the war, expecting to go to India, but was instead sent to France with the 1st Devons #9282. He was wounded in the hand in Oct 1914 in the battle of Lille and sent back to Plymouth for 21 days to recuperate. He had an uncanny ability to get wounded. 22 May 1915, 9 Aug 1916 and 7 Aug 1917 were dates of three subsequent injury records. On 29 Apr 1919 in SP he married Rosa Maud Date (Oct 1898 SP -1988) and was described as a 'Mons hero'. 1939 register they lived at Pinnex Moor Cottage, Tiverton. William's occupation was an Ag Lab. William died in Sep 1969 in Newton Abbot. William's brother Thomas NEEDS b 1889 Chevithorne, was in the RN.

NORRISH James John was the 7th child of Richard Stone Norrish and Jane Heard Chanin and younger brother to Richard Stanley (below). James was b 10 Apr 1890 at Fordlands, Tiverton. The family moved to Merrimeade House, Lower Town, in 1900 and James was a scholar in the 1901 census.

After he left school he did not join the family business but trained as a baker/ confectioner. In the 1911 census he was at Teignmouth, but by 1915 he had moved to Ventnor on the Isle of Wight – occupation Baker. He enlisted Dec 1915 at Newport, IOW but was not actually called up until Jan 1917 at Weston-super-Mare, Somerset. He joined the ASC and was posted to Bath (# S307526). He was demobilised Apr 1920 and moved to Brentwood, Essex where he was listed as a baker. In Dec 1926 he married the 41-year-old Agnes Mabel Rideout. They had no children and lived in Brentwood until his death in Dec 1972. Family tree: https: //www.ancestry.co.uk/family-tree/ tree/120247555/family

James John Norrish

NORRISH Richard Stanley b Apr 1888 at "Fordlands", 1.5m NE of Tiverton. He was the 6th of 9 children of Richard Stone Norrish (1857-1907) a wealthy farmer and owner of a Creamery and Jane Heard Chanin (1856-1932) who was the daughter of a Yeoman Farmer. The previous generations of both his parents were all wealthy farmers. The family continued to live at Fordlands until 1900 and then moved to Merrimeade House, Lower Town next door to the newly constructed and extensive creamery owned by his parents in Chains Road. His father died in 1907 and the creamery was then run by his elder brother, William Henry, where Richard continued to work as an employee in the 1911 census. Shortly afterwards he moved to London to carry on the business there, but in Dec 1915 he enlisted as a private in the 13th London Regiment – initial service number 5690, then #492586. He was on active service in the Somme Jun 1916 to Nov 1916 then took part in many battles in 1917, including the Cambrai operations in Nov 1917. There he suffered multiple gunshot wounds 7 Dec 1917 to his right leg, head and ankle. He was hospitalised and finally discharged from the army

The Norrish family at the back of Merriemeade House c 1904. From left to right, Richard Stanley, Alice, Ethel, Jane, Grace, Jane snr, William Henry, Richard Stone, Mrs Norris snr, Elsie, and James John.

4 Mar 1918 and awarded a Silver Award Badge 2 weeks later – given to men honourably discharged through wounds or injury. He recovered and went to live in Tamworth Street, Fulham, returning to the dairy trade. In Mar 1923 in Kensington he married Dorothy Alice Humphrey, 9 years his junior. The family moved to St Albans, Herts where their two sons were born in 1924 and 1925. Richard continued to work in Paddington, then in 1929 the family moved to Wandsworth and 2 years later moved out to Harrow. They stayed there until 1939 then moved 15 miles out of London to Rickmansworth on the 216 acre Shepherds Farm. He operated a dairy business there called "Dairy Farmers Milk Supply Ltd". He died aged 57 on 9 Dec 1945 at the farm, which then passed to his sons. The business was then sold to Express Dairies. The farm was demolished in 1961 and is now a housing estate with more than 800 houses. His wife Dorothy died in 1957 in Brighton aged 60. Family tree: https://www.ancestry.co.uk/family-tree/tree/120247555/family

OSMOND Albert John b 12 May 1887, Halberton, eldest of 10 children of John (1861-1944, Ag Lab) and Annie (1867-1933, née Osmant). In 1911 census he was a traction engine driver, single, lived with parents and nine siblings at Catfords Cottage and he worked at Catfords Farm (1m S of SP). In April 1913 he married Louisa Hawkins (b May 1885). They moved to Kings Cottages Lower Town (*2018: site of 5-7 Lower Town*), which was his home address when he enlisted 7 Jun 1916 on Short Service attestation to the army reserve at Exeter - #WR21181 where he gave his occupation as ploughman. He was mobilised on 6 January 1917, initially as a sapper for the 302nd Road Construction Company in the Royal Engineers, number 228255. However, on 31 January he was transferred to the 306th Road Construction Company, now with number WR 21181, also as a sapper, in which company he remained for the duration of the war. He embarked for France on 2 February 1917. Working initially as a Road Maker, he passed the test for a steam roller driver in March 1918, which gave him a small increase in pay. Albert was wounded in the leg while on active service. He was eventually demobilised to the Army Reserves on 12 November 1919. He returned to SP, living at 4

Albert John Osmond (left) and his brother Ted

Kings Cottages, Lower Town, occupation labourer, where he and his wife Louisa had 9 children (including twins). The family still lived there in the 1939 but later moved to Boobery. His granddaughter remembers him very fondly, describing him as quiet, but a beautiful man. Albert died in 1963 in Tiverton. Family tree: https://www.ancestry.co.uk/family-tree/tree/74614375/family

OSMOND William Henry b 23 Oct 1892, Brithem Bottom, Halberton, 2nd of 10 children of John and Annie, younger brother to Albert (above). He joined the Royal Marines on 11 Jan 1911, service number 15220, giving his parents' address as Little Catfords Farm. During WW1 he served on the Eclipse and the Orion and was on board the Orion while it was taking part in the Battle of Jutland (31 May to 1 Jun 1916), the biggest naval battle of the war. On 4 Mar 1919 in SP he married Alice Maud Morrell (b 7 Aug 1896), where his occupation was shown as private in Royal Marines. He was invalided out on 16 October 1919 after 8 months back in Plymouth. Three children were born while they were living in Waterloo Cross. In the 1939 register the family lived at Waterloo Cross Cottages, Pugham Crossing where William was a "Farm Carter". William died 8 Dec 1972, aged 80, and is buried in SP cemetery. Family tree: https://www.ancestry.co.uk/family-tree/tree/74614375/family

William Henry Osmond

William Henry Osmond, in back row, second left

PARKER William b 11 Jan 1889, bp 20 Mar SP – 2nd/5 children of John Richard 1866 (Hockworthy) -1908 (labourer) and Jessie Jones, b 1868 Holcombe Rogus. In 1911 census William was an Ag Lab living with his younger brother John Richard with their remarried mother Mrs Jessie Taylor and stepfather George Henry Taylor (a farmer) at Mount Pleasant, Whitnage Road, SP. His stepfather's son by his first marriage was William Henry Taylor, a Major in the Veterinary Corps who lost his life just after WW1 ended. There is more about him earlier in this book.

William Parker enlisted in the Devon Regiment in Exeter 4 Sep 1914, but whist initially accepted, he was discharged 7 weeks later on 23 Oct 1914 as he had hammer toes. However, in the SP 1918 ER, "military section" he lived at "Roberts" on Boobery (*2018: number 16*) with "NM" after his name, so we suspect he joined the military at a second attempt. In the Spring 1920 ER he was still living with his younger brother John at "Roberts", but left the village shortly afterwards. Family tree: https://www.ancestry.co.uk/family-tree/tree/69315156/family

PARKHOUSE Albert William George B 5 Jan 1891 and baptized 19 Apr 1891 in SP, he was 5th/9 children of Tom Parkhouse, shoemaker and Clara (née Ponsford), a dressmaker. In 1901, the family lived in Boobery (*2018: 3-5 Boobery*), but by 1911 they had moved to Royal Oak Cottages in Higher Town (*2018: the space between 14 and the school*). Albert, now 20, worked as an assistant boot-maker for his father. Albert WG Parkhouse had 2 service records: firstly as a private in the Worcester Regiment, no 203226; secondly as private in the Royal Engineers, no 362762. In Mar 1925 in Exeter he married Lillian Victoria Butt (b12 Feb 1901). They had one son born in 1926. In the 1939 register the family lived at Sidmouth St, Seaton where Albert was a "Boot and Shoe Repairer and Retailer". His elder brother Stanley (a baker) lived with them. Albert died Dec 1983 in Honiton, aged 92. Family tree: https://www.ancestry.co.uk/family-tree/tree/54003725/family

PARKHOUSE Stanley Tom b 9 Nov 1889 was 4th of 9 children of Tom (bootmaker) and Clara (dressmaker), elder brother to Albert William George (above). By 1911 Census Stanley Tom had moved to Gold St, Tiverton where he was employed as a baker. He enlisted 21 Feb 1916 at Devonport, M19015, as a cook's mate. He first saw service at Vivid I – a shore-based installation, then moved to "Suffolk" 17 May 1917. He was finally discharged 31 Jul 1919 and initially returned to live with his parents at Royal Oak Cottages, Higher Town (*2018: the space between 14 and the school*) until Spring 1923. He was employed as a bootmaker and postman. In the 1939 register he was a baker, living with his brother Albert at Seaton, Devon. He later moved to Torquay, but he did not marry and died Apr 1952, leaving estate £1,163 to his younger brother, Victor Eli Parkhouse (a boot dealer in SP). Family tree: https://www.ancestry.co.uk/family-tree/tree/54003725/family

PEARCE Edward Leslie was b 6 May 1887 in SP and baptized at St John's on 12 Jun. He was the youngest of three children of Edward Pearce 1855-1950 and Louisa Florence Dunning 1855-1956. Both of his parents had extraordinarily long lives. His father Edward was born in Uplowman and bought up on a series of large farms – his father Thomas was a Yeoman farmer with over 300 acres. In the 1881 census the family were living at Turberfield House, Lower Town, but still running their farm in Uplowman, as well as being lime burners. Edward married in 1884 in Creech St Michael, Somerset to Louisa Florence Dunning, one of 9 children of a gentleman farmer. The newlyweds had three children within 3 years of getting married – the youngest being Edward Leslie. The family lived at Boehill Barton, 1m to the north of SP where they were "gentleman farmers". In the 1911 census, Edward Leslie, aged 23, was managing the farm on behalf of his father who was temporarily abroad – in Rio De Janeiro, Brazil.

Edward Leslie enlisted with the Devons – private #45696, serving first with the 2nd Devons then later with the 8th Devons. He served in France. He was discharged from the army on 3 Mar 1919. He returned to the village and lived with his parents on their farm at Boehill - he was on E.R. Autumn 1919 to Spring 1925. In Jun 1926 Thakeham, Sussex he married Mildred Dunning Aysh - his first cousin. The married couple returned to Boehill by 1927 and his parents moved out to Morrells in Lower Town. Edward and Mildred left Boehill end 1929 and in 1930 ER were at Pullen's House, Lower Town whilst his parents had moved over the road to Turberfield House – returning to where Edward lived with his parents in 1881 census. Both Pearce families were still in the same houses in the 1939 register.

Edward Leslie retired from farming by 1950 and died 3 Dec 1961 in Sunnycroft, SP - probate £21,461 to Stanley Pearce and Wilfred Thomas Cook – 2nd cousins. His wife Mildred died 6 years later in 1967, also in SP. Family tree: https://www.ancestry.co.uk/family-tree/tree/117056639/family

PEDLER Walter George b 27 Nov 1871 SP, bp 1 Jan 1872, 4th/8 children of William Frederick Pedler (Yeoman, lived at The Barton, SP) and his wife Elizabeth Garnsey Pedler. In 1881 census he lived with his parents and siblings at Sampford Barton, where his father was a farmer of 350 acres. By 1891, aged 20, he had moved to Hay in South Wales where he was employed as a clerk. He is assumed abroad by April 1901 as he was nowhere in the UK census. He may well have been Sgt Walter George Pedler who served in Bulawayo in the S African police during the Boer War,

1899-1902. In 1906 he sailed to Quebec with brother Herbert – both show occupation as farmers. In Jun 1915 he left South Africa, which was now his permanent residence and returned to the UK where he enlisted in the ASC, then aged 44, as a sergeant DM2/117923. A September 1917 newspaper article reported that "Sergt W Pedlar, ASC, Sampford Barton" was home on leave. On 30 Aug 1919 he received the Victory Medal and also the British War Medal. He returned to Pretoria, South Africa after the war and made occasional trips to the UK where he stayed at Rock House, Halberton – where his sisters lived. His final journey back to England was in Apr 1953, aged 81. He died in the Tiverton area in Q3 1955. His probate showed £4k of assets in the UK but probate was managed in Pretoria, South Africa, where his main estate and permanent residence was situated. He remained single all of his life. Family tree: https://www.ancestry.co.uk/family-tree/tree/107786313/family

PEDLER Alice Agnes b 31 Aug 1873 SP, daughter of William Frederick Pedler (Yeoman) and Elizabeth Garnsey Pedler (née Pocock). They lived at Sampford Barton and farmed 350 acres. There were eventually 11 children. She and her sister Mary, pursued careers in nursing – Alice worked at various hospitals in the South East before becoming a trained nurse. She was a Red Cross Volunteer in July 1915. She continued nursing until 1921. She later moved to Rock House, Halberton to live with her sister Mary and they travelled Oct 1932 to South Africa, returning a year later. She died, a spinster, on 12 Nov 1942 in Rock House, Halberton aged 69. There is more about her in the chapter on Sampford Peverell women. Family tree: https://www.ancestry.co.uk/family-tree/tree/107786313/family

PEDLER Mary – b 7 May 1868 to William Frederick Pedler (Yeoman) and Elizabeth Garnsey Pedler (née Pocock) of the Barton, SP. She trained at the University College Hospital, London 1892-1898 and joined the Queen Alexandra's Imperial Military Nursing Service General Hospital in 1903 as a nursing Sister. She became Assistant Matron, in the same order. Her next position was Acting Matron at the Military Hospital, Magdalen Camp, Winchester. She received a Royal Red Cross Award, which was published in the London Gazette on 23/2/1917, and was decorated by HM King at Buckingham Palace on 31/3/1917. The citation stated that she already held both the South Africa medals. She retired Jan 1921 and lived at Rock House, Halberton with her sister Alice. They travelled together to South Africa for a year in 1932/33. She died at Rock House, Halberton 15 Mar 1955. There is more about her in the chapter on Sampford Peverell women. Family tree: https://www.ancestry.co.uk/family-tree/tree/107786313/family

PERRY Charles John – b Mar 1881 Holcombe Rogus 4th/7 children to James Perry 1849-1897 (Carpenter) and Jane Vickery 1857-1928. Charles was a furniture maker who lived in Holcombe in 1911 census. In Apr 1913 in SP he married Clara Dunn, youngest of 11 children of William Charles "Cocky" Dunn, a shoemaker who lived in SP. Charles and Clara settled in SP and he appeared in Boobery in the 1915 Electoral Roll. Their son William was born in SP in 1914. Charles appears to have been conscripted in May 1917 and joined the RFC as an airman #80638. A newspaper article of 7th Sep 1917 reported that he was home on leave from the RFC. In the 1918 ER he had moved to Higher Town, and they had another son in 1921. They lived there until the Autumn 1924 ER and then left the village. In the 1939 register the family lived at "The Greens, Bradfield, Willand" where Charles was the estate carpenter. Clearly the family later returned to the village as Charles died Mar 1960 in SP whilst his wife Clara died Jul 1970. Family tree: https://www.ancestry.co.uk/family-tree/tree/75095161/family

PILLAR William Henry b Jun 1892 Sampford Bridge, Burlescombe first son to William (Railway Packer) b1862 SP and Mary (née Young, b 1866). Their younger son, Arthur John Pillar, lost his life in France & Flanders aged 18 - just 2 months before the end of the war. The family lived at Jersey Cottage in the 1901 census census and had moved to Boobery (*2018: site of number 7*) by 1918. William signed up 5 Sep 1914 to the 5th Somerset Light Infantry Regiment – private 2364. He was discharged as medically unfit to continue to fight (section xvi) 7 Mar 1916 and sent back to the UK. He married Q2 1918 to a Winifred Esther Authers in Burlescombe. (Registered as ANthers in Wellington, Somerset). They had one son. In the 1939 register the family lived at Snow Cottage and William was employed by GWR. William died Sep 1967 in Exeter; his wife Winifred died in 1980 in Whiteball, Wellington, Somerset – where the family lived. Family tree: https://www.ancestry.co.uk/family-tree/tree/68538081/family

PONSFORD Arthur b 9 Nov 1889 SP, 3rd of 9 children of Jesse and Fanny, brother to Charles (below). In 1901 the family was in Higher Town (*2018: part of 30 HT*) and in 1911 he was a farm labourer on Batten's Farm, Halberton. He signed up with the 8th Devons as Private 17728, and was reported as "home on furlough from the trenches" in August 1917. On 25 Feb 1919 he was transferred to Z reserve. He was awarded the standard two medals – the British War Medal and the Victory Medal. He returned to SP to work as a labourer and in 1923 lived at Higher Town and by 1926 in Boobery. On 5 Jun 1928 in SP he married Evelina Pillar (b Oct 1893).

They lived in Higher Town until 1932 and then left the village. In the 1939 register Arthur and Evelina lived at Hopkins Cottage, Halberton, where Arthur was a Road repair man. Arthur died Dec 1964 in the Tiverton area. His wife Evelina died 5 years later in 1969 in Holcombe Rogus. The death was registered in Wellington. Family tree: https://www.ancestry.co.uk/family-tree/tree/75159961/family

PONSFORD Charles b 4 Mar 1887 SP 2nd of 9 children of Jesse Ponsford (1864 SP, Railway Packer, d 1909) and Fanny Hunt (1862-1918), Seamstress. In 1901 he was living at a Diocesan house boys home in Frome, Somerset. In 1911 census he was a gardener, living with his widowed mother and 5 siblings back in SP in a Lower Town cottage (*2018: site of 16 Court Way*). He enlisted into the 11th Somerset Light Infantry (Private 265413) and served in France. He transferred to Z reserves 9 Feb 1919. In 1923 he lived in Higher Town, SP, single, occupation labourer. In the 1939 Register he lived at 1 Turnpike Cottage - occupation postman. He had lodgers – his recently widowed sister Alice Scorse b 1891 and her son Charles – b 1916. Charles (Senior) died Dec 1949, aged 62, in SP, having never married. Family tree: https://www.ancestry.co.uk/family-tree/tree/75159961/family

PONSFORD Edwin William – b 30 Jul 1894 eldest son of Thomas William Ponsford (tailor and fly proprietor) 1849-1918 and Charlotte Westlake Greedy (1860-1917) and brother to Ernest (below). In 1911 census he was a baker's boy, living with his parents and two siblings at Turnpike Cottage (*2018: 1, Turnpike*), SP. He enlisted as William Edwin Ponsford in the 6th Devon Regiment, private 4979. He was then transferred to the 11th Somerset Light Infantry #275145 and then transferred again to the Northumberland Fusiliers #206249. He was awarded the standard two medals – the British War Medal and the Victory Medal. Both of his parents died shortly before the end of the war. He returned to the family home at Turnpike Cottage and lived there (per the electoral roll) from Spring 1922 to Spring 1929. In Mar 1929 he married Amy Stone (b Feb 1898) and they moved into Tiverton. In the 1939 register they lived at the stores in the Tiverton district with occupation Baker and Grocer. They did not however have any children. William died in 1971, his wife Amy died 1963. Family tree: https://www.ancestry.co.uk/family-tree/tree/75159961/family

PONSFORD Ernest – b Q3 1896 SP. as John Ernest Ponsford , he had dropped the 'John' by 1911. He was son of Thomas William Ponsford, a tailor and fly (carriage) proprietor and Charlotte Westlake née Greedy. In 1911 census he lived with the family at Turnpike Cottage (*2018: 1, Turnpike*). He enlisted in September 1914 at Tiverton, into the Devonshire Regiment, firstly as no 3769, then later as no 11891, where his occupation was given as coachman, and passed the medical exam. He was posted to France in September 1915, and then to the Mediterranean in September 1915. He contracted Malaria at Salonika in June 1916 and was hospitalised several times as a result - in Malta and elsewhere. After several recurrences of the malaria, he was despatched back to the UK in February 1919 to hospital in Epsom, then he was discharged from military service in April 1919. He returned to SP and lived initially in Higher Town, then moved to Turnpike by 1924. In Sep 1929, in Tiverton, he married Beatrice Ellen Channing (b 20 Nov 1900) and they moved to 9 Council Cottages (later named Beaufort Close) SP. They had 3 children in the 1930s. In the 1939 Register they lived at 2, Coronation Cottages on Lower Town. Ernest was a "general Mason". Ernest died aged 63 in Exeter in Sep 1959. Family tree: https://www.ancestry.co.uk/family-tree/tree/75159961/family

PONSFORD Herbert b Apr 1896 SP, 6th/9 children of Jesse and Fanny - younger brother to Charles and Arthur above who also served. In the 1911 census Herbert was a "Yard Boy" on a farm, but lived with his widowed mother and siblings in Lower Town, SP (*2018: site of 16 Court Way*). He enlisted early 1915 and joined 8th Devons (like his older brother Arthur). Private #10641. He first saw active service 25 Jul 1915 in France. In a newspaper report of 5 Nov 1915 he had been severely injured – shot 7 times but the bullets had initially hit a "pocket testament" which cushioned the impact into his body. He recovered and continued to fight in France, but in Feb 1917 he was reported to be home on leave with a poisoned hand. In Jun 1918 a newspaper reported that "Mrs F Ponsford, of Higher Town, Sampford Peverell, has received news from Germany that her son, Herbert Ponsford, who was previously reported missing, was a prisoner of war. On 17 Mar 1919 he was transferred to the Z reserve. He was awarded the standard two medals: the British War Medal and the Victory Medal. In Jan 1921 he emigrated to Australia. Family tree: https://www.ancestry.co.uk/family-tree/tree/75159961/family

RICHARDS Harold b 31 Oct 1899, Tiverton. Youngest of 5 children of Josiah and Edith (née Phillips). The family lived at Roberts Cottage, Boobery (*2018: 16 Boobery*), SP in the 1911 census where his father was a Prudential Assurance Agent. The family moved away shortly after the date of the census. Harold was called to colours 18 Jan 1918 RNAS as air mechanic (gave occupation on enlistment as fitter and turner). Transferred 2 Feb 1918 to Daedalus, Cranwell, which would become part of the newly formed RAF two months later. In the 1939 Register he lived at Park Street, Tiverton, working as a milkman and retail food dealer, living with his wife, Winifred, and at least one child. He died in 1949.

RIDLER Walter Sidney William, known as Sid – b 21 Dec 1898 in SP (but declared Dec 1897 as his birthday when he signed up!), 1st of 4 children of Walter John Ridler (Harness Maker) 1872-1942 and Thomazine (née Ashman) 1878-1968. In the 1911 census the family lived in Higher Town (*2018: in or near 40 HT*). He enlisted 31 Jan 1916, in the RN, #M18762, shortly after his "18th" birthday for a period of 12 years. He gave his occupation as "Baker". A newspaper article of September 1917 reported that "Cooks' Mate Sydney Ridler" was home on leave. He worked as an apprentice Cooks Mate on Vivid I (shore based) for 9 months then transferred to HMS Devonshire where he worked as Cooks Mate until May 1919. He then transferred back to Vivid I (shore based) where he was promoted to Cook, then Leading Cook. He then worked in many different vessels (20 in all) as a Cook until Feb 1927 when he was invalided out with Pulmonary Tuberculosis. He married Alice Maud Jarman in Tiverton in 1922 and they had two sons. Sid died in Mar 1931, aged just 33 – presumably TB. His niece told us that he was on the Atlantic convoys and was twice on ships that sank. He had his own hand-written recipe book, and he was good at painting. His widow Alice remarried (to Leonard Legge)

Sid Ridler

in 1934, and Sid's sons moved to Australia in the 1950s. Family tree: https://www.ancestry.co.uk/family-tree/tree/75041917/family

RUSSELL William Henry – b 1896 Uffculme, bp 1 Aug 1896 2nd of 4 children of William, (b Oct 1864 Uffculme, Ag Lab) and his wife Elizabeth Ann Payne (1865 Wiveliscombe – Apr 1917 SP). In 1911 census the family lived at Baileys Cottages (*2018: site of 9 Boobery*) and Henry William was described as a butchers boy (aged 14). He enlisted early in the war in the ASC and was in Egypt on 6 Jul 1915. His service record shows he held the rank of Corporal and was acting Staff Sergeant. He was mentioned in despatches on 14 Jun 1918. On the 1919 Absent Voters list for SP a William Henry Russell S/2/12026 Sgt 21st P.O.L. Sup. Co. RASC is listed. This may be a supply company for Petroleum, Oil, Lubricants. He was discharged 10 Jun 1920. He lived with his widowed father in Boobery according to the 1920 ER. His father William Russell continued to live in Boobery until 1925, occupation labourer, when he left the village.

Surnames S-Z

SALTER Edmund James - b 21 Apr 1892 SP to James Salter (1867, Uffculme -Butcher) and his wife Mary Annie (1865 – Oakford). In the 1911 census they lived at Paulett, Higher Town (*2018: number 9*) where Edmund was an assistant butcher to his father. On 11 Oct 1915 in Exeter he married Elia Mary Woodrow, a farmer's daughter from Wiltshire. He gave his occupation as cattle dealer. Served in the ASC and the Devonshire Regiment (Service Number 67142), including at least 2 years with the ASC in Egypt, as the Western Times reported on 12th April 1918: *"information has just been received by Mr and Mrs J Salter, butcher, of Paulett House, SP, that their only son, Pte. E.J. Salter, A.S.C., has just won a certificate and bronze medallion, and is now qualified as an Instructor, having passed all the necessary tests. Mr Salter has been in Egypt over two years"*. He was wounded and discharged on 3rd July 1919. Edmund returned to SP and lived at "The Cottage" on Higher Town. He and Ella had one daughter. He died 21 Feb 1929 in SP, aged 36.

SALTER Joseph – b Apr 1878 Washfield, Tiverton 2nd/3 children of Joseph Salter (farmer) 1835-1919 and his second wife Sarah Ann Langdon 1855-1941. The family moved around from farm to farm, but in 1891 census they were at Pitt Farm, just N of SP. In 1898 Joseph married Laura Kerslake (b Apr 1876), whose father managed Hill Kiln quarry. In 1901 Joseph (a quarry worker) and his wife lived at Smoke Alley, Boobery (*2018: 22-24 Boobery*). In 1911 they still lived at Boobery – at his mother-in-laws' house. He gave his occupation as Inn Publican - he was landlord of the Globe inn until 1916. No military record found, however he clearly did serve as he is shown on the electoral roll after the end of the war with "NM" after his name. He appeared to leave the village, but his wife Laura was on ER for SP in Boobery from 1921 to 1934 and was also there on the 1939 register, while Joseph was in Axbridge, Somerset. Laura died 1940 in Willand. He died Jan 1953 in Weston Super Mare, Somerset, aged 74. Family tree: https://www.ancestry.co.uk/family-tree/tree/74614375/family

SAUNDERS William Mark – b 22 Jan 1877 (bp 18 Feb) SP, eldest of 8 children of Robert (1850 -1937 SP, builder) and Ellen née Arthurs (1850 Uplowman). In 1911 census they lived at Bridge House, SP next to the Canal in Lower Town. William was a mason, assisting his father. He enlisted after his application in Mar 1916 to be "starred" was rejected. Service number 23168 in Devon Regiment, No 2 Devon Works Company at Wearde

Camp, Saltash, attached to E Surrey Regiment, then Larkhill Camp Salisbury. In the 1918 electoral roll he lived at Bridge House with "NM" after his name so was still away. He returned to Bridge House (4 Lower Town) where he worked as a mason, and the family were still there in 1934 Electoral Roll. In Sep 1928 he married Hilda Minnie Bass (b Jul 1901) in SP. They had a daughter in 1929 in SP. In 1939 Register he still lived at Bridge House, but with occupation Dairy Farmer. William died Dec 1955 in SP. Family tree: https://www.ancestry.co.uk/family-tree/tree/55070480/family

William Saunders

SAYER Herbert – b 27 Jun 1885 Stogursey, Somerset 11th/12 children of Joseph Sayer (farmer 1837-1887) and Charlotte Phillips (1837-1911). Herbert lived and worked in Somerset but on 17 Apr 1911 in SP he married Mary Ellen Russell (B Apr 1890 Uffculme) who lived with her parents William and Elizabeth Ann in Boobery (*2018: site of 9 Boobery*). Herbert gave his occupation as Chauffeur – in 1911! Herbert enlisted Jan 1915 into the ASC, occupation Driver - private M2/046421, seeing active servce in France from Feb 1915. He was discharged to Z reserves Mar 1919 and returned briefly to SP after the war, was included on the Spring 1919 ER with occupation Chauffeur and lived in Kiln Cottage from Autumn 1919 to Autumn 1920. He re-enlisted in the RASC and finally left 18 Jun 1930. Herbert and Mary Ellen had three children. In the 1939 register the family lived at Rumwell Park, Taunton where Herbert was a gardener. Herbert died in 1949 in Taunton.

SCORSE John – b 30 Jul 1889 SP 8th of 10 children of Charles Scorse (1844

Halberton-1910, Plate Layer GWR) and Elizabeth Scorse (née Trevellyan b1851 SP). In 1891 the family lived at Wink Cottage, Whitnage Road. By 1901 they had moved to Easton Cottage in Easton Lane – a property which no longer exists. Charles, the father died 1910 and his widow and three sons moved to Always Cottage on Chains Road (*2018: 1-3 Chains*), where John was employed as a railway worker. On 5 Apr 1915 John married Alice Ponsford (1888 SP) and gave occupation as plate layer GWR. He enlisted shortly afterwards in the Royal Engineers (#175210) and was later transferred to the 275th Railway Co – part of RE. He was a Corporal, but an Acting Sergeant at the end of the war. They had a son Charles John b 23 Nov 1916 and bp 4 Feb 1917, where father declared occupation as "Royal Engineers". He returned to SP and lived in Boobery until 1929 where they had two more children. In the 1920 Gregory's Directory his occupation is shown as (railway) packer. In 1930 the family moved to Turnpike Cottage which became the family home. John died 22 Jun 1937 in SP. John had two nephews, Arthur Scorse and Bertie Scorse, who both lost their lives in 1917 during the war – aged 19 and 21 (more details earlier in this book). Family tree:
https://www.ancestry.co.uk/family-tree/tree/75159961/family

SELWAY Albert – b 1 Mar 1884, only child of James Selway (ag Lab 1846-1909 Uffculme) and Eliza Taylor (1843-1913 b Cullompton, d SP). In the 1901 census Albert had left his parents and was working as an Ag Lab at Shutehanger, ½ mile S of SP, but technically in Halberton. By 1911 he was living with his widowed mother Eliza at Lower Turberfield Cottages, Moorend (*2018: on the road to the station*) where his occupation was shown as quarryman. His mother died in July 1913, one month before he married Florence Bristow of Ayshford (1879-1939) 7th/8 children of Noah Bristow and Elizabeth Buncombe. They had their first child, Albert J Selway, 1 Oct 1915 and he was baptized on 31 Oct where his father gave his occupation as labourer. He must have enlisted shortly afterwards, but it has proved hard to determine exactly which service record is his. Our best guess is CMT/2347 in the RASC. He was on leave from the trenches in 1917 according to a newspaper report. His first cousin Francis George Selway, b Apr 1892 Exeter, enlisted with the 2nd Battalion of the Dublin Fusilliers and lost his life in France & Flanders 21 Mar 1918.

Albert and his wife had a second child Hetty, b 2 May 1917 in SP. After the war, in Spring 1919 electoral roll, the family lived in Uffculme. In 1939 register Albert (widower) lived at Colliers Court Cottages, Honiton RD with his married daughter, Hetty Snow. Albert died in 1949 in Honiton, his wife

died 10 years earlier. Family tree:
https://www.ancestry.co.uk/family-tree/tree/109895825/family

SMITH Ernest James – b Jul 1887 Ash Thomas, Halberton 1ˢᵗ/5 children of James Smith (1865 Ash Thomas, Carter) and Caroline (1856, Upottery, Honiton) – this was Caroline's second marriage, her 1ˢᵗ husband (Mr Davies) d 1884, shortly after the birth of their second child, Tasmina. The family lived in the Ash Thomas/ Pigsfoot area, just S of Halberton. On 28 Dec 1903 Ernest, aged 17y 6m signed up for 6 years' service in the Militia – serving in 4ᵗʰ Battalion of the Devon Regt, #4446. He was however discharged 3 Jun 1907 as being permanently unfit for duty. In 1911 census Ernest James (and indeed his younger brother Samuel) were Traction Driver Steersmen. Ernest re-enlisted as private 468927 in the 697ᵗʰ Agric Co. He married Caroline Hodder (b 1892 Newton Abbot) in the Tiverton area in 1917 and in 1918 was listed on the ER in Higher Town as NM. In the Autumn 1919 Electoral roll for SP he was a lodger at Wink Cottage marked as NM, with Samuel and Eliza Selway (former neighbours from Ash Thomas) whose son Francis George was killed in action Mar 1918. Ernest left the village by Spring 1920 and lived at Five Bridges, Halberton but returned Spring 1923 with his wife Caroline and worked as a labourer. By 1925 they had moved to Pond Cottage in Higher Town and continued to live there until the end of 1933, then left the village. They had three children.

TREVELLYAN Alfred – b 18 Aug 1885, SP; 7ᵗʰ/9 children of George (1847-93 SP, Carpenter) and Caroline Walker (1849-1906). In 1891 the family lived at Always Cottage on Chains Road (*2018: 1-3 Chains Road*). His father died in 1893 and his mother remarried a John Hooper Parkhouse, an engine driver at the butter factory. The family stayed in Chains Road (number 8) and Alfred was a Stockman on a farm.

In 1904 he joined GWR and was a "Carman" based in Monmouthshire, but shortly after joining was given two weeks' notice as he was "deficient in reading". He returned to SP and lived at Chains Cottage with his elder sister Lily, who had married William Goffin, a RN "professional". Alfred was once again working for GWR, but this time as a labourer. On 20 Aug 1913 he married his second cousin Emma Trevellyan (b Apr 1878 in Burlescombe dr of James Trevellyan and Sarah Ann Saunders). They had a daughter Sylvia Annie, b Apr 1914 in the Wellington area. He enlisted in the Royal Engineers and joined the Railway regiment with rank Sapper, 104843. His brother-in-law Sidney Dunn died in the war (more details earlier in this book). In 1939 register he lived at 4 Mount Pleasant, Exeter and worked for GWR. He died

Dec 1968 in Exeter. Family tree: https://www.ancestry.co.uk/family-tree/tree/75014822/family

TREVELLYAN Walter George b Jan 1880 SP; 6th/9 children to George Trevellyan (1847-93 SP, Carpenter) and Caroline (née Walker) 1849-1906. Older brother to Alfred (above). In 1891 census they lived at Always Cottage (*2018: 1-3 Chains Road*). When his father died in 1891, his mother remarried John Hooper Parkhouse and they still lived in Chains Road. By 1901 Walter was a bricklayer and was living in Bedfordshire with his newly married sister Rosa – her husband was also a bricklayer. There is no definitive record for him in the 1911 census – there is a George Trevellyan living in SP as a servant b 1883, but this is probably the George Trevellyan b 1883 in Burlescombe. Walter enlisted but there are several possible military records and we cannot be sure which one is his. After the war he returned to the village, but never married. He died in Tiverton Hospital May 1929 and was buried 23 May in SP. Family tree: https://www.ancestry.co.uk/family-tree/tree/75014822/family

TREVELYAN George Charles (Charley) b 29 Jan 1899 SP; 2nd/4 children of William Edward (1871 SP, Labourer) and Mary Ann (née Radford) b 1869 Culmstock. They lived in a Lower Town cottage (*2018: site of 16 Court Way*). In 1911 census the family had moved out of SP to Whitnage, Uplowman. Charley enlisted in the army – RFA #135577. His elder brother Stanley lost his life at sea in the war and there is more information about the family in the section on him earlier in this book. On 24 Dec 1921 Charley emigrated to Australia, giving his occupation as 'motor driver' and his UK address as c/o Thorn & Baker, Cullompton. He died in Australia in 1973. Family tree: https://www.ancestry.co.uk/family-tree/tree/75014822/family

TREVELYAN Percy John b 6 Sep 1901 SP; 3rd/4 children of William Edward and Mary Ann. Younger brother to George Charles (above) and Stanley, who lost his life in WW1 at sea in Aug 1918. They lived in a Lower Town cottage (*2018: site of 16 Court Way*). In 1911 census the family had moved to Whitnage, Uplowman. Percy signed up to the RN in July 1917 initially as a cabin boy, but he later enlisted for 12 years starting 6 Sep 1919 (his 18th birthday). He first saw active service on HMS Impregnable # J74038 on 23 Jul 1917. However he was invalided out of the RN 20 Mar 1918, even before his "official service" started, with Emphysema. He was married Jun 1919 in Tiverton to Maud Pring and they had a daughter in 1921. At some stage he emigrated to Australia and saw active service with the Australian armed forces in WW2. He died in Perth, Western Australia on 28 Feb 1984. Family tree: https://www.ancestry.co.uk/family-tree/tree/75014822/family

TUCKER Herbert John b 10 Jun 1895, bp 14 Jul 1895 at SP; Herbert was the eldest of 6 children of Richard b 1862, Cheriton, Ag Lab and Elizabeth Jane Cottey b 1872, SP. His parents married 4 Jul 1894 at St Johns, SP. His younger siblings Frederick and Ernest both lost their lives during the war – there is more about them in an earlier chapter. His mother Jane died in Oct 1907 in childbirth and her 2-day-old son was buried with her in the same coffin. His father Richard remarried to Annie b 1863 Topsham. The family lived at Smoke Alley, Boobery, (*2018: 22-24 Boobery*) in both 1901 and 1911 censuses, but by 1911 Herbert had left home and was working as a farm boy (aged 15) for the Dennis family at Jurishayes, Withleigh, Tiverton. We know he served in the war as he was listed in the ER for Ayshford in 1918 as NM, but we cannot be sure which he was of several servicemen with the same name. The 1920 ER shows that he returned to live with his parents in Ayshford after the war. Family tree: https://www.ancestry.co.uk/family-tree/tree/74511558/family

WALLINGTON Lucy (née Harris) b 22 Mar 1889 Glamorgan, youngest of 8 children of William Harris (painter) and Lucy Rees, married William Claude Wallington (b Sep 1876) in Apr 1909 in Glamorgan and they lived in Cardiff. Her brother in law Charles Harold Wallington was a SP man who lost his life in 1917 in WW1 – there is more about him earlier in this book. Lucy joined the war effort as a Red Cross Volunteer nurse in 1915 – the same year as her husband William enlisted. She worked initially in Cardiff, but gave her home address as "Morrells, Lower Town, SP" (*2018: 3 Lower Town*) which was where her mother-in-law lived. At the end of the war Nov/Dec 1918 she worked at the Beaufort War hospital in Bristol. In the 1939 register she lived in Teignmouth. Her husband William also lived in Teignmouth but in the "Woodhall Household" – a nursing home. She died Dec 1969 in Newton Abbott, aged 80. Her husband William had died 15 years earlier in Exeter hospital. Family tree: https://www.ancestry.co.uk/family-tree/tree/74092134/family

WARE Albert Edwin was b 26 Nov 1885 in Bampton. Albert was the youngest of 8 children of Edwin Ware, a farmer b Apr 1848 in Halberton, and Emma, née Parker, who helped on the farm and was b Jan 1846 in SP. In the 1901 census, Edwin and Emma, together with Albert Edwin and a grand-daughter, Elsie Redwood Ware (the illegitimate daughter of another of their children, Annie Ware) lived at Blackdown Gate farm in Culmstock. By the time of the next census in 1911, the family had all moved to Holbrook, which is on the border of SP and Burlescombe. Albert, aged 26, was described as single, a joiner and carpenter employing others, whilst his parents continued to be farmers. Albert married Rosalie Morgan b 1890 Burlescombe, in Apr 1911 and by Sep 1911 they had their first child, Bessie May, who was bp at St John's church, SP on 15 Oct 1911 (died 1988). On 30 Dec 1913 they had a son, Edwin Albert, also bp SP, on 8 Jan 1914. The family moved into Baileys Cottages, Boobery (*2018: site of 7-11*) around the time of their son's birth and Albert is on the 1914 Electoral Roll. Boobery remained their home until 1920. Albert Edwin appears on the 1918 E.R. with NM appearing against his name. No service record survived for him, but from this one piece of evidence it does appear that he served during the War. In the 1939 Register, Albert Edwin Ware was the licensee of the Plymouth Inn, Crediton, living there with Rosalie. He died Dec 1970 in Exeter. His wife Rosalie died 10 years earlier.

WILLIAMS Albert John b Dec 1890, Tiverton; he was 5th /6 children of John Williams (b 1862 Tiverton-Mar 1931 SP), labourer and his wife Sarah Ann Kerslake (b 1860 Tiverton- Dec 1927 SP). His elder brother, William Henry Williams (see below), also served in the War. In 1891 census, aged 3 months, Albert lived with parents at Westexe, Tiverton. By 1911 census his family were in Back Street SP (*2018: 17-19 Higher Town*) and he had joined the army and was stationed at Aldershot where he was a driver with RHA (Royal Horse Artillery) - reg no 63083 with the 69th Battalion. He later transferred to RFA (Royal Field Artillery). He returned to SP after the war and he and his brother lived with their parents at Higher Town from 1919 to 1922 per the Electoral Rolls. Unable to trace him after he left the village around 1922.

WILLIAMS William Henry, b 27 Jan 1889, Tiverton; he was 4th /6 children of John Williams (1862, Tiverton) and Sarah (1860, Tiverton). His younger brother Albert John Williams also served (see above). In 1891 census family lived at Westexe, Tiverton. By 1901 they moved out to Little Silver, 3m S of Tiverton, but by 1911 the family were living at Back Street, SP (*2018: 17-19 Higher Town*). William Henry was shown as a steerman on a traction engine. He enlisted 19 Nov 1915 in the Duke of Edinburgh Wiltshire Regiment (#26227) where he gave his occupation as labourer, GWR. He was mobilised 15 Feb 1916 in the Royal Berkshire Regiment. On

13 May 1916, 3 months after being mobilised, he was promoted to Lance Corporal. Exactly a year later, on 13 May 1917 he was promoted to Corporal (94824) in the 159th Labour Corps of the Royal Berkshire Regiment. He returned to "Base Depot" 29 Jun 1919 and was discharged 15 Sep 1919. He returned to SP and lived with his parents at Higher Town from Autumn 1919 to Autumn 1921 (Per the electoral rolls). In the 1920 Gregory's Directory he was employed as a Chauffeur and lived in Boobery. He left the village 1921 and there's a William Henry Williams in Clayhanger in 1924 (Electoral Roll). In 1939 he was in Chelsea Terrace, Tiverton, with his wife Bessie Williams née Richards. His job was 'Permanent Way maintenance repair staff'. He died in the Tiverton area in 1964.

WILLIAMS Stanley b 20 Feb 1891, SP; 6th /8 children of William John Williams (b 1851 Uffculme) butcher and Eliza Wright (b 1856 Hemyock). He lived with his parents in 1911 census at Challis, Lower Town *(2018: 12 Lower Town)*, SP where he was a butcher working in the family business He enlisted as a driver in Dec 1915 in the RFA (Royal Field Artillery). He was in France for 18 months between 1917 and 1919. In 1914 he married Dora Elston (b Jan 1891) from Silverton and their first daughter, Stella, was born in 1915. After the war Stanley returned to SP and took over the family butchers business at Challis, Lower Town. He was part of the British Legion committee who set up the village hall in 1933. Stanley and his wife Dora moved to Moorend House before the start of WW2 where his occupation was shown as Farmer, Butcher and Cattle Dealer. He "retired" from the business during WW2 and handed it over to his daughter and her husband. Much more detail of the butchers business is given in a publication by the SP Society on village businesses. Stanley died in 1968, aged 77 and Dora in 1975, aged 84. Family tree: https://www.ancestry.co.uk/family-tree/tree/54003725/family

Bibliography

Peter Ayres, *Britain's Green Allies: Medicinal Plants in Wartime,* (Matador, 2015)

Denis Cluett and Sampford Peverell Society, *A Village Childhood : Memories of Living in Rural Devon before the Age of the Motor Car, Sampford Peverell Society Publication* (Great Britain: Charles Scott-Fox, 2007).

Todd Gray, *Lest Devon forgets : service, sacrifice and the creation of Great War memorials.* (Exeter, The Mint Press, 2010)

N. Thornton, *Led by Lions: MPs and Sons Who Fell in the First World War* (Fonthill Media, 2017).